The Smithsonian Guides to Natural America

THE ATLANTIC COAST
AND BLUE RIDGE

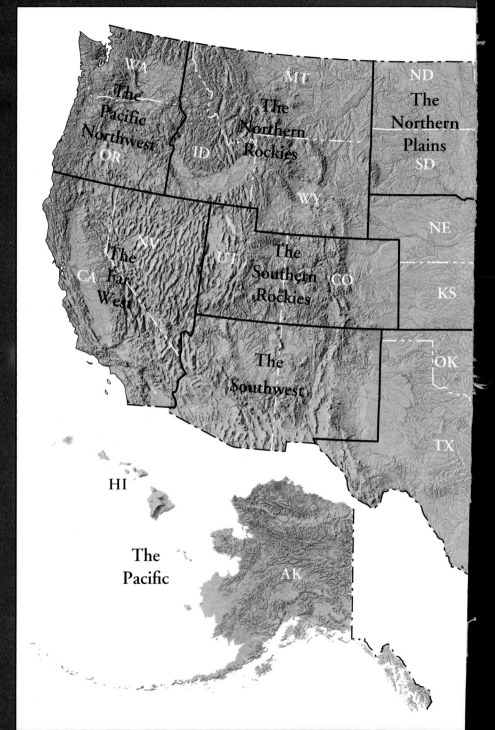

WA

The
Pacific
Northwest
OR

MT

The
Northern
Rockies

ID

WY

ND

The
Northern
Plains
SD

NE

NV

The
Far
West

CA

UT

The
Southern
Rockies

CO

KS

The
Southwest

OK

TX

HI

The
Pacific

AK

THE ATLANTIC COAST
VIRGINIA – MARYLAND – DELAWARE
NORTH CAROLINA

THE SMITHSONIAN GUIDES TO NATURAL AMERICA

THE ATLANTIC COAST AND BLUE RIDGE

MARYLAND, DISTRICT OF COLUMBIA, DELAWARE, VIRGINIA, NORTH CAROLINA

TEXT
John Ross

PHOTOGRAPHY
Bates Littlehales

PREFACE
Thomas E. Lovejoy

SMITHSONIAN BOOKS • WASHINGTON, D.C.
RANDOM HOUSE • NEW YORK, N.Y.

Front cover: Salt marsh, Eastern Shore, Virginia
Half-title page: Buckeye butterfly on goldenrod, Merchant's Mill Pond, North Carolina
Frontispiece: Flame azalea, Roan Mountain, North Carolina
Back cover: Atlantis fritillary butterfly; white ibis; mountain laurel blossoms

THE SMITHSONIAN INSTITUTION
SECRETARY I. Michael Heyman
COUNSELOR TO THE SECRETARY FOR BIODIVERSITY
AND ENVIRONMENTAL AFFAIRS Thomas E. Lovejoy
ACTING DIRECTOR, SMITHSONIAN INSTITUTION PRESS Daniel H. Goodwin

SMITHSONIAN BOOKS
EDITOR IN CHIEF Patricia Gallagher
SENIOR EDITOR Alexis Doster III
MARKETING MANAGER Susan E. Romatowski
BUSINESS MANAGER Steven J. Bergstrom

THE SMITHSONIAN GUIDES TO NATURAL AMERICA
SERIES EDITOR Sandra Wilmot
MANAGING EDITOR Ellen Scordato
SERIES PHOTO EDITOR Mary Jenkins
PHOTO EDITOR Sarah Longacre
ART DIRECTOR Mervyn Clay
ASSISTANT PHOTO EDITOR Ferris Cook
ASSISTANT PHOTO EDITOR Rebecca Williams
ASSISTANT EDITOR Seth Ginsberg
COPY EDITORS Karen Hammonds, James Waller
FACT CHECKER Jean Cotterell
PRODUCTION DIRECTOR Katherine Rosenbloom

Library of Congress Cataloging-in-Publication Data
Ross, John.
     The Smithsonian guides to natural America. The Atlantic coast and
  Blue Ridge—Maryland, Washington, D.C., Virginia, and North Carolina
  /text by John Ross; photography by Bates Littlehales; preface by
  Thomas E. Lovejoy
       p. cm.
     Includes bibliographical references (p 256) and index.
     ISBN 0-679-76314-7 (pbk.)
     1. Natural history—Atlantic States—Guidebooks. 2. Atlantic
  States—Guidebooks. I. Littlehales, Bates. II. Title.
QH104.5.A85R67 1995   95-1486
508.75—dc20   CIP

Manufactured in the United States of America
98765432

How to Use This Book

The Smithsonian Guides to Natural America explore and celebrate the preserved and protected natural areas of this country that are open for the public to use and enjoy. From world-famous national parks to tiny local preserves, the places featured in these guides offer a splendid panoply of this nation's natural wonders.

Divided by state and region, this book offers suggested itineraries for travelers, briefly describing the high points of each preserve, refuge, park or wilderness area along the way. Each site was chosen for a specific reason: Some are noted for their botanical, zoological, or geological significance, others simply for their exceptional scenic beauty.

Information pertaining to the area as a whole can be found in the introductory sections to the book and to each chapter. In addition, specialized maps at the beginning of each book and chapter highlight an area's geography and geological features as well as pinpoint the specific locales that the author describes.

For quick reference, places of interest are set in **boldface** type; those set in **boldface** followed by the symbol ❖ are listed in the Site Guide at the back of the book. (This feature begins on page **261**, just before the index.) Here noteworthy sites are listed alphabetically by state, and each entry provides practical information that visitors need: telephone numbers, mailing addresses, and specific services available.

Addresses and telephone numbers of national, state, and local agencies and organizations are also listed. Also in appendices are a glossary of pertinent scientific terms and designations used to describe natural areas; the author's recommendations for further reading (both nonfiction and fiction); and a list of sources that can aid travelers planning a guided visit.

The words and images of these guides are meant to help both the active naturalist and the armchair traveler to appreciate more fully the environmental diversity and natural splendor of this country. To ensure a successful visit, always contact a site in advance to obtain detailed maps, updated information on hours and fees, and current weather conditions. Many areas maintain a fragile ecological balance. Remember that their continued vitality depends in part on responsible visitors who tread the land lightly.

C O N T E N T S

PREFACE

Some of my earliest experiences with nature come from Maryland's Eastern Shore, where I spent a year at the end of World War II. At that time, there were no great bridges spanning the Delaware or the Susquehanna rivers, let alone the Chesapeake Bay. The Eastern Shore was a place where nature loomed large and was as tranquil as the gentle lapping of Bay waters. In this setting, it is little wonder that family memory has me interrupting my father and uncle, as they discussed an Edward R. Murrow broadcast, to request that we talk about "something interesting. . . like skunks and snakes and things."

A lot has changed since then. There are bridges now, of course, and on a good weekend the backup of cars waiting to cross the Bay can be very frustrating. The greatest of all estuaries—averaging only 21 feet (6.4 meters) deep—and a seemingly perpetually generous source of oysters, crabs, and rockfish (as striped bass are known there), the Chesapeake Bay has major problems. Even the "beautiful swimmers," as former Smithsonian Assistant Secretary William W. Warner termed the blue crabs in his exquisite book of the same name, are currently in decline. The oyster population, which once a week used to filter a volume of water equal to the entire Bay, has been so reduced that the oysters now take a year to filter the same amount. From the vantage point of a small airplane, it is no longer easy to discern where the oyster beds lie.

Not all the changes have been negative, however. Cooperation among the states of Maryland, Virginia, and Delaware has led to the recovery of the rockfish population and reinstitution of a rockfish season. Many sources of pollution have been brought under reasonable control, and various signs of recovery are evident. The principal problem remaining to be tackled is agricultural runoff from a vast drainage area, which includes large portions of both Pennsylvania and New York

---

PRECEDING PAGES: *Delmarva's brackish marshes and fields serve as the principal wintering grounds for the eastern population of Canada geese.*

states. Still, the Bay is at least a partial success story in what is now termed ecosystem management.

The Bay may be the single most dominant feature of this region, but the natural riches of coastal plain and piedmont are noteworthy in themselves. From White Clay and Brandywine creeks in the north to the Great Dismal Swamp, the Blue Ridge Parkway, and the North Carolina mountains in the south, interesting and wonderful nature abounds. On Maryland's Eastern Shore, the brown-headed nuthatch and loblolly pine exist at their northernmost limit. As we move southward into Virginia, the forest takes on a palpably lusher character. In the higher elevations, nurtured by substantial moisture, various kinds of rhododendrons and azaleas abound, and conditions in the North Carolina mountains support an amazing diversity of trees (130 species) and salamanders (27 species).

This region is also a great haven for birdlife. Waterfowl—swans, geese, and various ducks—are major features of the Bay and the Tidewater areas, and they share their habitat with great blue herons, bald eagles, ospreys, and many other water-oriented birds.

ABOVE: *Except for portions of Delmarva's eastern shore, the loblolly pine grows no farther north than the Potomac River.*

Farther north, Delaware Bay provides a great staging area from which to watch the spectacle of migrating shorebirds. Their spring migration coincides with the spawning cycle of Delaware Bay's horseshoe crabs—primordial creatures, with blood literally blue, a species that has survived virtually unchanged for hundreds of millions of years. The birds gorge on the horseshoe crabs' eggs, replenishing their fat reserves for the remainder of their journey.

OVERLEAF: *In early spring the brilliant white blossoms of the shadbush light up the shores of the Potomac River near Washington, D.C.*

A number of wildlife refuges and state parks dot the region, providing the opportunity for viewing our northernmost bald cypress swamps; carnivorous plants such as the Venus's-flytrap; fossils eroding out of Calvert Cliffs; the Virginia barrier islands; the outer banks and brown pelicans; the New River (actually one of America's oldest); and, at 1.1 billion years old, one of the world's most ancient peaks: Grandfather Mountain, highest point in the Blue Ridge.

Around the nation's capital, there are multiple opportunities to experience nature, thanks to visionaries such as U.S. Supreme Court Justice William O. Douglas, who had the foresight to protect the Chesapeake and Ohio Canal. On Roosevelt Island, site of a famous presidential skinny dip, native plants and migratory birds are within sight (and, unfortunately for the birds, hearing) of Washington's National Airport. At Black Pond, beavers go about their business oblivious to governmental stirring only a dozen miles away. Prothonotary warblers pass through in the spring, and every 13 years the cicadas erupt in a great spectacle that bemuses and/or terrifies newcomers to the area. A careful and patient hunt may be rewarded with a glimpse of wild turkeys or even the pale green of a luna moth, and June evenings are bespangled with fireflies, each kind with its own semaphore.

As I wrote this introduction from the heart of this region, a hermit thrush outside my window cocked an eye and gave me a vernal glance—as if to say, Nature is right here.... What are you waiting for?

—*Thomas E. Lovejoy*
Counselor to the Secretary for
Biodiversity and Environmental Affairs,
SMITHSONIAN INSTITUTION

LEFT: *Soaring over the rolling hills of North Carolina's piedmont, the craggy eminence of billion-year-old, 5,964-foot-tall Grandfather Mountain rises higher than any other Blue Ridge peak.*

xvii

ATLANTIC COAST AND BLUE RIDGE

25   0   25   50 Miles

25   0   25   50 Kilometers

WEST

VIRGINIA

Alleghe

KENTUCKY

APPALACHIAN

Blue Ridge Mts

81

TENNESSEE

Winston
Salem

40

Smoky Mountains

BLUE RIDGE PARKWAY

40   77

75

85

Asheville

19

221

64

Great

Charlot

64

85

GEORGIA

SOUTH
CAROLINA

1

INTRODUCTION:
THE ATLANTIC COAST
AND BLUE RIDGE

Springtime races into the Mid-Atlantic like a wildfire burning out of control. The first lick of color begins as small crocuses push aside winter's brown detritus and open their purple petals. Soon after, spring spreads quickly, torching forsythia bushes and groves of daffodils in electric yellow—slivers of sunshine fallen from the sky.

Alerted by the clarion call of spring, thousands of Canada geese leave their winter haunts on the shores of the Chesapeake Bay, heading north in large, noisy flocks. Inland, on the piedmont, meadows and river floodplains grow thick with countless bluebells, tiny wildflowers that droop with clusters of baby blue blossoms. Far to the west, in the Appalachian Mountains, legions of rhododendron and mountain laurel bushes produce large ripe buds, which will soon erupt into lavender, pink, and white flowers.

Springtime reveals itself across Delaware, Maryland, Virginia, and North Carolina in an almost unlimited number of guises, inspired by the diverse range of habitats, topographies, and climates that characterize this region. All within a day's drive of Washington, D.C., are many of the East Coast's premier natural features: Assateague, Chincoteague, the Virginia Coast Reserve, and the Outer Banks represent the most beautiful, longest, and relatively unspoiled examples of barrier island habitat in the East; the Chesapeake Bay is North America's largest and most productive estuary; many of North America's largest remaining tracts of virgin deciduous woodlands are found in the Great Smoky Mountains National Park and nearby national forests; at 6,684 feet, Mount Mitchell rises higher than any mountain east of South Dakota's Black Hills; and the 469-mile-long Blue Ridge Parkway connecting two of the country's most popular national parks, Shenandoah and Great Smoky Mountains, remains one of the world's longest and highest scenic highways.

There is such diversity within the Mid-Atlantic region that it's possible to

PRECEDING PAGES: *With a raucous cacophony, hundreds of ring-billed and herring gulls take flight over Delaware Bay near Port Mahon. These omnivorous scavengers have thrived in humanity's presence.*

sample just about every habitat that exists along the length of the eastern seaboard. Not only is the region a meeting ground of northern and southern species, but, stretching from west to east, it includes three exceedingly different physical provinces. Each of these provinces—the montane, piedmont, and coastal plain—have distinct topographical and biotic personalities, forged by variations in geology, climate, soil, human impact, and many other factors.

In all the Mid-Atlantic states except Delaware, which is entirely within the coastal plain, the montane region begins at or near the eastern continental divide, which separates the watersheds of the Gulf of Mexico and the Atlantic Ocean. The montane is a relatively thin sliver of rugged topography running southwest from Maryland's panhandle through the western regions of Virginia and North Carolina and bordering the mountain states of West Virginia, Kentucky, and Tennessee. These are the Appalachians, mountains once as tall as the Rockies but carved and muted by hundreds of millions of years of weathering and erosion. Long ago, this chain arose from titanic geothermal activities within the earth and the collision of land masses caused by continental drift.

In the northern section of the montane Mid-Atlantic, trails thread along the narrow crests of ridges, the mountainsides falling away steeply on either side. In the valleys between the ridges, which run from southwest to northeast, are peculiar formations of weathered limestone known as karst features. Above the ground arise a series of chimneylike pillars, numerous sinkholes, and a natural bridge arching high over a river gorge. Below the surface are large caverns, alien worlds filled with immense chambers, contorted rock formations, and miles of sinuous passageways. Even today, some of these caverns have not been fully explored.

Spreading from southern Virginia down through North Carolina are the southern Appalachians, a tangle of rugged ridges with broader peaks than those to the north. These are the great southern balds. Here, the mountains often soar higher than 6,000 feet but do so with rounded features. Capping many of these summits are mysterious open areas known as grass and heath balds and deep green stands of spruce and fir trees. On the flanks are moist cove forests—steep, vegetation-clogged ravines that rarely see the sun's direct rays or human footsteps.

The Blue Ridge Mountains, the easternmost fringes of the Appalachians, draw the boundary between the montane and the adjacent province, the piedmont. From this ridgeline the piedmont stretches eastward as far as the eye can see, an ocean of rolling hills, agricultural fields, and an occasional mountainous rise. These odd blips in the otherwise uniform piedmont plain are monadnocks, small, localized areas that have appeared not because of geological upthrusting but because they are partially composed of erosion-resistant rock and have withstood weathering better than the surrounding area.

The piedmont, or "foot of the mountain," is sandwiched between the mountains and the coastal plain and accounts for much of the total area of the Mid-Atlantic region. Of the three provinces, the piedmont—with its pleasant rolling hills—has suffered the most from human occupation. Three centuries of liberal ax-wielding, development, and cultivation have left few pockets of undisturbed habitat.

Opportunities to explore the natural world here lie in the edge communities, borders between second-growth forests and meadows or lakes, where bird and mammal life flourishes. Or they are found in forgotten environments, such as Maryland's Soldiers Delight, serpentine barrens where tenacious prairie flowers grow on broken beds of rock near strangely twisted blackjack oaks. Serendipity has also saved some of the thin floodplain corridors along the major rivers that cut southeast across the piedmont. Here, wildflowers grow in the rich alluvial soils, and songbirds stop for a rest while using these rivers as migratory corridors.

The piedmont rivers often drop through a series of rapids at the fall line, the zone where the hard metamorphic rocks of the piedmont covered by surface soil give way to the unconsolidated sediments of the coastal plain province. In the coastal plain, the rivers undergo sudden personality changes, growing slower and wider as they cut through sand, clay, and gravel. Nearing the sea, many of these rivers become estuaries, feeling the wash of freshwater at one end and the tidal pulse of salt water at the other.

In the Mid-Atlantic region, the low-lying coastal plain is defined by water and wetlands—not only by rivers and estuaries but also by salt and brackish marshes, cypress swamps, and shallow lagoons behind thin barrier islands. This is a land of tall marsh grasses, muskrats, bald eagles, and ospreys. In its distant past, the coastal plain was submerged by a series of shallow seas that helped deposit many of the sediments that now form the sandy

RIGHT: *Over the eons, North Carolina's hard Pilot Rock, a monadnock, resisted erosion as the surrounding piedmont weathered down.*
OVERLEAF: *Marshlands, such as this one near Delaware's Woodland Beach, are among the region's richest—and least understood—habitats.*

ABOVE: *A great egret perches in a loblolly pine. Plume hunters once devastated the population of these herons, which have made a strong recovery.*
RIGHT: *At Carolina Beach State Park, delicate white camas flowers are silhouetted against the dark tangle of a pocosin, a dense regional shrub bog.*

soils of the province. Large sharks' teeth and whale vertebrae, remains of these ancient times, erode out of river bluffs on Virginia's York River and cliff faces along the western shore of the Chesapeake Bay.

The Chesapeake Bay dominates the northern end of the coastal plain, its shores so interrupted by coves, creeks, and river mouths that its shoreline measures nearly three times that of the entire California coast. Bordering the bay and its creeks are marshes that are among the richest habitats in North America, each acre generating more than two times the organic material produced by an equivalent parcel of cultivated land. Flocking to these wetlands are some of the continent's most spectacular wading birds—herons, ibis, and egrets. Here, one might glimpse the elegant, four-foot-tall profile of the princely great blue heron, its grayish blue feathers lightly rippling in the wind as it surveys its marshy domain.

In the southern end of the coastal plain are the remains of once-vast wetlands: the Great Dismal Swamp, straddling the Virginia–North Carolina border, and North Carolina's Green Swamp. Each is filled with the primordial-looking shapes of the bald cypress tree, recognizable by the bizarre swell of its lower trunk and the profusion of knobby "knees" in the water around it. Not far away are other coastal plain wetlands, most notably the nearly impenetrable shrub bogs known as pocosins, one of the rarest and least understood wetland habitats in the East. On the fringes of the pocosins it is possible to find the Venus's-flytrap, a carnivorous plant that grows naturally nowhere else in the world. Peppering the southern coastal plain are Carolina bay lakes, pondlike depressions often filled with glade and swamp plants. All Carolina bays are elliptical or circular and line up along a northwest-southeast axis, suggesting a common origin, and although no theory has adequately explained these puzzling topo-

ABOVE: *Showy amanita mushrooms (left), part of a large, sometimes deadly family, brighten North Carolina's Raven Rock State Park. A song sparrow (right) blends into the brown reeds of a salt marsh.*

graphical features, several interesting ideas about their origin include wind erosion or meteorite impact.

Protecting both the northern and southern coastline from the fury of the Atlantic are a series of barrier islands, dynamic spits of sand that absorb the impact of storms, wind, and the pounding of waves and tides. Remarkably, the Outer Banks of North Carolina push out as much as 25 miles from the mainland, a slight spit of land that seems on the verge of being swallowed by the vast presence of the ocean. It is, paradoxically, the tenuous and ever-adapting quality of the barrier island that enables it to survive where the strongest human-made seawall would eventually fail.

Another curious aspect of the Mid-Atlantic region, one that contributes to its diversity of life-forms, is its position as a kind of biological Mason-Dixon line. No other area on the eastern seaboard contains so many northern and southern species at the extremes of their natural ranges. Part of this mixing has to do with the region's temperate climate. Other reasons provide more particular explanations. Along the shore warm waters from the south flow north up along the Atlantic coast to North Carolina, tempering the climate and enabling southern plant species such as palms to reach their northern limits here. In the cooler climate of the mountains, examples of boreal Canadian forests and cranberry bogs exist, the remains of northern plant communities pushed south by the advancing glaciers during the ice ages. Consequently, it's possible to wander in a cool grove of spruce and Fraser fir

Above: *Rare and spectacular, the pink lady's slipper (left) grows on a dry forest floor. A young red fox kit (right) nibbles on a fish head left on the beach at Delaware's Bombay Hook National Wildlife Refuge.*

trees and spot a snow bunting, a finch from arctic regions, then drive several hundred miles east (not south) and find a deep swamp where alligators live among cypress trees hung with Spanish moss.

Perhaps the Mid-Atlantic's most interesting nature experiences involve stalking the often dramatic crossover points between the physical provinces, northern and southern species, and the seasons. A well-timed hike up Virginia's Old Rag Mountain in late summer, for instance, begins amid the dense foliage of summer but crosses over to the crisp winds and changing foliage of fall near the top. A bike ride along Maryland's Chesapeake and Ohio Canal east from Cumberland toward Washington, D.C., reveals the striking change in the Potomac as it transforms from a lively piedmont river into a lazy coastal plain river after crossing the fall line.

By tracking the points where changeover occurs within this diverse region, the complex interrelationships between habitat, geology, the seasons, and climate become clearer. Study them, and the harmony that exists in the natural world verges on the magical. A kind of beauty emerges that transcends—and enhances—the excitement of discovering a pink lady's slipper or stumbling on a breathtaking view.

As summer wanes in the mountains, the skies grow stormy and cloudy and are filled with the silhouettes of hawks heading south. The uniform green cover of the mountainside transforms into splotches of brilliant reds, yellows, and oranges. Another dramatic change in the Mid-Atlantic has taken place and is here to savor.

13

MARYLAND · WASHINGTON DC

INTERIOR MARYLAND AND WASHINGTON, D.C.

Every warm weekend morning in suburban Maryland, a line of cars topped with large, cigar-shaped kayaks pulls into a dusty parking lot several miles south of Great Falls and a short walk from the Potomac River. The kayaks are transferred to shoulders, carried over the C & O Canal, down a steep embankment, and launched into the Potomac. Heading downstream, the kayakers reach Mather Gorge, where they snake into eddies, shoot by vertical gneiss and schist cliffs, and challenge the rushing white water. This slice of wilderness is a kayaker's dream.

Remarkably, this area is little more than a dozen miles from Washington, D.C.—and it represents some of the most challenging white water to be found near a major metropolitan area along the entire length of the East Coast. Despite the closeness of a large city and the proliferation of suburbs, a number of natural sites exist within a short drive from the district. For those willing to push farther afield, Maryland's wide range of topographies embrace numerous habitats and life-forms.

This chapter covers the entire state of Maryland except for the Eastern Shore (discussed in the following chapter). The route begins in the deciduous hardwood forests atop Maryland's highest peak, 3,360-foot-tall

PRECEDING PAGES: *Mule-drawn boats provide tourist excursions on the C & O Canal and towpath, a haven for hikers, bikers, and birders.*
LEFT: *Defining Maryland's southern border, the Potomac River curls below the heights of Green Ridge State Forest in the state's panhandle.*

Hoyes Knob on Backbone Mountain, on the westernmost border of the state, then traverses the state and ends at the western shore of the Chesapeake Bay. Moving from west to east, a series of five distinct physiographic provinces define Maryland's topography, helping to account for the state's wide diversity of habitats and life-forms. Maryland's narrow panhandle stretches 95 miles from the West Virginia border east to Hagerstown, cutting across the Appalachian Plateau province and the ridge and valley province. East from Hagerstown, the state swells in size, encompassing Maryland's narrow mountain ridges before widening even farther to the piedmont and, finally, the coastal plain.

One of the more interesting natural features of the region is a 185-mile-long linear preserve, the Chesapeake and Ohio Canal National Historical Park. Beginning in Cumberland, deep in Maryland's panhandle, the Chesapeake and Ohio (C & O) Canal shadows the Potomac as it flows east, defining the state's southern border with West Virginia and Virginia. With its wide, dirt towpath and many access points, the canal provides opportunities for scores of visits, from short walks to smell the spring air and hear the sweet call of migrating songbirds, to longer, overnight bicycling expeditions on which the traveler can experience the many guises of the Potomac on its long journey from the mountains to the coastal plain. Gone from this green corridor are some of the larger woodland denizens found in earlier times—elk, wolf, and mountain lion—but others appear with regularity: the swift red fox, flocks of wild turkeys that take off like cannon shot, and slider turtles sunbathing on logs.

The driving route picks up Route 219 near Backbone Mountain in the southwesternmost tip of the panhandle, heading north until it reaches Interstate 68 at Keysers Ridge. Along the way are examples of subarctic peat bogs, peculiar relict communities left during the last ice age, with carnivorous plants and sphagnum moss. The route then heads east along I-68 (formerly Routes 40 and 48) through the water gap at Cumberland, past Green Ridge State Forest with its dry forests, high ridges, and desert-like shale barrens to Sideling Hill, a highway excavation that exposes 850 million years of geologic history.

From Hancock, the route continues east along Route 70 past Hagerstown, crossing the Blue Ridge, the easternmost expression of the

---

OVERLEAF: *Sounding their distinctive "konk-ka-reee" cry and flashing brightly colored epaulets, a winter flock of noisy red-winged blackbirds cavort at Maryland's Blackwater National Wildlife Refuge.*

Appalachian Mountains in Maryland. It continues south on Interstates 70 and 270 to Washington, D.C., passing a number of bird-filled preserves along the Potomac. From the capital city, the driving route goes south on Route 5 toward southern Maryland, picking up Routes 301, 234, 238, and 5 on the way south to Point Lookout. This route passes by the large wetlands of Zekiah Swamp and near the wide mouths of the marsh-lined Nanjemoy Creek and Wicomico River.

ABOVE: *The exposed branches of a red maple make a perfect perch for the male northern cardinal, a common, vivid red songbird, to broadcast forth his loud, throaty whistle.*

RIGHT: *Each fall the rocky banks of the Youghiogheny River in Swallow Falls State Park turn electric with the fluorescent colors of red maples and white oaks.*

From Point Lookout, the western shore's southernmost tip, our course heads north on Routes 235, 2 and 4, and 301, generally paralleling the Chesapeake Bay, past tall eroding cliffs that reveal the fossil remains of ancient sea creatures. Not far from these cliffs, Hellen Creek Hemlock Preserve protects the southernmost stand of eastern hemlock on the coastal plain, a species far more prevalent to the west and north. Yet just a few miles away, at Battle Creek Cypress Swamp Sanctuary, is a sight one would expect far to the south: a swamp filled with towering bald cypress trees, each supporting curious clumps of offshoots known as knees. Maryland's interesting mix of southern and northern species can be explained by climate changes and the movement of a great continental glacier 50,000 years ago. As the climate cooled and the ice sheet crept southward to Pennsylvania, northern plants, such as larch, spruce, mountain holly, and wild raspberry moved south, preceding the glacier. When the ice sheet retreated thousands of years later and the climate warmed up, southern plants such as magnolia, papaw, bald cypress, and tulip poplar moved north. Remains of both population shifts are represented in Maryland today.

The route then continues north past Annapolis to Baltimore. Off a fast-food-outlet-choked highway northwest of Baltimore is a new park, Soldiers Delight Natural Environment Area, that encompasses a rare mi-

croenvironment known as a serpentine barren. It's not immediately apparent that the desertlike grassland underlain by broken rock is anything worth protecting. Once this area was considered so unremarkable that kids raced motorcycles here, and others used it as a trash dump. A few moments spent walking these grasslands, however, reveal a strange and beautiful world. Small prairie flowers cling tenaciously to life on a bed of broken rock. A rare fringed gentian might be in bloom, its hooded petals an eye-catching hue of regal purple. On the edges of the barren grasslands, nutrient-deprived blackjack oaks curl in arthritic poses, while Virginia pines bend in gravity-defying directions—extraordinary examples of how life-forms adapt to their environment.

The route continues north from Baltimore on Interstate 95 up to the Susquehanna River and the head of the bay. Draining a huge area extending well into New York State, the Susquehanna pours forth its large volume of water into the Chesapeake, the world's most productive estuary.

MARYLAND'S PANHANDLE: THE APPALACHIAN PLATEAU

The eastern continental divide runs across the western tip of Maryland, passing through Hoyes Knob on Backbone Mountain, Maryland's highest point. Snow and rain falling on the western slope of Hoyes Knob drain into the Youghiogheny River, which flows north through Maryland for more than 50 miles before turning west to the Mississippi basin and on to the Gulf of Mexico. Water falling on the mountain's eastern slope awaits a different destiny: It drains into the north branch of the Potomac, which heads east, defining Maryland's border first with West Virginia and then Virginia as it flows through Washington, D.C., and on toward the Chesapeake Bay and the Atlantic Ocean.

Although these rivers pass several miles from one another, they couldn't be more unalike. The Potomac in its long leisurely passage east is far more characteristic of Maryland's waters than the Youghiogheny is. On its short, tempestuous journey through the Appalachian Plateau of Maryland, the Youghiogheny, known locally as the Yock, runs through country that's far different from that found in most of the state—rugged mountains, high elevation, northern hardwood and coniferous forests, and pockets of unusual habitats, such as the mountain peatland, more characteristic of West Virginia than Maryland. The white-water stretches of the powerful Youghiogheny reflect this ruggedness.

Northbound Route 219 provides access to **Swallow Falls State Park❖**, one of the best places to see the Youghiogheny up close. Located eight miles northwest from Oakland on Herrington Manor Road in Maryland's oldest state forest, **Garrett State Forest❖,** Swallow Falls contains one of the state's most spectacular hikes: a one-mile-long trail that winds past both the cascading drop of Swallow Falls at the Youghiogheny and the 54-foot single drop of Muddy Falls on Muddy Creek, a tributary of the Youghiogheny. In places the cliff-shaded trail grows cool, damp, and primordial; ferns and mosses abound. On the faces of some fallen boulders are fossilized remnants of ancient fernlike plants, such as horsetail and club moss. The trail passes through a 40-acre grove of old-growth hemlock and white pine estimated to be 200 to 300 years old.

Swallow Falls probably earned its name from the thousands of cliff swallows that once inhabited Swallow Rock, a weathered pillar that stands on the edge of the Youghiogheny near the falls. Parking is limited, filling quickly on summer weekends, but those with mountain bikes can ride in from **Herrington Manor State Park❖,** three miles south of Swallow Falls on Herrington Manor Road. A connector trail between the two parks follows an old tramway line through hardwood forests, creating a leisurely 11-mile round-trip bike ride to the falls and

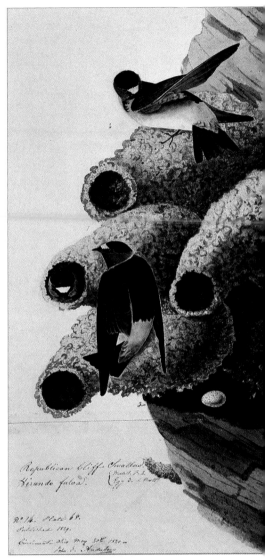

ABOVE: *In an 1820 watercolor, John J. Audubon captured cliff swallows frolicking near and sitting in their distinctive mud nests. Today these slight birds most often build their nests under bridges or barn eaves.*

25

back. Activity at Herrington Manor centers around an artificial lake, though the park does maintain six miles of hiking trails, which are groomed for cross-country skiing in winter.

The Youghiogheny River provides some of the East's best—and most challenging—white-water rafting. The water in this section is dam-released: A nearby utility company sends water through pipes to a spot two miles north of Swallow Falls, usually twice a week. On dry summer days before the dam is released, there are still spots where a person can stand. But in the springtime, when the water is running, the Youghiogheny turns

fierce. Near Sang Run at Bastard Falls, white water plummets at a rate of 116 feet per mile through class IV and V rapids with names like Meat Cleaver, Double Pencil Sharpener, and Powerful Popper. A number of area outfitters offer rafting trips.

Aside from the adrenaline rush, a rafting trip offers the best way to see some of the most pristine forest left in Maryland. These waters are the last haven for such animals as the hellbender, a rare, aquatic salamander that sometimes reaches 29 inches in length and has a flattened, oarlike tail. Lucky kayakers may see one sunning on rocks in or along the river. Hellbenders have been known to live for 55 years in captivity, but pollution has virtually extirpated this creature from the state's waters.

ABOVE: *Golden spore capsules of star moss rise above a tangle of sphagnum, grasses, and mushrooms in Cranesville Swamp Nature Preserve.*
RIGHT: *The Cranesville preserve is also home to the skunk cabbage, which exudes a rank odor when its leaves are bruised.*

One mile south of Swallow Falls is the mouth of Deep Creek, which flows east to Deep Creek Lake, which Route 24 crosses north of Thayerville. Farther downstream, the creek's waters were dammed in 1924 for hydroelectricity, creating six-square-mile Deep Creek Lake, Maryland's largest lake. The lake is accessible at **Deep Creek Lake State Park❖** on its northwestern shore, northeast from Route 219 at Thayerville. Best avoided during the warmer months, when crowds of teenagers throng the passel of vacation cottages lining its shores, Deep Creek Lake makes a worthwhile detour between November and April, when migratory loons, grebes, and other waterfowl, including American

wigeon, teal, pintail, and mergansers, are much in evidence. The state park is headquarters for the Deep Creek Lake Recreation Area, which includes the corridor surrounding the Youghiogheny.

Back on the western side of the Youghiogheny toward the West Virginia border, Herrington Manor Road, off Route 219, continues north past Swallow Falls State Park toward one of western Maryland's most unusual habitats: the peat bog. Off Cranesville Road is the **Cranesville Swamp Nature Preserve❖,** a Nature Conservancy sanctuary and the source of Muddy Creek, which runs into the Youghiogheny near Swallow Falls. Walking along the 1,500-foot-long boardwalk into the bog is like traveling back in time 18,000 years to the Ice Age, when vast ice sheets covered large portions of North America and northern plant species crept far south of their normal range. Once the glaciers retreated north as the climate changed, all but a handful of these plants disappeared. At Cranesville and several other bogs in western Maryland, special cold microclimates known as frost pockets sustain relict communities of northern forest and bog. These pockets occur in high-altitude depressions where cold air sinks and is trapped.

Larch, a deciduous conifer far more common up north in Canada and Alaska, lives here, the farthest southern limit of the species. Also found here are other northern plant species such as white-tufted cotton grass, cranberry, and the small, round-leaved sundew, an insectivorous plant that traps insects with sticky fluid it exudes from special glands.

The peat bog imposes its own extreme conditions on the flora. The compacted, partially decomposed plant remains, or peat, form an acidic and nutrient-poor base. Continually wet from poor drainage, these conditions create a habitat hostile to most trees. Sphagnum moss, sedge meadows, shrub swamps, and stands of conifers dominate this world. (Sadly, nearly 50 percent of western Maryland's peat bogs have been destroyed, mostly because of strip mining for coal.)

Maryland's largest bog, the **Glades❖,** is located north of Deep Creek Lake, two miles west of Bittinger off Route 495 (or five miles east of Route 219 at McHenry), at the headwaters of the North Branch of the Casselman River. Access to the Glades, a Nature Conservancy preserve, is limited. Call ahead for information about possible visits. Few tall shrubs or trees interrupt this wide-open bog land, kept wet mostly by rainfall. An especially good time to visit is in late August and September, when the white tufts of cotton grass contrast richly with the green and scarlet colors of the bog. Not only are the unusual plants of this bog interesting—the cranberry, carnivorous bladderwort, and the bog club moss are examples—but large mammals such as black bears and bobcats frequent the area, building their dens nearby. Wild turkeys often bring their young to the open, sandy edges of the bog to feast on grasshoppers. Around the cranberry plants are bog copper butterflies, first discovered in Maryland at this site. The bog copper caterpillar feeds only on cranberry leaves.

Another notable bog is located in the northeastern corner of Garrett County, east on I-68, then north on Route 546 from the Frostburg exit. Sitting in a shallow depression between Big and Little Savage mountains, **Finzel Swamp❖,** another Nature Conservancy preserve, is an excellent example of a shrub swamp peatland, covered almost entirely in a dense thicket of speckled alder, winterberry, wild raisin, and great laurel. Good views of the swamp and its resident flora are available from a short dirt road running across the southern tip of the preserve. Of particular note are the larches and the wild calla herb—one of the few species of calla found in western Maryland but not in nearby West Virginia. Rare this far south, wild calla has large, heart-shaped, glossy green leaves; it produces a white flower in the spring and a large cluster of red berries in the summer. Northern waterthrushes and alder flycatchers nest in the dense shrub of the swamp, and purple finches are found in the scattered clumps of conifers.

Maryland's largest state forest, **Savage River State Forest❖,** covers much of the eastern area of Garrett County south of I-68 and is a strategic watershed surrounding the Savage River Dam. Forty-six miles of trails wind through deeply cut ridges, thickets of rhododendron, and forests of hickory and red and white oak, and along mountain ridges with rocky outcrops—rugged country for Maryland. The 17-mile-long Big Savage Mountain Trail traverses the crest of the mountain, offering wonderful views. It runs from the Savage River Dam to the vicinity of I-68 and makes the basis of a good backpacking trip. At the northern end of the forest is **New Germany State Park❖,** renowned for cross-country ski trails in the winter, where one can glide in solitude amid a forest of deep green conifers.

To the south of New Germany, **Big Run State Park❖** surrounds the 350-acre Savage River Reservoir, a good spot for catching rainbow trout and smallmouth bass. Outtake from the reservoir converts this portion of the Savage River into a world-class white-water kayaking course.

To the east of Savage River Reservoir, off Route 36 from the Midland exit at I-68, or via Route 657 to Route 36, **Dan's Mountain Wildlife Management Area❖** is a mountainous hardwood forest of more than 8,000 acres with 15 miles of dirt roads. Although the area is managed primarily for hunting, a visit to 2,898-foot-tall **Dan's Rock,** just outside the

ABOVE: *Delicate flowers crowd the leafless branches of the eastern red-bud in early spring, turning the understory of Rocky Gap State Park*

preserve, provides long vistas to the east. It used to be a popular site for hawk hunting, but, fortunately, hunting these birds of prey is now illegal. Hawk watchers, though, continue to visit the rocky outcrop to search the skies for hawks on fall days. Other avian residents include golden-winged warblers and mourning warblers.

At Cumberland, western Maryland's largest town, Wills Creek has eroded a deep gorge known as the Narrows, forming a natural break, or water gap, in the Appalachian Mountains. From Lover's Leap the cliffs drop 800 feet to the water. I-68 passes through the **Cumberland Gap.** In the nineteenth century, Cumberland served as the eastern terminus of the Cumberland Road and the western terminus of the Chesapeake and Ohio Canal, a transfer point for coal and other materials shuttling between the Ohio Valley and the Atlantic coast.

Twelve miles east of Cumberland on I-68, **Rocky Gap State Park❖** sits in a natural saddle between Martin's Mountain to the east and Evitts Mountain to the west. In this designated wilderness are 14 miles of trails and 243-acre Lake Habeeb, which attracts many waterfowl during migration. From a small wharf and the paved Touch of Nature Trail, which runs along the lake's western edge, it is possible to glimpse mallard, common loons, grebes, blue-winged teal, ring-necked ducks, mergansers, and a

pink with color. Often planted as an ornamental, the small, slender tree occurs naturally along moist slopes and stream bottoms.

host of other avian visitors—birds more usually seen on the Chesapeake Bay, well to the east. Perhaps the most spectacular feature of the park is Rocky Gap Run, which flows through a deep, mile-long valley faced at places with steep cliffs, a testament to the erosive powers of water. The valley serves as a nesting site for ravens. No trails wind along Rocky Gap Run, but a rock scramble is possible for the adventurous, starting out from where Rocky Gap Road crosses the river on a small bridge.

MARYLAND'S PANHANDLE: RIDGE AND VALLEY PROVINCE

The Appalachian Plateau, Maryland's westernmost physiographic province, ends just west of Cumberland, turning into the ridge and valley province, which continues east to about Hagerstown. Because it is in the rain shadow of the Appalachian Plateau, this area is the driest in the state. One extreme example of this phenomenon, helped by particular soil conditions, is the microenvironment known as the shale barren, the closest thing to a desert in Maryland. Several good examples exist in Maryland's second-largest state forest, **Green Ridge State Forest❖**, 20 miles east of Cumberland off I-68.

Most often found on steep, south-facing slopes undercut by a stream or river (such as the Potomac), the shale barrens consist of exposed beds of

ABOVE: *In Maryland's Green Ridge State Forest, pussytoes, a hardy wildflower whose clusters resemble a cat's paw, survives in a dry shale barren, formed from deposits left 400 million years ago.*
RIGHT: *Seven oak species and a complement of red and sugar maples guarantee a brilliant fall spectacle at Green Ridge State Forest.*

Devonian shale, a dark, flaky rock that holds little water and grows very hot on sunny days. Consequently, the barrens areas attract a tenacious group of fleshy-stemmed, spiny, and narrow-leaved plants with deep roots, such as evening primrose, shale ragwort, and Kate's mountain clover. Few bushes or shrubs grow, but Virginia pine, various oaks, shagbark hickory, and black locust trees are evident. Although a shale barren might not look like much at first view, a careful observer will begin to realize how delicate the interplay of plant and animal life is in this xeric, or dry, habitat. Scrounging through the shale talus for a meal of insects may be a five-lined skink (a striped brown lizard). Breeding males have striking red-orange heads, while juveniles often possess bright blue tails. Other animals found here are timber rattlesnakes, wood turtles, pine and prairie warblers, white-eyed vireos, and Carolina wrens.

The 27-mile **Green Ridge Trail** hugs one of the narrow ridges found throughout the state forest, providing clear vistas of the banks of the Potomac River as it makes a number of snakelike bends. The trail begins near the Pennsylvania border and works south all the way to the towpath at the C & O Canal. For the less active, Green Ridge Road also traverses the ridgetop, and a series of other back roads cut through the forest, where bird-watchers can hear the drumming of a grouse or the call of a wild turkey if they leave their windows open and drive slowly. On Carroll Road, **Point Lookout** provides excellent views of the Potomac from 400 feet above. The multitude of dirt roads traversing the state forest are open to

mountain bikers—several organized races are held here each year.

The Green Ridge Trail combined with the C & O Canal towpath makes an enjoyable 45-mile circuit. It passes through the **Paw Paw Tunnel**, a feat of determined engineering grit when it was built between 1836 and 1850. To avoid a 6-mile bend in the river, the canal builders hewed this 3,118-foot-long tunnel through the solid rock of a small mountain. A trail leads over the top of the tunnel for views of the Potomac and the Paw Paw bends.

Near the bends, the Potomac heads to the northeast, bringing the Maryland–West Virginia border north until it nearly touches Pennsylvania at Hancock. A half dozen miles before I-68 hits Hancock it runs through the **Sideling Hill Cut❖**, a 340-foot-deep excavation created for the highway, which exposes 850 feet of rock face. At this unusual park, the geology of the ridge and valley physiographic province unfolds graphically from vantages at the visitor center and a suspension bridge that crosses the highway. Exhibits explain that sediments laid 330 to 345 million years ago were later buckled into tight folds by geologic forces. The characteristic topography of the area formed as erosion ate away areas underlain by soluble limestone and erodible shale to create valleys, while the ridge areas were left intact because they were capped with erosion-resistant sandstone.

While at the cut, take a walk along Sideling Hill Creek into the **Sideling Hill Wildlife Management Area❖**, one of the best places in Maryland to see wild turkeys. Wildflowers bloom here in the spring, including the rare crested iris with its lavender petals.

In the valleys of central Maryland, the limestone foundations create what is known as karst topography: the caves, sinkholes, haystack hills, and bold cliffs that result when limestone weathers and dissolves. An example of a karst feature in Maryland is **Crystal Grottoes Caverns❖**, located two miles south of Boonsboro on Route 34, well to the east of Hancock on I-70. The only commercial cave operation of its kind in Maryland, these caverns feature small, twisting passages that lead visitors past formations resembling horse blankets hanging in disarray from the ceiling.

The **Appalachian National Scenic Trail❖**, the interstate trail that follows the Appalachian Mountains from Maine south to Georgia, crosses I-70 not far from Boonsboro. In Maryland, most of the trail lies in **South Mountain State Park❖**, a narrow, 41-mile-long preserve that runs along the generally north-south crest of South Mountain Ridge from the Pennsylvania-Maryland border in the north to Harpers Ferry in the south. On the western fringe of the piedmont, South Mountain and, to the northeast, Catoctin Mountain comprise the Maryland portion of the Blue Ridge Mountains, the easternmost ridge system of the Appalachian Mountain chain. On South Mountain, wind-blown outcrops formed by erosion-resistant quartz, known as Weaverton quartzite, offer views of the Hagerstown Valley to the west. The mountain descends from 2,000 feet at the Pennsylvania border to 200 feet at the West Virginia border east of Harpers Ferry.

Harpers Ferry National Historical Park❖, reached by taking I-70 east, then Route 340 southwest from Frederick, is worth visiting. Here, the Shenandoah River, approaching from the southwest, adds its great volume to the Potomac. In the middle of the V formed by the two rivers sits Harpers Ferry, most famous for the rebellion of antislavery crusader John Brown before the Civil War. Maryland Heights, some 1,000 feet above the Potomac atop Elk Ridge, has the best views of the area. The Grant Conway Trail ascends Maryland Heights and continues up to the ridge where a Civil War–era stone fort and several batteries are visible.

At the first exit off Route 340 northeast of Harpers Ferry, Route 67 leads north to Rohrersville and **Mount Briar Wetlands Preserve❖,** a tiny jewel of a wetland. Boardwalks, interrupted by three observation towers, traverse the area for a length of eight football fields. Unusual insects, such as the leaf moth, which camouflages itself as a fallen leaf, are found here.

Northeast of this area, off Route 15 out of Frederick, lie Catoctin Mountain, the easternmost extension of the Blue Ridge in Maryland, and a number of great hiking spots. **Catoctin Mountain Park❖** and its contiguous neighbors **Cunningham Falls State Park❖** and **Gambrill State Park❖** occupy the mountain, a broad, long, flat-topped ridge like South Mountain. Catoctin is home to **Camp David,** the presidential retreat. On the ridge of Catoctin are outcrops of Catoctin greenstone, a metamorphic rock also known as metabasalt, which resulted from a lava flow some 600 million years ago. In Catoctin Mountain Park, trails lead high up to rock ledges, most notably **Chimney Rock** and **Wolf Rock,** with good vistas of nearby mountains and the piedmont to the east. These rock ledges contain fissure caves—narrow, deep trenches created by erosion.

Gambrill State Park, the southernmost of the Catoctin Mountain parks, offers five miles of hiking trails, including the **Lost Chestnut Trail,** a self-guided nature trail. From the overlook atop 1,600-foot-tall High Knob, South Mountain is visible to the west. At Cunningham Falls State Park, south of Catoctin Mountain Park, **Big Hunting Creek** tumbles 78 feet through a hemlock-shaded gorge, creating **Cunningham Falls,** Maryland's highest waterfall. The creek, which originates from springs in Catoctin Mountain, has some of the best trout fishing in the state. Only conventional

North America's largest moth, the cecropia (right) emerges from its chrysalis. The exquisite blue crested dwarf iris (top left) blooms in April and May; summer brings the spotted, recurved Turk's-cap (bottom left), the region's largest and most colorful native lily.

fly tackle can be used in this catch-and-return creek. A 29-mile-long trail traverses the mountain, beginning at Mount Zion Church, just outside Catoctin Mountain Park, and finishing at Gambrill State Park in the south.

South past Frederick on Route 270, **Sugarloaf Mountain❖** towers above the rolling plains of the piedmont to the west. Beyond the reach of the Blue Ridge, Sugarloaf is an anomaly known as a monadnock, a mountain composed of erosion-resistant rock. Although only 1,280 feet high, its wide, flat summit is more than an acre in size, providing vantages of surrounding farmland and good hawk watching in the fall and spring. Lower down its slopes, migrant thrushes and many warblers appear, especially on gray days when the summit is obscured by clouds. The nonprofit organization that owns the land supports research programs, including an attempt to develop a blight-resistant strain of American chestnut, a tree species that was common on the mountain before a fungal disease decimated the chestnuts earlier in the twentieth century.

CHESAPEAKE AND OHIO CANAL

Shortly after its completion in 1850, the C & O Canal was eclipsed by the railroad, and it never quite realized its grandest commercial goals. It has,

The fishlike markings on its leaves earned the trout lily (top left) its name. Blooming in early spring, pink round-lobed hepatica (bottom left) thrives in dry, rocky woods. The vivid eastern tiger swallowtail (right) sips nectar from spotted joe-pye weed.

however, left an unintended legacy of enduring value for those who enjoy the natural world. Most lengths of the canal are dry today and in many places are filled with trees and bushes. But the wide, packed dirt and sand towpath remains intact from the time when harnessed mules walked it, dragging barges slowly behind them. Today, the 12-foot-wide towpath, the thin corridor of canal, and the Potomac embankment are all part of the **Chesapeake and Ohio Canal National Historical Park❖.** Cutting 185 miles through the largely unspoiled Potomac Valley from Cumberland all the way southeast to Washington, D.C., the canal offers unparalleled opportunities for nature study. Many have traveled the length by foot or bike, watching how the Potomac picks up tributaries and grows, changes form, rolls through the piedmont, then crashes over the fall line onto the coastal plain on its way to the Chesapeake Bay.

Southwest of Frederick, Route 15 crosses the Potomac near Point of Rocks, 137 miles along the canal towpath from Cumberland and only 48 from Washington. Here the river flows out of the last ripples of the Blue Ridge and enters the rolling hills of the piedmont. Under the bridge at Route 15 is the put-in for the 17.5-mile-long **Potomac Crossroads Canoe Trail,** a leisurely two-day trip. This section of river passes by small, often

flooded islands to Edward's Ferry at lock 25 of the C & O Canal. About six miles downstream, the Monocacy River flows in from the east. At the confluence is the **Monocacy River Aqueduct,** made from white granite quarried from nearby Sugarloaf Mountain, visible four miles to the east. The Monocacy, an Indian name that translates as "stream of many big bends," is also worth exploring by canoe. During the summer, wading birds such as great blue herons and snowy egrets can be seen.

Farther down the Potomac at Seneca, the **McKee-Beshers Wildlife Management Area❖,** accessible by heading south from Gaithersburg toward Seneca and Hunting Quarter Road, provides some of the best bird-watching opportunities in the greater Washington, D.C., area. The hedgerows, crop fields, fallow meadows, and swampy woods of the area, locally known as Hughes Hollow, appeal to a wide assortment of bird species, especially during spring and fall migrations. Three impoundments attract a number of ducks and breeding populations of white-eyed vireos, red-winged blackbirds, least bitterns, willow flycatchers, and marsh wrens. Springtime brings the mating rituals

LEFT: *At Great Falls, the Potomac plummets dramatically, 76 feet in a quarter mile, crashing and tumbling across the fall line from the piedmont to the coastal plain.*

39

of the woodcocks, whose amorous displays send them shooting high up in the air, then hurtling back to earth.

Off MacArthur Boulevard, north of Washington, D.C., at **Great Falls,** the Potomac River hits the fall line at a series of large rapids, where the hard underlying bedrock of the piedmont yields to the soft, easily eroded sediments of the coastal plain. From the canal towpath, narrow bridges cross to **Olmstead Island,** spanning chutes of white water stirred by a drop of 76 feet in a quarter mile. The 35-acre island has an unusual and fragile landform, known as a bedrock river terrace. A thin layer of soil atop a table of gneiss and schist supports rare plants, including hairy wild petunias, erect water hyssops, and tall tickseeds. Occasionally a white-tailed deer stirs in the underbrush. Approximately 150 species of birds can be seen here at various times of the year. The boardwalk ends on a rocky outcrop equipped with a fence, with breathtaking views of the falls and of Virginia on the far side.

All along the C & O Canal towpath, numerous trails cut down to the banks of the Potomac and rich alluvial wetlands, often overwashed by the

LEFT: *After a day at the National Zoo, nattily attired turn-of-the-century visitors enjoy Washington's newly opened park on Rock Creek.*

RIGHT: *Within view of the spires of Georgetown, the thick foliage of 88-acre Theodore Roosevelt Island hides a warren of hiking trails and several different natural habitats.*

river. Some areas are small swamps with a profusion of skunk cabbage and fern species. Off the towpath just north of the historic Great Falls Tavern is a concrete overlook for views of the falls. From the platform's northwest corner, visitors can sometimes see a pair of bald eagles nesting on an island in late winter and early spring.

A half mile south of the tavern is one of the premier hikes of the Washington, D.C., area—the **Billy Goat Trail.** The rugged, two-mile trail scrambles over boulders and along narrow ledges, dramatically skirting the Potomac, high atop gneiss and schist cliffs overlooking Mather Gorge. On almost any warmish weekend, kayakers are visible plying the eddies and ripples below. All along the trail are aspects of riverine geology. Perhaps the most dramatic are the potholes, great holes formed when the river swirled rocks with such force that they ground smooth, round holes in the gneiss and schist over which it flowed. Away from the river are small beaver ponds and, in spring, an abundance of jack-in-the-pulpit and other wildflowers.

A major tributary of the Potomac, **Rock Creek** begins near Gaithersburg and travels 30 miles south through a thin corridor of protected parkland into Washington, D.C., where it feeds into the Potomac near Georgetown and the end of the C & O Canal. Both Maryland's **Rock Creek Regional Park**❖ and Washington's **Rock Creek Park**❖ are heavily used by the urban population, not only as recreational areas but also as a commuter route. Yet, within the 2,000 acres of the D.C. section are 12 trails leading up and down the often steep, wooded banks, where it is easy to escape the commotion of the city. Many of the trails are also open to horses, and a paved bike path runs alongside the bubbling creek. In spring, the woods come alive with the songs of ovenbirds, wood thrushes, least flycatchers, scarlet tanagers, and northern waterthrushes, and the "drink your tea!" calls of rufous-sided towhees.

For wilderness in an urban setting, it's hard to top **Theodore Roosevelt Island❖,** located in the Potomac off George Washington Parkway and near Memorial Bridge. Looking from the Kennedy Center across the river, the skyscrapers of Rosslyn, Virginia, seem to grow directly out from the island's low-lying expanse of oak, hickory, elm, sycamore, dogwood, maple, and ash. Yet this unusual 88-acre island holds a tidal freshwater marsh with cypress trees on its southern end and a stand of eastern hemlocks in its center. Everything from wood ducks and wood thrushes to red foxes and beavers inhabit the island, and finches often winter near the bridge. Runoff from farming and building has filled the Potomac with sediment, causing Theodore Roosevelt Island to grow in length and width as the sediment is deposited on its southern edge.

THE PATUXENT RIVER AND SOUTHERN MARYLAND

Originating near Mount Airy, more than 30 miles north of Washington, and meeting the Chesapeake Bay at Solomon, the **Patuxent River** is the longest and deepest river running entirely in the state of Maryland. On its way from Maryland's piedmont to the coastal plain, the river passes through several parks and preserves. Near the river's headwaters, about 20 miles north of D.C. and reachable by taking Route 97 (Georgia Avenue) from the Capital Beltway (I-495) north past Sunshine, the **Patuxent River State Park❖** includes 12 miles of the river's course as it flows through rolling farmland. The Patuxent runs by the Triadelphia and Rock Gorge reservoirs, which provide drinking water for much of the immediate area and are open for swimming and boating. Twenty-eight miles of horse trails wind along ridges, through meadows, and across the river and its tributaries.

Farther downriver, near where the Patuxent crosses the fall line, northeast of D.C., is the **Patuxent Environmental Science Center❖,** the nation's first and foremost wildlife research center. Operating for more than 50 years, the center pioneered influential studies on the effects of DDT and other contaminants on wildlife—studies that ultimately formed much of the basis of Rachel Carson's book *Silent Spring.* More recent work has included research on the captive propagation of endangered species such as the whooping crane and threatened bald eagle. Both the research center and the **National Wildlife Visitor Center❖** off Powder Mill Road, two miles east of the Baltimore/Washington Parkway, are run by the National Biological Survey.

Moving downstream, the Patuxent cuts through the sandy sediments of the coastal plain, leaving eroded banks. From the Capital Beltway east toward Upper Marlboro on Route 4 (Pennsylvania Avenue), then south on Routes 301 and 382 to Croom Airport Road, is the **Patuxent River Park, Jug Bay Natural Area❖,** one of the best bird-watching spots near D.C. Some hundred nesting species have been counted here, and more than 150 other bird species have been sighted. Before narrowing again, the Patuxent widens into a bay about a mile wide and three miles long lined with freshwater tidal marsh. The rich variety of aquatic plants is dominated by wild rice, a plant that grows up to ten feet tall and blooms with a shimmery gold color in early August. Wild rice, millet, and smartweed seeds ripen in late August or early September, coinciding with the southward migration of red-winged blackbirds, bobolinks, sora and Virginia rail, and ducks. Red-winged blackbirds can often be spotted hovering near wild rice seedheads and pecking at them.

A nature trail and boardwalk lead to the edge of the wild rice marsh and to an observation tower, from which bald eagles and ospreys are sometimes visible. Atop another observation tower at the area headquarters, bird-watchers have identified 29 species of waterfowl. But the best way to view Jug Bay's rich avian fauna is by canoe (the area rents canoes by reservation).

A trip to Jug Bay is incomplete without visiting adjacent **Merkle Wildlife Sanctuary❖** (just south of Jug Bay on Route 382, off Saint Thomas Church Road), with its large wintering populations of Canada geese. Conservationist Edgar Merkle reintroduced Canada geese into the area, starting in 1932 with several breeding pairs. He encouraged large populations to winter here by leaving fields planted with winter wheat, corn, and orchard grass. Today, as many as 10,000 Canada geese flock to the marshes, fields, and freshwater ponds, the largest wintering ground of this species on the western shore of the Chesapeake Bay.

Good vantages of the geese are available from the two-story windows of the visitor center. Ospreys and bald eagles also inhabit the area.

OVERLEAF: *Wild rice and other freshwater marsh vegetation flourish in Patuxent River State Park, where they provide a rich source of food for red-winged blackbirds and a variety of migratory waterfowl.*

A native annual that blooms in May, wild rice (top left) grows six to ten feet tall in freshwater and brackish marshes. The raccoon (bottom left), a sweet-faced nocturnal prowler, spend most nights foraging along streambanks. A crow-sized green-backed heron perches on cattails (right); this wading bird thrives in fresh and salt water habitats.

Eastern bluebirds, purple martins, and wood ducks nest in structures specially built for them. A short nature trail leads through a small wooded area, crossed by a small stream, where papaws grow. Identifiable by its long rounded leaves, this shrub or small tree bears an edible green fruit, much loved by opossums, squirrels, raccoons, and birds.

One of the best times to see Jug Bay and Merkle is on Sunday afternoon, the only time the **Chesapeake Bay Critical Driving Tour** is open to the public. Beginning at Patuxent River Park and traveling for four miles across Mattaponi Creek and into Merkle Wildlife Sanctuary, the tour passes an observation tower, and there are many places to pull off and watch wildlife.

One of southern Maryland's most extensive wilderness areas, the 70,000-acre **Zekiah Swamp❖** stretches 16 miles from Cedarville south to Allens Fresh. The state's largest freshwater swamp, it occupies the valley of the Wicomico River, becoming tidal wetlands of the river at Allens Fresh. Densely vegetated, the swamp is filled with numerous insects, from the caddis fly to glass shrimp beetles, making it a prime location for entomologists collecting for the Smithsonian's Insect Zoo at the National Museum of Natural History.

Most of the swamp is privately owned, but **Cedarville State Forest❖**, located off Cedarville Road and Route 301 at the swamp's headwaters, offers a glimpse. Several streams and a pond feed the boggy land here, and more than 20 miles of hiking and horse trails wind through the forest of Virginia pine, sycamore, willow, oak, and tulip poplar. A host of bog plants thrive, including the carnivorous pitcher plant.

Two creeks to the west of the Wicomico is the Nanjemoy, home of the largest great blue heronry on the East Coast. At **Nanjemoy Creek Great Blue Heron Sanctuary,** about 900 pairs of great blue herons build nests in the tops of tall beeches, tulip poplars, and Virginia pines. For 50 years, herons have returned to this spot around Valentine's Day. Eggs are laid in March, and the young hatch by mid-April. Nesting herons are easily disturbed, even by just a few careless visitors, so the Maryland chapter of the Nature Conservancy restricts all public visits.

Some of the best spots for views of great blue herons and bald eagles are along the shores of the Potomac River, where these large birds prey on the rockfish that come to spawn. One site worth visiting is **Purse State Park❖,** a small property with river frontage, which is managed by Smallwood State Park to the north. The park, which requires a walk-in, is located west of the town of Nanjemoy, reachable via Route 301 to Route 6, then south on Route 224.

THE WESTERN SHORE OF THE CHESAPEAKE BAY

Point Lookout occupies the tip of land at the very southern end of Maryland's western shore, overlooking the meeting of the Potomac and the Chesapeake Bay. **Point Lookout State Park❖,** reached by following Route 301 to Route 234 to Route 5 south, offers marshes and jetties, ponds and stands of pine. It is an ideal spot for watching a wide variety of bird species, especially during the spring and fall migrations. Warblers, thrushes, and waterbirds abound, and great horned owls live in the pine trees.

Some of the East Coast's best fossil hunting is found north of the point, along the stretch of beach between Chesapeake Beach and Cove Point off Route 2. (Take Route 235 north, then cross the Patuxent on Route 4 to reach combined Routes 2 and 4.) High, crumbling clay cliffs erode under

the constant surge of the bay, releasing tantalizing secrets of life during the Miocene epoch some 15 million years ago, when the area was covered by a shallow sea. Most popular with fossil hunters are sharks' teeth, some as long as five inches, from the giant predator *Carcharodon megalodon,* an extinct relative of the modern great white shark. The vast number of sharks' teeth fossils—far more common than fossilized whale, porpoise, or crocodile teeth—is probably due to the fact that sharks shed their teeth rather frequently, replacing each tooth as often as every seven or eight days.

The best spot to search for fossils is at **Calvert Cliffs State Park❖,** located just north of the small town of Bertha off combined Routes 2 and 4. A two-mile hike through a sandy forest of pine, beech, and oak ends at a small beach, lapped by the brackish waters of the bay and adjacent to tall cliffs eroded by the Chesapeake. On the lip above the cliff is the forest itself, where full-size trees perch precariously on the edge, eventually falling into the bay as erosion progresses. Fossil collecting is best after a winter storm, when the bay has further eroded the cliff face and fossil remains wash up on the beach. Other fossils can be found in addition to sharks' teeth—including shark vertebrae, coral, barnacles, gastropods, brachiopods, and the dental plates of rays.

Four miles north of the park on Routes 2 and 4, **Flag Ponds Nature Park❖** also has fossils along the beach. Accreting sand from other parts of the bay has added to the shorefront over many hundreds of years, cutting off two saltwater inlets to form Duncan and Todd ponds. A fishing shack, once located on the shore, is a startling reminder of the speed of accretion—now several hundred yards of forested land separate it from the water. Trails and boardwalks penetrate the forest, offering occasional views of shy woodland denizens: muskrats, otters, turkeys, foxes, and deer. The park earned its name from the blue flag iris that blooms here between May and July in wetland areas.

On the other side of Routes 2 and 4, toward the Patuxent River, **Hellen Creek Hemlock Preserve** is an area of steep bluffs, ravines, and marshes. It protects the southernmost stand of eastern, or Canada, hemlock on the eastern coastal plain. Identifiable by their blunt, dark green needles with two narrow white bands underneath, the hemlocks are probably a relict community from the last ice age. Also prevalent is the climbing fern, usual-

LEFT: *A pair of ospreys construct their nest on a tall piling at Point Lookout, Maryland. These fish-eating raptors will return to the same nest each year, building it higher and higher until it rivals an eagle's in size.*

ABOVE: *The tiny spring beauty grows from a potatolike tuber, once considered a delicacy by Indians and colonists.*

LEFT: *The water-loving blue flag, a handsome native iris, blooms each summer in swamps, marshes, and coastal areas.*

RIGHT: *Strangely animated and peculiar, the "knees" of the bald cypress tree probably serve as part of an aerial root system.*

ly found in Appalachian forests well to the west. Other plants of particular interest are the cardinal flower, marshmallow, and trailing arbutus.

Several miles away, up Routes 2 and 4 just past Port Republic, Route 506 heads west to **Battle Creek Cypress Swamp Sanctuary❖** and one of the northernmost stands of bald cypress in the country. Scientists still puzzle over why these trees, some as tall as 100 feet and with trunks 4 feet in diameter, survive here and nowhere else on Maryland's western shore. From the boardwalk, the cypresses' aerial roots, or knees, are clearly visible. Among the many spring wildflowers seen here are pink lady's slipper, purple orchids, and spring beauties. Bald cypresses only propagate under a very limited set of seasonal conditions that are rarely met; sometimes many years pass between successful generations before a raft of seedlings can take root. This accounts for the recognizable generations of trees in the swamp.

Follow Route 4 to rejoin Route 301 at Upper Marlboro. Take Route 301 to Route 50/301 east. Just before Route 50/301 crosses over the Bay Bridge to the eastern shore is one of Maryland's premier bird-watching spots, **Sandy Point State Park❖.** Peregrine falcons nest on the bridge and riotous crowds of gulls converge on the beach; it's also a good place to watch the hawk migrations during the fall or to search in the marsh for elusive rail. The jetty near the bridge offers views of ducks that winter here, such as canvasbacks and greater and lesser scaup. Great horned,

barred, and long-eared owls are found in the large stand of pines. Although it gets crowded during the summer, most people keep to the beach, leaving much of the other marsh habitats free for nature study.

This exploration of Maryland now turns back inland, heading west on Route 50 to 97, then north to Interstate 695. Northwest of Baltimore, off Route 26 (Liberty Road) from I-695, is **Soldiers Delight Natural Environment Area❖.** This unusual desertlike microenvironment set in the normally lush woodlands of the piedmont is known as a serpentine barren. Exposed and weathered serpentinite bedrock, a metamorphosed igneous rock containing greenish serpentine minerals, creates a nutrient-poor soil full of magnesium, chromium, iron, and nickel, toxic to most plants. Soldiers Delight is the largest of only four such sites—rare throughout the world—remaining in the state.

The hot and dry grasslands known as barrens together with the surrounding woodlands harbor a large number of rare or isolated plant species, which have either developed adaptations to the harsh conditions or are unable to compete in richer habitats. True prairie grasses, such as little bluestem, purplish three-awn, and Indian grass, thrive here. Little bluestem prevents water loss by rolling its long, narrow leaves inward; other species have developed hairy leaves and stems that reflect heat but trap humidity. Wildflowers also grow here: blazing stars, federally endangered fringed gentians that display delicate purple blooms in the fall, and pink-blossomed fameflowers, which open their flowers for only a few hours on sunny summer days. Only three tree species can survive— blackjack oak, post oak, and Virginia pine—and these are often scraggly, stunted, and bent from poor nutrition.

Nineteenth-century chromium mines, from which chrome ore was extracted, are still visible. With a little searching, rocks with small black specks, known as bird's-eye chromium, can be found.

Interior Maryland and Washington, D.C.

Northeast from Baltimore on Route 40 (Exit 35 off I-695), 15,000-acre **Gunpowder Falls State Park❖** lies along the banks of the Big Gunpowder Falls and Little Gunpowder Falls rivers as they flow across the piedmont, cross to the coastal plain, join, and feed into the Chesapeake Bay near Joppa. The park is scattered in five separate sections: one lies near the bay, the other four upstream. At the Hammerman–Dundee Creek Area, near the mouth of the Gunpowder River, freshwater tidal marshes and sandy beaches provide bird-watching opportunities throughout the seasons. Species to see include owls, wintering waterfowl and sparrows, least bitterns, whip-poorwills, and bald eagles. The best way to tour the area is by canoe.

The remote **Hereford Area** of the park, 20 miles to the northwest near Interstate 83, is quite different—more typical of a piedmont river valley with rocky bluffs and forest slopes of oak and hickory. All told, some 98 miles of hiking and horse trails cross the park. One 21-mile stretch runs along the former right-of-way of the Northern Central Railroad from the Maryland-Pennsylvania border south to Ashland along Big Gunpowder Falls, Little Gunpowder Falls, and Beetree Run. The railroad trail was created after Hurricane Agnes washed out bridges and made the line impassable in 1972. Suitable for hiking or biking, the trail also provides access for fishing and tubing on the river.

I-83 south bends back to I-695 and I-95 north. Off I-95, five miles north of Forest Hill on Route 24 near the town of Rocks, **Rocks State Park❖** features a number of towering rock outcrops and sheer rock faces above Deer Creek. The highest of these formations is the 190-foot King and Queen Seat, probably named after the Susquehannock chieftains who held council meetings here. From high atop these outcrops, it is possible to

watch red-tailed hawks and turkey vultures wheeling and soaring effort-lessly in the rising thermals.

Northeast from Baltimore, toward Delaware, I-95 crosses the **Susquehanna River** near the river's mouth at Havre de Grace. Here, the Susquehanna adds its vast waters to the Chesapeake—all told, it supplies 50 percent of the freshwater from all sources that feed the bay. One of the best spots to see this vast waterway is **Susquehanna State Park❖,** lo-cated on the river's west bank, off Route 155 from I-95, then northeast from the town of Level. High bluffs flank the river, offering good vistas and a chance to see an osprey winging across the wide expanse of the river on a fishing expedition, unmistakable with its white head and the characteristic dark brown line running across its eye.

DELMARVA

THE DELMARVA PENINSULA:
DELAWARE AND THE EASTERN SHORES

C ome spring each year, more than a million shorebirds descend on the sandy shores and muddy flats of the Delaware Bay, exhausted from flights of thousands of miles from Suriname, Argentina, Paraguay, and Tierra del Fuego. As though divinely guided, the half-starved birds arrive exactly during the peak of the horseshoe crabs' mating period, in time for a lifesaving feast of crab eggs.

Every year around the first full moon in May, thousands of helmetshaped horseshoe crabs—a species that has remained unchanged for the past 300 million years—clamber ashore. The female lays 80,000 pea-green eggs the size of BBs in the sand, and the male then fertilizes them. Sanderlings, red knots, ruddy turnstones, and semipalmated sandpipers flit among the ponderous crabs in a feeding frenzy that doubles their body weight in about two weeks. By June, most of the shorebirds have continued on the next leg of their journey, 3,000 miles to their breeding grounds in the Canadian Arctic. Delaware Bay's spring influx of shorebirds is recognized as one of the largest in North America, second only to a mass spring migration to Alaska's large Copper River Delta.

This chapter covers an area known as the Delmarva Peninsula, so named because it includes all of Delaware and the Eastern Shore counties of Maryland and Virginia. The northern end of this immense sandbar, a

PRECEDING PAGES: *The source of the Chesapeake Bay's unrivaled productivity lies in the hundreds of miles of salt marsh lining its shores.*
LEFT: *Hog Island, one of Delmarva's thin barrier islands, acts as a buffer between land and sea, muting the violence of Atlantic storms.*

mere 70 miles across at its widest point, begins near Wilmington in northern Delaware and runs about 200 miles south to Virginia's Cape Charles. To the east, the peninsula borders the Delaware River, the Delaware Bay, and the Atlantic Ocean. To the west, Delmarva fronts the Chesapeake Bay, the world's largest and richest estuary.

Across the peninsula from the Delaware Bay, the Chesapeake Bay has its own wondrous spring ritual: Countless thousands of female blue crabs begin to molt, miraculously squeezing out of their shells prior to mating. By mid- to late summer, these crabs will head south to the mouth of the bay, where each will release up to two million larvae. In the years to come, this new generation of crabs will support much of the bay's large commercial fishery. All told, the Chesapeake contains the most plentiful concentrations of fish and shellfish of any bay in North America.

The entire Delmarva falls in the ecosystem known as the coastal plain, with the exception of a small, crescent-shaped area of the higher piedmont country in northern Delaware. This chapter's route begins near Wilmington and explores several sites in the piedmont before heading south along the Delaware River on Route 13, crossing over the east-west–running Chesapeake and Delaware Canal. In addition to connecting the Delaware River and the Chesapeake Bay for commercial and recreational boat travel, the canal also serves as an informal dividing line between the heavily developed land to the north and the more rural farmland to the south, where the countless acres of fields planted with soybean and corn are interrupted every so often by tidy farmhouses in small groves of trees.

The route continues south along Route 1, branching off toward the Delaware Bay shore and Route 9 near Odessa. As the Delaware River broadens, it becomes Delaware Bay, an estuary that feels the tidal surges of the ocean. Between Route 9 and the bay are the tidal, brackish marshes favored by many species of migratory birds along the Atlantic Flyway. A trip to Delaware's inland region begins at Dover and offers opportunities to see examples of some of the area's only remaining Delmarva, or Carolina, bays, curious pondlike wetlands of unknown origin that often support a number of unusual plant species.

The main driving route continues south along Routes 9 and 1. At Cape Henlopen the bay ends and the Atlantic Ocean begins; wide, sandy beaches

---

OVERLEAF: *At Bombay Hook National Wildlife Refuge, flocks of gregarious American avocets patrol the tidal marshes, poking the mud with long, up-curved bills as they hunt for insects and small crustaceans.*

PENNSYLVANIA

Brandywine
River

BRANDYWINE CREEK SP

896

2

Newark

I-295

WALTER S. CARPENTER JR SP
WHITE CLAY CREEK PRES
ELK NECK
DEMONSTRATION FOREST

Wilmington

NEW
JERSEY

Pea Patch Island

Glasgow

IRON
HILL
PARK

FORT DELAWARE SP

Delaware City

C&D CANAL WILDLIFE
MANAGEMENT AREA

95

MARYLAND

ELK NECK
SP

272

Elk
Neck

LUMS
POND
SP

AUGUSTINE WILDLIFE
AREA

40

9

213

13

1

WOODLAND BEACH
WILDLIFE AREA

BLACKBIRD
STATE FOR

Baltimore

445

20

Rock
Hall

EASTERN NECK
NAT WILDLIFE
REFUGE

50

301

Grasonville

6

Smyrna

BOMBAY HOOK
NATIONAL WILDLIFE
REFUGE

PORT MAHON PRESERVE

1

DOVER

LITTLE CREEK WILDLIFE AREA

301

NORMAN G. WILDER
WILDLIFE AREA

Little
Creek

Viola

PRIME HOOK
NAT WILDLIFE
PRES

Delaware Bay

HORSEHEAD WETLANDS
CENTER

Kent
Island

Wye
Mills

TUCKAHOE
SP

Felton

113

KILLENS POND
SP

384

WYE OAK SP

480

Queen
Anne

Denton

13

Milford

BEACH PLUM
ISLAND NATURE PRESERVE

WASHINGTON DC

WYE ISLAND NATURAL
RESOURCES AREA

50

Easton

MARTINAK
SP

16

Ellendale

1

Lewes

CAPE HENLOPEN
SP

33

16

484

Greenwood

18

REDDEN
STATE FOR

30

24

Rehoboth
Beach

Chesapeake

CHOPTANK
WETLANDS

331

Seaford

9

DELAWARE
SEASHORE
SP

Cambridge

16

NANTICOKE
WILDLIFE AREA

Bethel

26

TRAP POND
STATE PARK

Bethany
Beach

ROBINSON NECK/
FRANK M EWING PRES

Laurel

DELAWARE

54

GREAT
CYPRESS
SWAMP

ASSAWOMAN
WA

Bay

Taylors
Island

BLACKWATER
NAT WILDLIFE
REFUGE

50

MARYLAND

Assawoman

FENWICK
ISLAND SP

Bay

528

Salisbury

Berlin

Ocean
City

13

SAXIS WATERFOWL MGT
AREA & REFUGE
DEAL ISLAND WILDLIFE
MGT AREA

363

Princess
Anne

12

Snow
Hill

611

ASSATEAGUE I
STATE PARK

113

Bloodsworth
Island

Deal
Island

413

364

NASSAWANGO CR
PRES

POCOMOKE R
STATE PARK

POCOMOKE RIVER
STATE FOR

JANES I
SP

Smith
Island

Pocomoke
City

MARTIN NAT
WILDLIFE REFUGE

Crisfield

695

Chincoteague I

175

CHINCOTEAGUE NAT
WILDLIFE REFUGE

Temperanceville

VIRGINIA

13

Parramore
Island

Nassawadox

639

Cape
Charles

Cheriton

Ship Shoal Island

VIRGINIA COASTAL RESERVE

13

Smith Island
MOCKHORN ISLAND WILDLIFE
MGT AREA

EASTERN
SHORE OF VA
NAT WILDLIFE
REFUGE

FISHERMAN'S ISLAND NAT
WILDLIFE REFUGE

THE DELMARVA
PENINSULA

25   0   25 Miles

25   0   25 Kilometers

ABOVE: *Each spring an army of horseshoe crabs invades Delaware's muddy coast to lay millions of BB-shaped eggs, most of which are eaten by migrating shorebirds such as this semipalmated sandpiper.*

and barrier islands characterize the coast south through the remaining leg of Delaware, across Maryland, and all the way to Cape Charles, Virginia, including the remote islands of Assateague, Chincoteague, and the Nature Conservancy's Virginia Coast Reserve. Behind the barrier beaches are shallow saltwater marshes, protected from the fury of the ocean but inundated with salt water during high tides and storms.

From the tip of the Delmarva Peninsula at Cape Charles, the route backtracks north up Route 13, splitting off to the west near Pocomoke City, Maryland, then north to Salisbury into Chesapeake Bay country.

Route 50 presses northwest to Cambridge, then north to Grasonville. The western side of the peninsula is Chesapeake Bay country, some 5,000 miles of twisting coastline, home to hundreds of channels, river mouths, inlets, guts, and creeks. Here the route becomes a series of detours into, out of, and around these waterways. The pulse of the tidal waters leaves floodplains along rivers, where rich brackish marsh ecosystems thrive. Upstream, along rivers such as the Choptank and Nanticoke, the brackish waters eventually turn fresh, supporting freshwater marshes of wild rice and arrow arum and life-forms even more diverse than those of the saltwater marshes. At the heads of some rivers are dark and mysterious black-water swamps, some filled with primordial-looking stands of bald cypress and sweet gum.

To the untrained eye, the vast wetlands on the edges of the Chesapeake and Delaware bays appear inhospitable, even worthless—pockets of pestilence with hordes of biting insects, wet muck, and searing heat during the summer. Biologists now know, however, that the wetland is one of the most fertile ecosystems on earth. Each acre produces about ten tons of organic material each year, more than twice that of a cultivated hayfield. In the salt marshes breed the blue, ghost, and fiddler crabs, flounder, oysters, clams, and striped bass on which the commercial fisheries depend.

In fact, the Chesapeake and other estuaries are nutrient traps: The freshwater that flows in from rivers brings organic material, while the ocean washes in with a supply of salts and important minerals. The grasses and aquatic plants of the estuarine wetlands capture these materials, turning them into organic material that supports the food chain.

The Chesapeake's shallow waters account, in part, for its unparalleled richness among all estuaries of the world. Averaging only 21 feet in depth, the bay supports a vast and healthy population of aquatic plants because in many areas the sun can penetrate and warm its waters all the way down to the bottom.

This chapter ends at the head of the bay, near the mouth of the Susquehanna River.

NORTHERN DELAWARE

The **Delaware River** begins in the Catskill Mountains of New York, far north of the state that shares its name. It wends its way south, describing the eastern border of Pennsylvania before cutting inland near Trenton, New Jersey, and flowing by Philadelphia and then Wilmington, Delaware. The river crosses over the fall line, a geological transition from the piedmont to the coastal plain, around Wilmington, and its waters slow and widen, eventually spilling out into the Atlantic.

Where the Delaware flows past Wilmington in northern Delaware, two much smaller rivers join it: the Christina River from the southwestern coastal plain and the Brandywine from the northern piedmont. The Brandywine was harnessed by industrialists in the eighteenth and nineteenth centuries as a source of water power for grinding materials, most notably gunpowder. Some of the only undeveloped spots among the rolling hills of this urban and suburban area are the former estates of industrialists, such as the du Ponts, who deeded 433 acres of the 850-acre **Brandywine Creek State**

Park❖ over to the state. Three miles north of Wilmington at the intersection of Routes 100 and 92, the park contains rolling hills, largely untouched for the past 200 years, that gracefully descend to the banks of the Brandywine.

A boardwalk runs through a nontidal freshwater marsh in the park's southeastern section, home to wild rice and a large, but secretive, population of Muhlenberg bog turtles, a rare species of reptile. Especially during spring and fall, sparrows and warblers abound. During the autumn, many bird-watchers converge on the park's high ground, known as **Hawk Watch,** for the migratory parade of raptors.

A three-mile nature trail leads to a magnificent stand of 100- to 190-year-old tulip poplars, which rise more than 100 feet high. Neither tulip nor poplar, these trees are a relative of ancient magnolias, among earth's first flowering trees. Named for the large green and yellow tuliplike flowers that bloom high in its crown, the tulip poplar grows larger than any other tree in eastern North America: Horses were once stabled in the hollow interiors of some specimens that reportedly measured more than 12 feet in diameter.

Beginning again at Wilmington, take Route 2 west to Newark. Three miles northeast of Newark on Route 896, in the western end of Delaware's small crescent of the piedmont, the densely wooded **White Clay Creek State Park**❖ covers the stream valley of White Clay Creek and its tributaries. Wissahickon schist, which underlies the area, shows itself in a large outcrop in the park's northern section. One of Delaware's only rock outcrops, it contains bits of orange-colored feldspar. Pieces of milky quartz and pegmatite debris are found on the forest floor. White-tailed deer are so plentiful in the park that hunting is sometimes allowed during the winter, though never on Sundays.

Adjacent to the state park, the bistate **White Clay Creek Preserve** contains more than 600 acres of forest. Designed to protect an upstream watershed along with native wildlife and plants, the preserve has not been developed for recreational use. Five miles of the 187-mile **Mason-Dixon Trail** runs along the creek, however, on its loop west and north into Pennsylvania, offering access for fishing, canoeing, and hiking. For bird lovers, White Clay is the best spot in the state to spot numerous upland species, such as flycatchers, warblers, and sparrows.

South from White Clay Creek on Route 896, three miles past the center of Newark, Delaware, a small mountain comes into view to the west. Made of gabbro, a type of granular, igneous rock, it rises 270 feet above the coastal plain sediments. Geologists remain puzzled by the presence of this volcanic rock amid the generally uniform layers of unconsolidated sediments that define the topography of the coastal plain. The area, now preserved as **Iron Hill Park❖,** was mined by Paleo-Indians for jasper, a brownish, crystalline silicate that they chipped into implements. Later miners extracted iron ore from shafts: weathered pieces of ore still remain in the hillside pits that cover the Iron Hill's flanks. A museum atop Iron Hill contains a selection of Delaware's rocks and minerals.

To reach Route 13, continue on Route 896 south to Glasgow, then west on Route 40. Route 13 sweeps down from Wilmington paralleling the Delaware River, passing through industrialized areas and suburbs. Tugs and large ships ply the Delaware, while the skyscrapers of Wilmington are never far from view. In the midst of this urbanization is **Pea Patch Island.** Its huge heronry, the largest north of Florida, is a testament to the resilience of nature. Off the coast of Delaware City, reached by taking Route 72 and then Route 9 east from Wrangle Hill Road at Route 13, Pea Patch Island is entirely protected by **Fort Delaware State Park❖.** More than 12,000 breeding pairs of 9 species of herons nest on this tiny, low-lying island surrounded by mud flats: great blue herons, little blue herons, tricolored herons, black-crowned night herons, yellow-crowned night herons, cattle egrets, snowy egrets, great egrets, and glossy ibis. The largest nests, belonging to the great blue herons and great egrets, perch on the topmost part of the trees, while others build below—a division of nest building that helps reduce site competition in this crowded environment. All the herons share similar anatomical features: long legs, which are good for wading, and sharp beaks, which along with long necks are effective tools for catching fish and frogs.

Marshlands separate the heronry on the northern end of the island from the publicly accessible southern part of the island, reached seasonally by ferry from the park office in Delaware City. With the help of binoculars, spectacular views are available from a short wooden tower, especially during nesting season, from mid-March to mid-July, when the large nests are full of young birds and the underbrush is literally alive with birdlife. Each year, Brandywine Creek State Park leads a small number of trips to the heronry, though never during breeding season, when the birds are easily disturbed.

Many of the herons, egrets, and ibis that flock to Pea Patch during the summer find their way over to the Dragon Run Marshes on the mainland near Delaware City. Just north of the light on Clinton Street in Delaware City is **Dragon Run Park,** which has good views of Dragon Run Creek. **Battery Park** has views of the marshes, where there are nesting populations of wood ducks, American and least bitterns, and pied-billed grebes.

65

Pea Patch Island supports a huge heronry. Among the species in residence are black-crowned night herons (above left), nocturnal hunters; great blue herons (above right), which stand four feet tall and have a seven-foot wingspan; and great egrets (right), which are noted for their brilliant all-white plumage.

CHESAPEAKE AND DELAWARE CANAL

Delaware City lies on the northeastern corner of the **Chesapeake and Delaware Canal,** which runs east-west across Delaware and into Maryland, cutting across the narrowest part of the northern Delmarva Peninsula and connecting the Delaware River with the Chesapeake Bay. Earth dredged to create the canal was piled along the banks, creating steep bluffs. Dirt roads run parallel to the still-busy canal, permitting foot traffic along the edge. Back from the canal, parts of the land and marsh belong to the **C & D Canal Wildlife Management Area❖.** Despite the constant evidence of human engineering and industry, a hiker might encounter swallow nests in the embankment, find an ancient marine fossil, or watch a great blue heron move across the water with great cumbersome wing beats.

Toward the western end of the C & D Canal on Route 71, southwest from Tyabouts Corner at Route 13, is Delaware's largest freshwater pond, created from an abandoned feeder pond used in the 1800s to control canal water levels. The only commerce today at **Lums Pond State Park❖** is a busy swimming beach, a large population of basking turtles, and anglers fishing for largemouth bass, bluegill, crappie, and catfish. Nature trails loop around the lake, through fields and woods of beech, oak, and river birch. Lums contains all three of eastern North America's mimic thrushes: northern mockingbird, gray catbird, and brown thrasher. One of the best spots for bird-watching is on the wharf, looking toward a forested area flooded by the rising water of the impoundment. On the numerous snags, logs, and stumps are eastern kingbirds, belted kingfishers, woodpeckers, and other species.

Route 896 runs south from Newark along the western edge of the state park, crossing the canal at Summit Bridge, so named because it sits near the divide between the Chesapeake and Delaware watersheds. Running east along the canal for the next mile and a half is the area known as **Deep Cut,** named for the high sand and silt bluffs that rise as much as 60 feet above the canal on the north side. While excavating the canal, the U.S. Army Corps of Engineers cut through the embankments, exposing layers of marine sediments from the Upper Cretaceous, a geologic period between 65 and 135 million years ago. Patient collectors might find sharks' teeth, ancient clams, snails, and other fossils in the midden that has dropped from the cliff. Many of the fossils are *Steinkerns*, a German term for molds left in the sediment long after the original fossil has decomposed. Regulations permit collecting only from the remains that have fallen from the cliff face.

To the west of Route 9 after it crosses the canal is **Thousand-Acre Marsh,** the largest freshwater marsh in Delaware and once a prime muskrat-trapping area. Muskrat lodges, made of mud and soft-stemmed grasses, are especially visible in the winter. The once-abundant muskrat population has dwindled in the last several decades, mostly because of the encroachment of phragmites, an exotic (nonnative), stiff-stemmed weed that muskrats find hard to penetrate.

East of Route 9, south of the canal, the 1,500-acre **Augustine Wildlife Area** stretches along the shores of the Delaware down to Bay View Beach. It is managed mostly for hunting. Off Augustine Creek, the private conservation organization Delaware Wild Lands owns **J. Gordon Armstrong Heronry,** where many great blue herons nest 100 feet above the ground in a mature forest of oaks, beech, and hickory. The nests are crowded so thick that shrubs and ground cover are stunted from the

OVERLEAF: *At Blackbird State Forest, a shallow Carolina bay supports lush wetland vegetation. The origin of these strangely uniform circular depressions, which dot the Delmarva Peninsula, remains a mystery.*

herons' droppings. Special permission is required to visit the heronry.

Farther south off Route 13, Blackbird Forest Road leads to the Tyabout Tract, one of six separate areas that make up **Blackbird State Forest❖**. It contains four unusual topographical features known as Delmarva, or Carolina, bays—shallow, pondlike depressions that support vegetation different from the surrounding forest, often glade and swamp plants that are rare elsewhere. Named for similar features found throughout the region, these bays align on a northwest-to-southeast axis and all are circular or elliptical, suggesting a common origin. Several hundred of these bays once existed within a 50-mile radius in Delaware and Maryland; development and cultivation destroyed most of them. Theories about their creation range from the fantastic to the geomorphic: One proposes that groups of stranded whales created them by vigorously flailing their bodies; another blames a shower of meteors; a third suggests that underground aquifers created sinkholes.

These poorly drained habitats are often quite wet, so it is best to view them from the edges. Among the wildlife there are wood ducks, immediately identifiable by their beautifully colored heads. They are attracted to the bays by buttonbush, a wetland shrub bearing round fruit. The bays also provide the water that frogs and toads need during their breeding season.

THE DELAWARE BAY

At Smyrna, Route 6 cuts east from Route 13, heading across flat farmland toward the Delaware River. Where Route 6 meets the river is the **Woodland Beach Wildlife Area❖,** managed for hunting. However, the preserve does offer good opportunities to watch migratory shorebirds, especially from the watchtower. The salt marshes of Woodland and Bombay Hook (see below) are filled with guts, small, twisting saltwater creeks that feed into larger tidal creeks. Before it reaches the water, Route 6 crosses Route 9.

Several miles south on Route 9 is **Bombay Hook National Wildlife Refuge❖,** one of the premier bird-watching spots along the entire East Coast. Along with adjacent preserves, it occupies two dozen miles of coastline, where the Delaware River spreads out into the Delaware Bay. It attracts migratory waterfowl and shorebirds as no other place on the Delmarva Peninsula does. Approximately 16,000 acres are covered with land ideal for wintering or resting birds—salt marsh; fields planted with corn, wheat, clover, and other crops; and freshwater impoundments filled with aquatic foods birds love. At times, it is virtually impossible to look in any direction and not see birdlife.

In one of nature's most impressive spectacles, thousands of geese return at dusk each day during the winter months, filling the air with the sound of honks and flapping wings and the sight of their rapid yet graceful descents. At peak periods, especially in October and November, more than 100,000 Canada geese, greater snow geese, and dabbling ducks (mostly black ducks, mallard, pintail, and green-winged teal) may occupy Bombay Hook at one time. May, August, and September are the best times to see shorebirds such as dunlins, turnstones, black-bellied plovers, red knots, sandpipers, and stilts; wading birds; and songbirds. All told, 314 bird species have been sighted here, including the most famous avian residents, a nesting pair of bald eagles, often visible on Parson Point in **Shearness Pool.**

Much of the preserve is salt marsh, inaccessible by foot, but 12 miles of roads weave around freshwater impoundments. In addition, several trails skirt the marshes, and three observation platforms and a boardwalk enable glimpses of this extraordinarily animal- and plant-rich environment. Watching a half-dozen great blue herons standing near some ivory-colored egrets as a pair of ducks fly overhead—all visible from the window of a car—will make a bird lover out of anyone. Also present in the preserve are white-tailed deer, beavers, muskrats, and northern diamondback terrapins. During the summer, mosquitoes and biting flies make extended walks uncomfortable.

South on Route 9 at Little Creek, Port Mahon Road heads east to the southern end of Bombay Hook and vantages of the small but species-rich **Port Mahon Preserve❖,** an undeveloped marshland run by the Nature Conservancy. In early summer four species of shorebirds—black-bellied plovers, ruddy turnstones, sanderlings, and red knots—arrive to feed on the millions of horseshoe crab eggs that litter the beach. When disrupted, all members of a flock will take to the air in unison, turning and veering with breathless speed and coordination. The preserve also serves as a breeding and wintering ground for five species of rail, the short-eared owl, the northern harrier (also known as the marsh hawk), and the rough-legged hawk.

To the south is **Little Creek Wildlife Area❖,** a preserve managed by the state mostly for hunting. Two large, brackish-water impoundments attract a great number of migratory waterfowl and shorebirds. Walking the dikes around the impoundments is easiest in the fall and spring, when the reeds have not grown tall. Northern harriers, gulls, falcons, and rough-legged hawks hunt here. A boardwalk leads to an observation tower overlooking the southern impoundment, the larger of the two, which is the best place to watch migratory waterfowl. Little Creek, along with Bombay Hook, is the northernmost point on the East Coast where black-necked stilts nest regu-

larly. At this point, one can choose to visit Delaware's inland areas, taking Route 13 south and rejoining the main route at Milford, or continue south on Route 1/113 to Milford.

DELAWARE'S INLAND SOUTH

At Dover, Route 13 branches off from Route 1/113 and heads south, keeping to an inland route. At Viola, Route 108 leads west to the **Norman G. Wilder Wildlife Area❖,** a coastal plain forest with mature stands of white oak, chestnut oak, and willow oak, with some trees rising more than 100 feet. At only 60 feet above sea level, these narrow highlands are a tall enough feature on the flat Delmarva Peninsula to divide the watersheds draining into the Chesapeake and Delaware bays. The area also supports one of Delaware's most extensive growths of club moss, remnants of ancient forests that look like miniature evergreen trees with tiny cones. Club mosses grow about a foot tall and cover the forest floor. Dense undergrowth makes the area almost impenetrable during the sum-

ABOVE: *Vigilant even while asleep, Canada geese frequent Delmarva's tidal rivers, fields, and open bays during the winter, spring, and fall.*

LEFT: *Swamp rose-mallow (marsh hibiscus) brings a burst of color to the fringes of the freshwater marsh at Bombay Hook National Wildlife Refuge during the dog days of July and August.*

mer, although a series of fire roads do provide limited access.

Continuing south on Route 13 beyond Felton, Route 384 cuts east 1.2 miles to **Killens Pond State Park❖,** surrounding an old mill pond created when part of the Upper Murderkill River was dammed. High nitrate levels from fertilizer runoff and animal waste have forced the state to close the pond to swimming, but it is open year-round for canoeing and small boat use, and largemouth bass, pickerel, crappie, and bluegill still thrive in the pond's waters, while otters and raccoons roam the water's edge. They can be seen by the patient observer on the 2.5-mile Pondside Nature Trail. During the winter, pairs of tundra swans and Canada geese often stop here for a rest.

ABOVE: *Common but often elusive, the boldly colored wood duck nests high above the ground in tree cavities or nest boxes.*

LEFT: *A strikingly patterned eastern black swallowtail butterfly shares the nectar of a colorful bull thistle with a honeybee.*

RIGHT: *Ancestors of the present-day club moss thrived in earth's primitive forests. This evergreen perennial herb now grows best in moist and shady locations.*

The largest example of Delaware's coastal plain forest is found in the little-visited **Redden State Forest❖,** located south of Milford and Ellendale on Route 113, which can be reached by taking Route 16 east from Route 13 at Greenwood. A wetland forest of southeastern trees, Redden has a mix of sweet gum, maple, white oak, Virginia pine, short-leaf pine, and some of the northernmost stands of loblolly pine. In the wet areas, sphagnum moss grows.

South of Redden State Forest, take Route 9 southwest to Laurel. To the west, at **Nanticoke Wildlife Area❖,** along the Nanticoke River, are tell-tale signs of a freshwater tidal marsh: spatterdock, pickerelweed, arrow arum, and broad-leaved cattail. Near the southwestern corner of Delaware, where Broad Creek feeds into the Nanticoke, the area is located five miles west of Laurel, off Route 492. One of Delaware's only rivers to drain south into the Chesapeake Bay, the Nanticoke twists 36 miles from its headwaters above Seaford to the bay. Throughout its length it feels the bay's tidal pull, which continually recycles nutrients into the area, supporting one of the East Coast's richest ecosystems. It is probably the least-developed major river valley in Delaware.

The best way to appreciate the riches of the Nanticoke is to canoe its waters. One good put-in is **Phillips Landing,** located on Broad Creek where it feeds into the Nanticoke, several miles west of Bethel off Routes 493 and 496. Across from the landing grows the state's largest stand of wild rice, sometimes reaching ten feet in height. The seeds are eaten by red-

winged blackbirds, bobolinks, and a number of duck species, including mallard and blue-winged teal, during the summer. In the spring, male blackbirds carve the marsh into small territories, usually a quarter of an acre or less, challenging any transgressors with a "song-spread": Either from a perch or at the end of a short flight, the male displays its red shoulder patches, sometimes vibrates them, then spreads its wings and tail—all while singing its song. In the fall, thousands of red-winged blackbirds use the Nanticoke as a migratory flyway.

The forestland bordering Broad Creek includes loblolly, Virginia, and pond pine, and Atlantic white cedar. Here also grows the rare and endangered box huckleberry, a low-lying shrub with branches that root where they touch the ground. A single individual can survive longer than 500 years and cover an acre of open woods.

Ten miles east of Broad Creek's mouth at the Nanticoke are the creek's headwaters in **Trap Pond State Park❖,** five miles east of Laurel off Route 24. In winter the one-mile walk around the pond might reveal a fairy-tale scene of tall bald cypress trees locked in ice. The bald cypresses that crowd the water's edge and the swamp at the headwaters are the northernmost individuals of this southern-growing species. Surrounding a former mill pond is a dense forest made up of 12 species of oak, including blackjack oak, which is not usually seen near swampy ground. The poor drainage of the coastal plain sediments accounts for the close proximity of these oaks to the swamp. A number of turtles (eastern painted and spotted), frogs (bullfrogs and green tree frogs), and water snakes live in the pond. In May, swamp azaleas bloom, while June brings a burst of large pinkish white clusters of mountain laurel. A mile to the west, **Trussum Pond** also has a small stand of bald cypress. White water lilies bloom here in the spring.

One of the largest stands of bald cypress in this immediate area once grew to the east of Trap Pond, at the headwaters of the Pocomoke River. What remains today of the **Great Cypress Swamp**, an 11,000-acre preserve, is located several miles west of Selbyville on either side of Route 54. The word *pocomoke* comes from an Algonquian word for "black water"; the

LEFT: *A totally different species from the gray squirrel, the endangered Delmarva fox squirrel probably evolved in this area because of the peninsula's relative isolation.*

RIGHT: *Towering bald cypress trees dominate sunlit Trussum Pond near Laurel. Not a cypress at all, this species is related to California redwoods and drops its needles each fall.*

color comes from the organic detritus that fills swampy areas and darkens the water. Geographers describe a black-water river as a southern river with black water that has a narrow floodplain and a drainage system within the coastal plain. Unfortunately, human activity has dramatically altered this swamp, which once contained 50,000 acres of bald cypress and Atlantic white cedar. One late-eighteenth-century observer here described bald cypress trees that stood 140 feet high and had knees 8 to 10 feet tall. Extremely resistant to rot, both cypress and cedar were logged significantly in the eighteenth and nineteenth centuries, opening up large holes in the treetop canopy. The sun dried the peat bogs through these openings, making the area vulnerable to fire. One fire in the 1930s burned for eight months.

As a result, stands of cypress are few and far between, the forest given over to pond and loblolly pine, sweet gum, black gum, swamp cottonwood, and red maple. Still, the swamp offers a large area of undeveloped wilderness. One resident is the carpenter frog, also known as the bog frog because it prefers sphagnum wetlands of cypress swamps; its call sounds like a hammer hitting wood. The swamp is a favorite bird-watching spot for those searching for elusive Swainson's warblers, the northernmost population of these swamp-loving warblers. This is one of the least-known birds in North America because it mostly frequents dense, swampy ground. To continue with the main driving route, go east on Route 54 to Route 113, then north to Milford.

THE DELAWARE BAY COAST
Route 1 splits off from Route 1/113 east near Milford and heads southeast, passing by **Prime Hook National Wildlife Refuge❖** after 12 miles. The

refuge provides a haven for great numbers of migratory birds and nesting habitat for wood ducks, black ducks, mallard, and gadwalls. Endangered and threatened species such as the bald eagle, peregrine falcon, and Delmarva fox squirrel also live here. Unlike Bombay Hook National Wildlife Refuge to the north, Prime Hook is not accessible along dike-top roads.

A seven-mile, self-guided canoe trip down Prime Hook Creek is the best way to sample the preserve from its narrow headwaters to the open marsh at the end. Sweetbay magnolia line the creekside upstream, giving way downstream to red maple, resplendent in fall and spring. The rare seaside alder, which has small red fruits and miniature pinecones, winter-berry, sweet pepperbush, blueberry, and bayberry also line the shores. A half-mile boardwalk winds through a wooded swamp, and three other short trails offer access to the refuge. For migratory birds, try the middle of March and early November. Songbirds and shorebirds may be most popu-lous in April and May. Because the refuge allows hunting on certain dates, check before setting out (Sundays are always safe).

Adjacent to Prime Hook, off Broadkill Beach at the end of Route 16, **Beach Plum Island Nature Preserve❖** is the only barrier island on the western shore of Delaware Bay. A four-mile round-trip hike goes along a windswept beach past dunes and an inland tidal marsh. The small red berries of the beach plum, a low-lying shrub, make a tart but delicious jelly. The waxy bayberry's small fruit was used by colonists to make candles. The only distractions in this otherwise exceptional area are the vehicles of surf fishers; the ruts they create often mar the sand during the summer.

Longshore currents created the island by washing sand from Delaware Bay beachfronts to the north. Known as a transgressive barrier island, Beach Plum is gradually moving inland across the marshes of Canary and Old Mill creeks as the Delaware Bay erodes the beach and washes sand over to the marsh side.

DELAWARE'S ATLANTIC COAST

On any map of Delaware, the curled peninsula that divides the shores of Delaware Bay to the north from the Atlantic Coast beaches to the south is instantly recognizable. The coastline sweeps southeastward along the bay, hits the thumblike projection, then drops south along a series of beaches and barrier islands. Just east of Lewes on Route 9, **Cape Henlopen State Park❖** occupies all of the cape. The site of a military facility during World War II, it is now an area of great natural diversity, providing an inkling of what Delaware's sand dunes and beaches looked like before develop-

PRINCE BOOKS

109 E. MAIN STREET NORFOLK 622-9223

105383	Reg 1 1:00 pm 01/11/96	

S DEATH OF COMMON S	1 @ 18.00	18.00
DISCOUNT - 20%		-3.60
S SMITHSONIAN GT AT	1 @ 19.95	19.95
DISCOUNT - 20%		-3.99
SUBTOTAL		30.36
TAX		1.37
TOTAL		31.73
CASH PAYMENT		40.00
CHANGE		8.27

Mon-Fri 9-8, Sat 10-8, Sun 11-5

ment. Back from the wide beach, an extensive series of dunes is covered with beach grass, beach heather, broomsedge, and switchgrass. Behind the dunes are salt marshes and forests of pine, oak, cherry, and cedar. The **Pinelands Nature Trail** passes by small cranberry bogs inhabited by insect-eating sundew plants.

On the ocean side, the shape of the spit is in a gradual but continual state of change as the Atlantic pounds it, currents shift it, and winds buffet it. On the quiet bay side, sand gradually accretes from gentle wave action. From the parking lot in the north, stretches of the dunes are roped off as breeding areas for easily disturbed piping plovers, least terns, and other beach nesters. A nearby platform bears an osprey nest.

Nature trails pass through walking dunes, so called because they shift southward at a rate of 6 to 15 feet each year, covering anything in their path with sand. The coastal dunes rise 80 feet, making them the tallest between Cape Cod, Massachusetts, and Nags Head, North Carolina. The best views of the area are from the observation platform, built atop an old military bunker. The first landfall from Cape May, New Jersey, the park provides shelter and food for numerous birds, including hawks and songbirds migrating south. The **Seaside Nature Center** features a series of aquariums filled with local fish.

South from the cape along the shore are a series of resort beaches. Off Route 1, two miles south of Rehoboth Beach, is **Delaware Seashore State Park❖,** a six-mile stretch of narrow sand reef with dunes separating the Atlantic Ocean from Rehoboth and Indian River bays. A half mile from the northern end, tree stumps emerge like ghosts at low tide, evidence of the westward advance of the sea, which has gradually overtaken the land.

Ospreys are much in evidence here: The area supports the region's largest colony of these magnificent raptors, identifiable by a distinctive brown stripe across the eyes. Compact plumage and strong wings aid the osprey as it hovers before splashing feet-first into the water to snatch a fish in its strong talons. The crashing sound of bird hitting water can sometimes be heard quite a distance away. A white underside camouflages the raptor from its unsuspecting quarry. In June, it's easy to spy an osprey flying across Delaware Seashore State Park with a fish in its talons, returning to its nest in a channel marker, dead tree, or human-made plat-

OVERLEAF: *For thousands of years, the Atlantic Ocean has carved and sculpted the dunes and coastline of Delaware's Cape Henlopen by a combination of strong longshore currents, stiff breezes, and crashing waves.*

form. Its call is a whistlelike "cheep-cheep" or a "yew-yew-yewk."

South along Route 1 is **Fenwick Island State Park❖,** a stretch of sandy beach and dunes separating the ocean from Assawoman and Little Assawoman bays. Although often crowded in the summer, the undeveloped beach provides numerous opportunities to observe animals of the Atlantic beach environment, from pods of bottle-nosed dolphins playing offshore and strings of brown pelicans flying parallel to the shore to boat-tailed grackles, black skimmers, and, of course, gulls and terns.

On the western shore of Little Assawoman Bay, at the end of Route 364, southwest of Bethany Beach, **Assawoman Wildlife Area❖** represents an effort by the State Division of Fish and Wildlife to restore marshes drained for mosquito control in the 1930s and 1940s. Freshwater impoundments have brought back migratory shorebirds, often visible from the observation tower. Brown-headed nuthatches and pine warblers also nest here.

Near the Maryland-Delaware border, Route 1 becomes Route 528 and continues south to Ocean City. There, one can take Route 50 west to Route 113 to rejoin the main driving route. To access the barrier islands of Assateague in Maryland take Route 611 off Route 50. Continue south on Route 113 to Virginia to get to Chincoteague, which is south on Route 13 and east on Route 175.

ASSATEAGUE AND CHINCOTEAGUE

For pure wilderness on the Delmarva Peninsula, nothing can beat the ever-changing landscape of beach, dunes, back dunes, and shallow saltwater marshes of Assateague Island. This thin barrier island, broken from the continent near Ocean City, Maryland, stretches for 37 miles, two-thirds of it in Maryland, the other third, joined by Chincoteague Island, in Virginia. As no public roads span the island, long stretches of wild beachfront are intact.

The Maryland end includes all of **Assateague Island State Park❖,** which covers two miles of shoreline, and part of the much larger **Assateague Island National Seashore❖.** Both are reachable via Route 611 south from Route 50, which connects Route 113 and Ocean City. Waves, winds, and tides continually resculpt the island's topography, often from one day to another, most dramatically after large winter storms. Such conditions have made it difficult for human habitation—a

---

RIGHT: *The rich marsh grasses at the Chincoteague National Wildlife Refuge offer ideal grazing for its famous herd of wild ponies, first hidden here in the 1600s by European settlers trying to avoid taxes.*

blessing for naturalists. Wild ponies roam many of Assateague's various habitats. Legends claim the animals arose from ancestors that escaped from a wrecked Spanish galleon, but historians have determined that the ponies descend from livestock hidden there in the 1600s by mainland colonists trying to avoid taxation. Another exotic species, the sika deer, introduced from Japan in the 1920s, now boasts a larger population than the indigenous white-tailed deer. During the summer months, the wild ponies often keep to the beach, where the winds keep the swarms of mosquitoes at bay. A stop on the Atlantic Flyway, Assateague also offers shelter for thousands of wading birds, shorebirds, and waterfowl. Adventurous travelers can take a 26-mile backpacking trip along the beach, stopping off at the two park-maintained, backcountry campsites located behind the primary dune off the ocean. This is not a trip to be undertaken lightly; the sun, insects, and walking on sand can take their toll. Yet Assateague is one of the rare places on the East Coast where an outdoorsperson can enjoy long hikes and spend several overnights in an unspoiled beach environment. The park also operates four canoe-camping sites on the bay side, good points from which to explore the shallow saltwater marshes in Chincoteague Bay on the western edge of Assateague.

Chincoteague National Wildlife Refuge❖ is managed largely for migratory waterfowl. Fourteen freshwater impoundments offer haven for ducks, Canada geese, and greater snow geese, which crowd these waters from October to March. Waterfowl also winter here, because of the mild climate and the salt marshes. Concern over dwindling habitats for snow geese, identifiable by their white bodies and black wing tips, helped establish the refuge in 1943. A total of 316 bird species and 44 mammal species have been identified in the refuge.

Sandy beaches, dunes, tidal marshes, and pine and hardwood forests offer opportunities to see much other birdlife. The refuge supports nesting piping plovers and is one of the best places on the East Coast for sighting peregrine falcons. Vital to this birdlife are the salt marshes filled with cordgrass and their attendant mudflats and tidal pools. Here many species of shorebirds, rail, herons, and egrets, along with grackles and sparrows, feast on a rich diet of mollusks, crustaceans, and insects. The distinctive call of the local shorebird, the willet, is unmistakable: "pul-wil-willet." Also visible at the refuge is the federally endangered Delmarva fox squirrel, which is larger than its common gray cousin and less inclined to run up a tree when startled.

ABOVE: *Imported from Japan in the 1920s to both Chincoteague and Assateague, the spotted sika deer is now more populous than its indigenous cousin, the white-tailed deer. Here a doe nuzzles her fawn.*

OCEAN CITY TO THE
VIRGINIA COAST RESERVE

Several miles south of Route 50 and Berlin, Route 113 meets and roughly parallels the Pocomoke River. Pockets of bald cypress trees—so called because they shed their needles each fall—extend along much of the length of the Pocomoke River from its headwaters in Delaware's Great Cypress Swamp to the Muds, where it empties into Pocomoke Sound, feeding into Chesapeake Bay. Scientists still puzzle over why cypresses grow along the Pocomoke and not along other nearby river systems, such as the Wicomico River to the west.

On Route 113, northeast of Pocomoke City, **Pocomoke River State Forest❖** encompasses more than 13,000 acres of Pocomoke River swamp and agricultural fields that have been taken over by stands of loblolly pine. The swamp is the northernmost of the great southern riverine swamps. Most of the area had been cleared by the 1930s, so the bald cypress is sec-

OVERLEAF: *Straight as an arrow and towering as high as 90 feet, loblolly pines are reflected in a still stretch of water in Chincoteague's fertile marshes, which provide a welcome haven for migratory waterfowl.*

ond-growth forest. After all the migrant birds have left, the swamp is quiet—except for the sound of the barred owl, which hunts at dusk and hoots "who-cooks-for-you…who-cooks-for-y'all."

Formerly separate state parks, Milburn Landing, on the west side of the river (off Route 364 from Pocomoke City), and Shad Landing, on the east side (off Route 113), were joined to form **Pocomoke River State Park.** Shad Landing has a boat launch, camping facilities, and the one-mile Trail of Change nature path. A more enjoyable hike into the swamp is the one-mile Baldcypress Trail at Milburn Landing. It skirts the swamp and passes fine ex-

amples of second-growth bald cypress. In the late summer and fall, Indian pipes grow near the swamp edges. These odd-looking plants do not contain chlorophyll, so their erect shoots are white, yellow, or red rather than green. They survive by living off organic matter in the humus. The best means of experiencing the swamp firsthand is by canoe—rentals are available in Snow Hill, a town farther north along the river, and at the Shad Landing marina.

An enjoyable side trip is to **Nassawango Creek Preserve❖,** an area running along Nassawango Creek, a tributary of the Pocomoke that joins it halfway between Snow Hill and Shad Landing. This small area, owned by the Nature Conservancy, is reachable from Snow Hill, north on Route 12, then left on Old Furnace Road. The one-mile Paul Leifer Trail begins at Furnace Town—the remains of an old iron-smelting facility—and works its way south along a boardwalk into a swampy bald cypress forest, situated between an old canal and Nassawango Creek.

ABOVE: *Although often confused with fungi, the Indian pipe belongs to the rhododendron family. Called a saprophyte, it grows on decaying wood in the soil.*

RIGHT: *Cleverly camouflaged by the foliage, a group of turkey vultures —black eagle-sized scavengers—roost in a large bald cypress in Pocomoke River State Park.*

Just south of the Maryland-Virginia line on Pocomoke Sound, **Saxis Waterfowl Management Area and Refuge❖** offers haven for some 3,000 breeding American black ducks. It can be reached by driving south from Pocomoke City on Route 13, then west on Route 695 and south on Route 788 near Temperanceville. Other dabbling ducks, such as mallard, American wigeon, pintail, and teal are also found here. Diving

ducks such as sea ducks, canvasbacks, redheads, scaup, and common goldeneyes are present nearby, on the open waters of Messongo Creek. Dabbling ducks are distinguished from diving ducks by their surface feeding habits; they dip only their heads and necks below the surface in shallow marshes and ponds to feed on wigeon grass and other vegetation. Diving ducks often immerse their entire bodies under water to forage for food in deeper waters. Champion divers, such as the canvasback, can descend up to 25 feet in search of clams. Diving ducks have larger feet and legs that are positioned closer to their tails than those of the dabblers. Consequently, diving ducks are more cumbersome walking on land—often a dead giveaway for birders trying to distinguish between dabblers and divers.

Michael Marsh Refuge❖, part of the Saxis area to the southwest, is best explored by boat. In addition to ducks, grebes, loons, herons, and egrets, many shorebirds and songbirds are found here.

From Assateague Island near the Maryland-Virginia border south to the mouth of the Chesapeake Bay at Cape Charles, Virginia's Atlantic coastline is protected by a series of barrier islands, most of which are owned by the Nature Conservancy as part of the **Virginia Coast Reserve❖.** Consisting of all or parts of 14 separate seaside islands and parts of the main peninsula, the reserve is the largest section of unspoiled barrier-island coastline in the country: some 45,000 acres of beach, marsh, lagoon, scattered pine forest, and wax myrtle scrub. All but Parramore, Shipshoal, and Revel islands are open for hiking, bird-watching, and fishing. Although many barrier islands retreat because of wave action and overwash, it appears that the Virginia barrier islands' rate of lateral migration (42 to 49 feet a year) is faster than any along the Atlantic Coast. Recent storms have sometimes doubled this annual rate in the course of two days. Consequently, the barriers are not hospitable to human habitation over the long term; the once-common houses, hotels, and lodges are now virtually all gone, leaving the beaches to thousands of black skimmers, terns, gulls, and plovers.

High saltwater cordgrass marshes lie behind the islands. In the spring, brown pelicans, numerous heron species, great and snowy egrets, night herons, American oystercatchers, willet, and royal, Forster's, and common terns are present. The fall brings brant, common loons, horned grebes, black ducks, red-breasted mergansers, scoters, peregrine falcons, and merlins. Because the islands' ecosystems are fragile, potential visitors must contact the reserve's office in Nassawadox before arriving. The Conservancy also operates trips to the islands with naturalists, probably the best way to enjoy the riches of the reserve.

Near Smith Island, the southernmost island in the Virginia Coast Reserve, **Mockhorn Island Wildlife Management Area❖** consists of tidal marsh. Only about five percent of the land remains above the high-tide mark, making it accessible only by boat from the Oyster Boat Ramp, just off Route 639 at Cheriton.

South on Route 13 at the tip of the Delmarva Peninsula is Cape Charles, the site of a former Air Force station, now the **Eastern Shore of Virginia National Wildlife Refuge❖.** It lies near the north tollgate of the Chesapeake Bay Bridge-Tunnel and serves as a frequent resting and feeding stop for southward-flying migratory birds. In the fall, many will wait out a strong northwesterly storm or other adverse weather conditions before setting out across the 19 miles of open bay water to the mainland. Migrating monarch butterflies also use this area as a resting spot.

One stop for migratory birds between Cape Charles and Norfolk is **Fisherman Island National Wildlife Refuge❖,** a low-lying, isolated barrier island consisting of 1,000 acres of brackish marsh and beach that is transected by the Chesapeake Bay Bridge-Tunnel. Double-breasted cormorants and Bonaparte's gulls, among others, stop here in numbers. Peregrine falcons, piping plovers, bald eagles, Atlantic loggerhead sea turtles, and tiger beetles are some of the endangered and threatened species using this area, and ospreys have built nests on several of the towers and piers of the abandoned naval station. Access is limited to guided four-mile hiking tours, which are by reservation only from the Eastern Shore of Virginia National Wildlife Refuge. The island is off limits during prime nesting season in late spring and early summer, when terns, ring-billed gulls, and shorebirds lay eggs in nests along the beach.

To explore the next area, follow Route 13 back north of Pocomoke City and continue northwest to the junction at Route 413, then head south.

MARYLAND'S EASTERN SHORE

For generations, the watermen of Maryland's Smith Island and other nearby communities have reaped the rich harvest of Tangier Sound, the epicenter of Chesapeake Bay and one of the most productive fishing grounds in the country. Blue crabs, oysters, clams, fish, eels, diamondback terrapins, and waterfowl live and proliferate here in large, but certainly not unlimited, numbers.

At the mouth of Crisfield Harbor, the region's center for processing

LEFT: *Vividly colored head feathers, among other features, distinguish the showy male mallard from the mottled brown female.*
RIGHT: *This aerial view encompasses just a fraction of the 500,000 acres of wetlands that surround the Chesapeake Bay, creating a particularly rich habitat for wildlife.*

blue crabs, lies **Janes Island State Park❖.** The mainland area of the park, Hodson Memorial Area, located off Route 358, has a boat launch and other facilities. During the summer, the state operates a ferry to Janes Island, a 3,000-acre, undeveloped marshy land with a sandy beach on its western coast facing Tangier Sound. A walk south along the four-mile **Flatrock Beach,** where a small stream must be waded, leads to a 50-foot chimney and the rendering vats of an old, abandoned fish factory. Tracks with two parallel furrows—signs of the diamondback terrapin—are often visible. These turtles have gray heads and necks, peppered with black, and diamond-shaped marks on their shells. Each turtle's markings are different. Birds include seaside sparrows, marsh wrens, boat-tailed grackles, and red-winged blackbirds.

In the southern bay, relatively high salinity and tidal conditions make life difficult for all but a few hardy plant species. Largely featureless saltwater-marsh islands form a line south from the tip of Dorchester County to the mouth of the bay. Some islands, such as Bloodsworth, contain no dry land at all, just cordgrass marsh dominated by one or two species. On islands with slightly higher elevation, where other plants can get a purchase, loblolly pines and wax myrtle grow, and some islands are occupied by herons and egrets. The people who live on Smith and Tangier islands are accustomed to flooded lawns and streets, so low is the land.

Out in the bay about ten miles west of Crisfield is Smith Island, actually a cluster of small islands. Occupying the northern island is **Martin National Wildlife Refuge,** an unspoiled salt marsh that shelters migratory waterfowl, black ducks, and a major osprey nesting area. Many species of herons and egrets and the glossy ibis also nest here at several rookeries.

Despite its name, **Deal Island Wildlife Management Area❖** is not on Deal Island but on the mainland, opposite the island off Route 363, 10 miles west from Route 13 and Princess Anne. It includes **Dames Quarter Marsh,** impounded marshland that feeds a large number of waterbirds, such as herons, glossy ibis, and Forster's terns, along with clapper rail, common gallinules, ducks, and geese. The marsh also serves as an important breeding ground for the black duck and the blue-winged teal.

ABOVE: *About a third of the nation's population of spectacular, all-white tundra swans winter in the brackish marshes of Delmarva. A large group gathers on Chesapeake Bay between the Chester and Choptank rivers.*

The construction of dikes and channels has opened up what had been mostly needlerush vegetation to a combination of salt-marsh bulrush and salt grass. Interspersed with small ponds, the marshland is now more hospitable to birds. Providing good vantages of waterfowl in the late fall, winter, and early spring, a ten-mile round-trip hike starting near the boat ramp crosses several bridges and circles the entire impoundment. Especially dramatic during the winter are the raptors: northern harriers, bald eagles, peregrines, short-eared owls, and red-tailed, rough-legged, and sharp-shinned hawks.

At Salisbury, take Route 50 west and north, parallel to Maryland's Eastern Shore and through southern Dorchester County, filled with mile upon mile of marsh—tidal flats with meandering creeks, stands of two-foot-tall grass known as Olney three-square, and occasional islands of trees. Winding through the marshes is the Blackwater River, which flows from three swamps—the Gum, Kentuck, and Moneystump. These marshlands, bordered by stands of the loblolly pine so characteristic of the South, are the most extensive in the bay area. At the center is one of Maryland's premier natural spots, the 20,090-acre **Blackwater National Wildlife Refuge❖,** located 12 miles south of Cambridge on Key Wallace Drive. Among the Canada geese and more than 20 species of ducks, on winter days some 50,000 shorebirds are visible from the road, which follows a dike that overlooks freshwater impoundments and marsh. In winter, thousands of Canada geese fly off in formation around sunset, in search of corn-stubble fields on which to feed—a spectacular sight.

No less thrilling than the sight of numerous migratory birds are the views of bald eagles. About ten nesting pairs, the largest concentration of bald eagles on the eastern seaboard north of Florida, make their home in tall trees within the refuge. Because bald eagles use them season after season, their nests can grow as big as 8 feet wide and 15 feet tall and weigh as much as two tons.

Two short trails, one with a boardwalk, are available to the hiker. However, refuge managers believe that visitors in cars cause less disturbance to the birds, possibly because the vehicle acts as a blind. A nice day trip for bikers starts at the visitor center and runs 22 miles down Maple Dam Road to the Blackwater River and back.

The refuge hosts the largest population of the endangered Delmarva fox squirrel, a mammal with a longer tail and a larger and lighter body than the common gray squirrel. Sometimes visible is the nutria, a beaver-sized rodent that is a South American immigrant. Unfortunately, the overall acreage of marsh is diminishing, mostly due to natural factors, including overgrazing by geese and muskrats.

On the other side of Blackwater NWR, toward the bay, off Route 16 near the town of Taylors Island, the **Robinson Neck/Frank M. Ewing Preserve❖** is half pine forest and half brackish tidal marsh. The preserve shelters migrating songbirds and waterfowl, and wildflowers sprout in the spring. A nature trail leads through loblolly pines to the tidal marsh of Slaughter Creek. Because poison ivy is one of the most common ground plants here, the best time to visit the preserve is between January and March, when it has lost its foliage.

Of the 21 rivers that feed into the Chesapeake Bay along the Delmarva Peninsula, the Choptank is the largest, running some 70 miles from western Delaware to the Chesapeake. The river twists and turns, forming marshes on the inside corners and bluffs on the outside of each bend. Upriver, the Choptank is a small-boater's paradise, with many guts and side creeks to explore. A number of good landings are left over from colonial times, when the area saw a brisk trade in tobacco. About 25 miles north of the city of Cambridge is a good put-in, **Martinak State Park❖,** located on the upper reaches of the Choptank. The park is off Route 404 near the town of Denton, 14 miles east of Route 50.

Downstream, about five miles east of Easton off Route 331, the Nature

OVERLEAF: A hummock of loblolly pines serves as the backdrop for a great blue heron and a flotilla of mallard that browse the bulrush and cattail marsh of Maryland's Blackwater National Wildlife Refuge.

95

Conservancy runs the **Choptank Wetlands Preserve❖,** a tidal marshland where Kings Creek feeds into the Choptank River. A half-mile-long board-walk with instructional signs and an elevated platform provide views of the wetland filled with switchgrass, cattails, phragmites, and the triangular leaves of the arrow arum. Although overland access is limited, a dock at the preserve enables visitors to reach the area by canoe. Up Kings Creek by canoe, the high, wooded banks obscure the agricultural fields from the river, engendering a feeling of real isolation and wilderness. River otters often play in the creek and are visible to the quiet and patient observer. The Choptank's strong tides are not to be taken lightly: Depending on the time of day, it might be better to put in upstream at the Kingston Road Bridge rather than the dock.

Tuckahoe Creek also feeds the Choptank River from the north, halfway between Choptank Wetlands and Martinak State Park. The twisting creek is worthy of exploration by canoe. Upstream is **Tuckahoe State Park❖,** nearly 3,500 acres of wooded marshland north of Queen Anne near the junction of Routes 404 and 480.

Poplar Island, in the bay, remains a strong reminder of the severe erosion that plagues the coastline along Maryland's Eastern Shore. In 1608, Captain John Smith described it as a single island, 1,000 acres in size. Located west of the town of Sherwood off Route 33, Poplar today consists of four islands totaling less than 50 acres. Osprey and blue heron nest here and a few white-tailed deer still roam.

Nearby **Wye Oak State Park❖,** a small, 29-acre park, off Route 662 south of Wye Mills (reachable via Route 50), is devoted to maintaining a 440-year-old white oak tree, the nation's largest and finest example of this species. Its crown measures 102 feet across.

To the southwest, along the Wye River, the **Wye Island Natural Resource Management Area❖** contains School House Woods, a 30-acre tract of 250-year-old white oaks, red oaks, hickory, and gum trees—one of the only stands of mature timber left on the Eastern Shore. Where the Wye River system splits off from the Miles River, it divides north and east into two rivers, the Wye and the Wye East. They rejoin at Wye Narrows, thus surrounding Wye Island. The rest of the 4.4-square-mile island consists mostly of soybean and corn fields, separated by hedgerows, and 30 miles of shoreline along which ospreys often nest. The Wye River is a watercourse worth exploring by small boat. Quite different from the Choptank with its long length and gradual salinity gradient, the Wye is short and brackish, winding by a series of lovely old farms and houses.

Near Grasonville, across from Kent Island off Route 18 and close to the Chesapeake Bay Bridge (which carries Routes 50 and 30), the Wildfowl Trust of North America runs **Horsehead Wetlands Center❖.** Set up to provide viewing of migrating wildfowl and shorebirds on 310 acres of marsh, woods, ponds, and meadows, the center includes an enclosed viewing area with a window wall, towers, bird blinds, and footpaths. Wood duck, black duck, gadwall, and blue-winged teal—the four duck species that nest and breed in the Chesapeake Bay—are raised here for release. It's hard to find a better place to see waterfowl up close. From the center, do not cross the Bay Bridge to the west; rather, continue northeast on Route 301 or on the slower, more scenic Route 213.

At the mouth of the Chester River, south of Rock Hall (take Route 20 south off Route 213, then head to the end of Route 445), **Eastern Neck National Wildlife Refuge❖** is a protected island with a good system of trails that has avoided the congestion and development seen on Kent Island. The refuge is best known for its wintering tundra swans, which arrive here after a nonstop flight from their summer haunts in the Arctic. Resident mute swans are visible on the mud shoals, from the boardwalk and observation tower at Tubby's Cove, as are red-breasted mergansers and buffleheads. The refuge is also a good place to see raptors year-round, but especially during the fall hawk migration. A strong population of Delmarva fox squirrels lives here as well. In keeping with its commitment to preserve wildlife, the refuge closes certain areas to visitors during various seasons.

To the north, at the head of the bay, the wedge-shaped peninsula known as Elk Neck is mostly public property. At the tip, reached by Route 272 (accessible via Route 40 west from Route 213), **Elk Neck State Park❖** features a variety of topography, from heavily wooded bluffs overlooking the North East River to sandy beaches and marshlands—easily accessible by more than seven miles of trails. Some of the forests include oaks and mountain laurel more typically found in the piedmont region rather than the coastal plain. Wild turkeys and great black-backed gulls are among the many bird species seen here.

Inland, in the neck's arid uplands, the **Elk Neck Demonstration Forest❖** is a state forest in which scientists experiment with tree hybrids, such as a cross between loblolly and pitch pines, to improve timber growth in sandy soils. The sandy soil provides an abundance of wildlife prints, and an afternoon can easily be spent following the tracks of a deer or raccoon. Often the quarry is not seen, but the search invariably reveals unexpected glimpses of other woodland animals and the quiet charm of even arid regions.

VIRGINIA'S PIEDMONT AND COASTAL PLAIN

From Virginia's border with Maryland near Washington, D.C., it's possible to drive southeast and feel the influence of the North waning and the flavor of the South taking over. The oaks of the rolling piedmont, so prevalent in the Mid-Atlantic, begin to give way to sandy soil and loblolly pines, their six-inch needles bobbing in clumps from branches attached to arrow-straight trunks.

In the far southeastern corner of the state, southwest of Norfolk near the North Carolina border, Route 17 cuts through the eastern edge of the Great Dismal Swamp National Wildlife Refuge. The southern character here is unmistakable. Bald cypress trees, the bases of their trunks swollen, stand in still water, their branches draped with Spanish moss. Some 20 species of vines twist or climb their way up tree trunks into the canopy. Patient observers might catch a glimpse of a marsh rabbit, a Creole pearly eye butterfly, or a salamanderlike lizard known as a green anole—just a few of the many animals that reach the northernmost ends of their natural range in this refuge.

This chapter covers the eastern two-thirds of Virginia, which consists of two distinct physiographic provinces, the piedmont and the coastal plain. Each province runs the length of the state from Maryland to North Carolina and is separated by a zone commonly called the fall line. This zone, a line

PRECEDING PAGES: *Before leaves appear in the early spring, eastern red-bud flowers paint the forests pink near Virginia's Great Falls Park.*
LEFT: *Against a backdrop of autumn leaves, lacy cascades tumble over waterfalls along Scotts Run near Dranesville in Virginia's piedmont.*

paralleled on a map by Interstate 95 from Alexandria south to Fredericksburg, Richmond, and Petersburg, describes the line where the hard, metamorphic rocks of the piedmont give way to the softer, sedimentary rocks of the coastal plain. Rivers crossing over the fall line frequently form rapids: Historically, these sites were selected for establishing settlements by both Native Americans and, later, Europeans. The varied geology around the fall line has fostered a number of different microenvironments, which in turn have supported a wide variety of plants and animals.

The driving route for this chapter is a loop that begins and ends near Washington, D.C. It starts at the northern edge of the piedmont in Alexandria, and travels up the Potomac River, which serves as a border between Maryland and Virginia. It then heads southwest through the piedmont on Route 29, east to Richmond on Route 6 (or by canoe on the James River), south to the border with North Carolina on I-95, then east to the coastal plain via Route 58. The route then follows the coastal plain north up Route 17 to Fredericksburg, and parallels the Potomac north to Alexandria.

At its start near the border with Maryland, Virginia's piedmont forms a narrow wedge of land as little as 45 miles wide, sitting snugly between the rise of the Blue Ridge Mountains to the west and the fall line at Alexandria to the east. The piedmont's girth swells to 180 miles by the time it meets the North Carolina border, as the mountains of the Blue Ridge angle to the southwest.

Out on Route 29, the hills of the piedmont bear witness to several hundred years of human habitation. Logging, along with clearing for agriculture, has left few stands of virgin trees. In the wake of this activity are croplands, abandoned fields, pastures, hay fields, artificial ponds, and scattered stands of second- and third-growth red oak, white oak, chestnut oak, and Virginia pine.

Despite the evidence of human effort, the edge communities, where pasture meets forest or lake meets forest, are rich in wildlife. Hedgerows provide safe havens from which birds can venture into fields in search of food. For the patient observer who steals away to the remote side of one of the piedmont's artificial lakes, such as Beaver Lake or Holliday Lake, the rewards are rich. At night, raccoons, opossums, and an occasional bobcat poke around the edge of a lake to slake their thirst and search for

---

OVERLEAF: *Spring's lavish exuberance carpets the moist forest floor of Bull Run Regional Park with thousands of Virginia bluebells. Budding in March, they burst into spectacular bloom by early April.*

VIRGINIA'S PIEDMONT AND COASTAL PLAIN

25 Miles
25 Kilometers

food. During the day, a muskrat might be seen swimming across a lake, part of its dark brown back exposed as it swims. Gnawed tree stumps and lodges tell of the presence of beavers. Bullfrogs and sliders sun themselves on snags, and kingfishers perch, scanning the water for small fish.

South of the James River, the deciduous forest gives way to coniferous, as pines become more abundant and black oak replaces red oak. East across the fall line into the coastal plain, the topography grows flat and wet, crossed by dark waters of the Nottoway and Blackwater rivers. Species of the southern forest—longleaf pine, pond pine, and loblolly— emerge. Along rivers and in the Great Dismal Swamp, the pines yield to red maple, bald cypress, tupelo, and black gum.

On Virginia's Atlantic coast, a sandy barrier island protects the expanse of Back Bay, with its wetland islands and surrounding marsh, from the relentless beating of the Atlantic. North of Norfolk, the coastline escapes the buffet of the open ocean, feeling only the relatively gentle lapping of the Chesapeake Bay. Here, the coastline is influenced by the four large estuarine rivers that flow southeast across the coastal plain to the bay: the James, York, Rappahannock, and Potomac. They cut the upper Virginia coast into three large peninsulas, each covered with a piedmont forest of oak and pine.

Along the banks of these estuarine rivers are rich marshlands that attract millions of migratory waterbirds each spring and fall. These same fertile waters lured European settlers up the James to establish the settlement of Jamestown on a small alluvial island. A far more ancient history is revealed on the sides of high bluffs, where the waters of the James and York have eroded the sediment: Huge whale vertebrae and still-sharp sharks' teeth emerge from the sand, mute evidence of geologic episodes five and nine million years ago when the coastal plain was covered by a shallow sea.

Despite the grand geologic and climatological forces that have formed the coastal plain over the past several million years, no changes have occurred more quickly or with greater impact than those caused by human development in the last three centuries. Perhaps most paradoxically of all, the natural symbol of the United States, the bald eagle, was nearly eliminated on the East Coast by DDT and other pesticides, hunting, and a shrinking habitat. The recent recovery of this species is a testament to the land's capacity to regenerate when helped, not hindered, by humankind. Perhaps no sight is more dramatic than watching one of nature's grandest predators fly across the edge of a marsh in a preserve only a half-hour drive from Washington, D.C.

NORTHERN VIRGINIA

Each afternoon, thousands of commuters race over Chain Bridge and pass high over the Potomac River, crossing from Washington, D.C., into Virginia. Few pause on their homeward dash to gaze upstream to a narrow stretch of white water, where the immense flow of the Potomac is suddenly crammed into a narrow rock chute. Here, many first-class canoeists have dumped their boats and shot downstream like a cork popped from a bottle of champagne. Little Falls and its big brother Great Falls, about ten miles upstream, form the most spectacular rapids at the fall line, where the Potomac flows from the hard, metamorphic rocks of the piedmont to the soft, easily erodible sediments of the coastal plain.

Georgetown Pike (Route 193) passes the entrance to **Great Falls Park❖,** four miles northwest of the Capital Beltway (I-495). Great Falls is the best place to witness the fury of the Potomac as it drops 76 feet in a quarter-mile sprint of seething white water. From safely atop the exposed rock along the edge of this melee, outlining a route a kayaker could take involves much imagination. Although no one is now permitted to make the attempt, in the past a handful of world-class paddlers have challenged the falls successfully by sneaking along a channel on the Virginia side of a rocky island in the middle of the river.

Trails from the overlooks, one of which reveals the high-water marks from past storms, when the water level has risen almost three times its normal depth, lead to **Mather Gorge,** a straight and narrow canyon carved by the river over millions of years along a fault in the rock. The cliffs drop 65 vertical feet, making them popular among rock climbers. Cowhoof Rock offers one of the best vistas of the gorge, from about 100 feet above the water.

Slightly inland, a small swamp occupies an old bed of the river. Skunk cabbage, its broad green leaves abundantly exuding the rank smell for which it is named, and spring-blooming jewelweed thrive in the wetter spots, while pin and willow oaks and some red maples grow in the drier areas.

The wet bottomlands along the Potomac and on its islands form some of the richest habitat in the piedmont, fortified by the dark, alluvial soil deposited by the river. Largely inaccessible to developers, the steep bluffs along the river's edge have remained mostly untouched. A quiet paddle along the Potomac reveals a world unchanged by modern civilization (with the exception of jet traffic high above). Great blue herons, ospreys, red-shouldered hawks, and wood ducks haunt the river, its banks lined with oaks and sycamores. Alders also hug the river's edge, their slim dark trunks and oval leaves hung with catkins—droopy, tassel-like flowers heavy with

109

pollen. River wash of flotsam and jetsam piles up on small alluvial islands, forming organic sculptures, and the rich smell of river mud hangs in the air.

Such is the diversity of the bottomland habitats that 110 animal species have been sighted at **Fraser Preserve❖,** a relatively small area owned by the Nature Conservancy five miles upstream from Great Falls Park along Routes 603 and 755. Rocky bluffs, thickets, mature hardwood forests, and floodplain forests that drop precipitously to alder swamp at river's edge provide nesting habitats for the red-shouldered hawk, ruby-throated hummingbird, downy woodpecker, scarlet tanager, and blue-gray gnatcatcher. Patient observers may uncover a wood turtle, two-lined salamander, or

southern leopard frog. Springtime brings in a chorus of wildflowers—on the order of 300 species, at last count by the conservancy. Because of the fragility of the area, the Nature Conservancy requires visitors to call ahead for permission to visit.

Farther upstream from Fraser off Route 15, Virginia recently established **Ball's Bluff Regional Park❖** around Ball's Bluff, one of the nation's smallest national cemeteries. The explosion of Virginia bluebells, the state flower, brings this small, undeveloped park alive in the springtime with fields of blue, touched by the pink of unopened buds. Other piedmont wildflowers also appear here, including jack-in-the-pulpit, wild ginger, white trout lily, and harbinger-of-spring.

ABOVE: *Like tiny licks of flame, delicate scarlet flowers turn the bursting-heart on fire every spring. The scraggly shrub grows up to eight feet tall.*

RIGHT: *At Virginia's Great Falls Park, the Potomac River crashes over the fall line, a point where the piedmont gives way to the flatter coastal plain.*

Bald eagles are known to nest and roost in **Mason Neck Management Area,** a stubby peninsula sticking out into the Potomac that includes the **Mason Neck National Wildlife Refuge❖,** a state park, Gunston Hall Plantation, and some undeveloped regional parkland. Eighteen miles south of Washington, D.C., off Virginia Routes 242 and 600, the neck contains two marshes; in the refuge is 245-acre Great Marsh, one of northern Virginia's largest, and in the state park is Kane Creek Marsh. The marshes provide food sources for a rich variety of birdlife, including bald eagles, which are often visible off the

three-mile **Woodmarsh Trail** that loops to the edge of the Great Marsh. The trail wanders through a deciduous forest where the large, noisy pileated woodpecker is sometimes heard and seen. All sorts of waterfowl collect here on their migratory run south down the Atlantic Flyway: canvasback ducks, mallard, black ducks, teal, mergansers, and scaup. In the state park, during the winter when Belmont Bay freezes over, bald eagles and waterfowl sometimes perch on the ice. In the summer, Mason Neck sustains one of the state's largest great blue heron colonies, numbering more than 1,000 nests.

Although **Huntley Meadows Park❖** is not located directly on the Potomac, the impact of the river on the park is just as significant as on Mason Neck. Located on Lockheed Boulevard, three miles south of the Capital Beltway (I-95) on Route 1, Huntley Meadows lies in wet lowlands that long ago were a channel of the Potomac. The river is now several miles to the east, but these lowlands support freshwater marshes interspersed with beaver ponds and remain one of the prime bird-watching spots in the Washington area. From a vantage 19 feet above a 60-acre wetland in the park's observation tower, bird-watchers have counted some 204 species, including five resident species of woodpecker and the elusive yellow-crowned night heron.

ABOVE: *A denizen of the shrubby open fields of the piedmont, the indigo bunting rises to the highest perch and fills the air with song.*

LEFT: *The marshes, ponds, and forests of Virginia's 1,200-acre Huntley Meadows Park serve as prime habitat for the king rail as well as various songbirds, herons, and ducks.*

As the sun sets on spring evenings, a chorus of frogs and toads fills the air like a discordant symphony. The resounding bass belongs to the bullfrog, while the diminutive spring peeper squeaks out a piccolo. The chorus lasts from dusk to midnight for about six weeks starting in March. During this time, naturalists lead a popular "frog romp" through the park and along the half-mile boardwalk. Another good time to visit is in June, when the marshland erupts in the pink bloom of swamp rose, buttonbush, and lizard's tail.

A favorite bird-watching spot of Washingtonians is **Dyke Marsh Wildlife Preserve❖,** a long and narrow park sandwiched between the Potomac and

113

ABOVE: *Generally abroad at night, the green frog (left) frequents shallow water and the edges of still ponds. The spotted salamander (right) lives mainly underground but migrates to wetlands to breed.*

George Washington Memorial Parkway south of Hunting Creek and the Belle Haven Picnic Area, not far from Alexandria. Commercial dredging for sand and gravel in the early 1950s devastated the area, but it was later restored by the National Park Service. Bird-watchers have counted more than 250 species here, mostly during the fall and spring when the area is flush with migrant species. A three-quarter-mile dirt trail leads through the woods from the picnic area. Another point of access is the bike trail paralleling the highway on its way to Mount Vernon. On a bright spring day the roar of jets from nearby Washington National Airport and other signs of the city dissolve with a glimpse of a double-breasted cormorant perched on a snag or log at the edge of the Dyke Marsh. Perhaps it just finished diving into the Potomac for a meal. With graceful, deliberate movements, it dries its sleek, dark wings by stretching them in the breeze.

THE PIEDMONT

An excellent spring wildflower display occurs to the west of the Potomac River, at a site reached by traveling southwest from Arlington on Route 29 to Centreville, just before Manassas. Downstream along Bull Run from the Manassas National Battlefield Park, **Bull Run Regional Park❖** spans a thou-

ABOVE: *An eastern box turtle caught the fancy of John White, official artist of the 1585 Roanoke expedition and the first Englishman to paint the natural life and native peoples of the North American continent.*

sand acres of woods and meadows. The one-and-a-half-mile **Bluebell Nature Loop** passes through a wet forestland teeming with thousands of Virginia bluebells in mid-April. Clusters of the baby blue flowers, each shaped like a trumpet, hang from each stem. The annual Bluebell Walk, led by park rangers, is one of the oldest nature walks in the area.

Heading southwest from Manassas toward Warrenton, Route 29 traverses the flat topography of the Culpeper Basin, consisting of thick sediments laid down by rivers during the Jurassic and Triassic periods, when dinosaurs walked the land. At New Baltimore, just shy of Warrenton, the topography grows more rugged to the west, a sign of an underlying, weather-resistant rock known as Cactoctin greenstone. The nearby long, low ridge of the Bull Run Mountains appears to be the foothills of the Blue Ridge Mountains; in fact, it is a monadnock, a height of land containing more erosion-resistant rock than the surrounding area. The rock around the monadnock, and covering most of the piedmont, weathered over time, leaving a thick layer of unconsolidated sediments known as saprolite. This layer has left few rock outcrops over the piedmont, making it difficult for geologists to sort out the complex history of the region. Route 29, which runs parallel to the western edge of the piedmont, passes other monadnocks on its way south, including the Southwest Mountains near Charlottesville, all dry ridgetops covered with chestnut oak and heath forests.

Off Route 29 at Opal, Route 17 heads southeast to Goldvein, a small town named for its many gold-bearing quartz veins. These were mined from the 1830s to the 1930s—not only for gold but also for pyrite, or fool's gold, which is processed to make sulfuric acid. Along the north shore of Lake Anna, to the south of Goldvein and accessible from Route 29 at Culpeper by taking Route 522 south and Route 208 east, **Lake Anna State Park❖** has gold-mining exhibits at Gold Hill, a part of the Goodwin Gold Mine during the peak mining years of the 1840s.

Lake Anna did not exist until long after the last gold was extracted from a zinc mine here in the 1940s. Engineers dammed the North Anna River in 1971 to form a lake that would serve as a water coolant for Virginia Power Company's nuclear power plant. Birdlife abounds among the lake's many fingers. Route 208 crosses the lake, where it's possible to glimpse common loons, ducks, and common mergansers from the bridge or the marina located on the northwestern end.

Lake Anna is one of a number of artificial lakes that dot Virginia's interior piedmont. Four state parks, arrayed like a squashed diamond between Route 29 to the west and Richmond to the east, contain lakes inside state forests. The northernmost park, **Bear Creek Lake State Park❖** in **Cumberland State Forest❖,** is located east on Route 60 from Route 29 at Amherst. Its small lake was created by the damming of Bear Creek, a tributary of the Willis and James rivers. A five-mile trail loops around the 40-acre lake, passing a swimming beach, camping sites, and evidence of beaver activity and through a large grove of tulip poplars.

For more ambitious hikers, Bear Creek Lake State Park provides access to the **Willis River Trail,** a 16-mile trail running through alluvial floodplain forests of tall oaks, river birch, papaws, and sycamores, and sometimes following the Willis River or its creeks. The only designated trail in any of Virginia's state forests, the Willis trail passes through the gently rolling Cumberland State Forest, where wild turkeys, deer, many songbirds, doves, and bobwhite abound. The trail also runs through **Rock Quarry Natural Area,** near a small canyon at Horn Quarter Creek, and includes overlooks of Winston Lake. Rock ledges along Bear Creek support liverworts, nonvascular plants related to the mosses that cling to bare rock.

Willis Mountain, a thin, rocky ridge to the southwest of the state park along Route 15, between Sprouses Corner and Sheppards, is another monadnock. The holes in the rock face result from mining kaolinite, a whitish clay used in industrial ceramics such as those needed for spark plugs. To the west of Willis Mountain, south from Sprouses Corner on Route 640, **Holliday Lake State Park❖** is nestled in **Appomattox-Buckingham State Forest❖,** not far from Appomattox Court House, the spot where Confederate general Robert E. Lee surrendered to Union forces during the Civil War. A concession stand at Holliday rents canoes for the short aquatic trail to the western side of the lake for a close look at lake ecology. A buoy marks a freshwater reef created by the Virginia Department of Game and Inland Fisheries from the remains of old Christmas trees. The reef feeds snails, sponges, and aquatic insects, which, in turn, feed the fish beloved by anglers—both human and raccoon.

A common denizen of Holliday Lake's shore and clear waters is the northern water snake, a copper-colored reptile with a pattern superficially resembling that of the poisonous copperhead. Unlike the copperhead, however, it takes willingly to the water and is harmless. It often basks in the sun on rocks near the water's edge, anticipating its next meal of sala-mander, turtle, crayfish, or minnow. This is probably the piedmont's most common snake, inhabiting streambanks as well as lakeshores.

THE JAMES RIVER

Not unlike the Potomac to the north, the James River defies generic descrip-tion as it cuts across the breadth of five physiographic provinces in Virginia, draining some of the Mid-Atlantic's most fertile agricultural land and traveling some 200 miles east from the West Virginia border to Richmond. From there it turns into a wide estuarine river; its banks were once home to Captain John Smith and Virginia's earliest European settlers. During the Pleistocene epoch, both the James and Potomac were tributaries of the glacial Susquehanna River system; consequently, they share similar fish species.

For those who savor a gentle canoe float on a bright spring day with fish-ing rod at the ready, the section of the James from Bent Creek, east along Route 60 from Route 29 at Amherst, to Goochland, two dozen miles west of Richmond, offers many excellent spots. (For those traveling by automobile, Route 6 partially parallels the James. Take Route 6 west from Route 29, near Faber; it first joins the river at Scottsville, about 30 miles north of Bent Creek.) For smallmouth bass, the James cannot be beat. Whether by trolling or fly-fishing, more trophy fish have been caught here than on any other river in the area. In May, the water warms and the bass shake off the sluggishness from the long, cold winter and regain their appetites. They move to pre-spawning spots along the shoreline where anglers await, lines cast.

117

On the river between Bent Creek and Wingina are a number of islands, including the Smith Islands, privately owned but open to the public. Notable is **Helena's Island Preserve❖,** owned by the Nature Conservancy, rich bottomland forest that was once farmed but is now wild. It has a sizable population of black walnut trees, perhaps the largest grove in Virginia. One of the scarcest of the native hardwoods, black walnut wood is prized for use in furniture and gunstocks. The fruit, or nut, is edible and delicious.

The James undergoes an abrupt personality change once it crosses the fall line at Richmond, where it forms white water ranging from class II to V rapids, depending on the time of the year. Although the water here won't rattle bones like a spin down the New River or the Youghiogheny, it does offer an impressive trip, dropping across ledges, broken-down dams, chutes, and holes—then ending with vistas of the Richmond skyline and a river otter's view of old factories that line the banks. Richmond raft companies offer eight-mile day trips.

As the river runs through western and central Richmond, it passes the riverside and island parkland of the 450-

RIGHT: *A native morning glory grows along the lush banks of the James River, which cuts a green corridor to the Atlantic through the rolling farmlands of Virginia's piedmont.*

ABOVE: *Like old-fashioned pantaloons hung on a clothesline, the fragrant white flowers of Dutchman's breeches dangle from leafless stems.*

acre **James River Park System❖.** In spots the rumble of the James drowns out the traffic and, for a few long moments, the sounds and sights of the city disappear. On early spring mornings on the southern bank of the James, at a place called Pony Pasture upriver near Williams Island, the air is often filled with the sweet harmonies of migrating warblers, thrushes, and other songbirds for which the James acts as a migratory highway. The alluvial floodplain, created by deposits of waterborne sediment from the rich farmlands to the west, bears sycamores, tulip poplars, and red maples. Wildflowers grow in abundance: morning glories, Virginia bellflowers, trout lilies, Dutchman's-breeches, saxifrage, foamflowers, mist flowers, soapworts, and papaws. The occasional daffodil also sprouts here, perhaps from a garden bulb washed out through a storm drain. Downriver, near Belle Isle, the short **Geology Interpretive Trail** runs along the granite rocks of the fall line. Riverbeds are among the only places to see exposed bedrock in the piedmont, which is mostly covered with saprolite, the weathered remains of bedrock. At water's edge, the smooth Petersburg granite is pockmarked with rounded depressions, potholes ground into the bedrock over the eons by the agitation of cobbles tossed about by the strong currents of the James River.

Diverse textures of granite range from uniform to homogenous to streaked to coarse-grained pegmatite—all once molten about 330 million

ABOVE: *White, petal-like bracts surround the small green flower of the blooming dogwood, adding bursts of spring color to Virginia's woodlands.*

years ago. Differences in cooling times may help explain the variety of textures. Large topaz crystals—measuring 11 inches long and weighing up to 9 pounds—were found in a granite pegmatite 10 miles west of Richmond, about halfway between Midlothian and Powhatan. Southwest from here, on Route 360 near Amelia, some property owners permit collectors to rummage for gems such as moonstone and amazonite in the mine dumps and abandoned quarries left over from commercial mining of granite pegmatites.

Exposed beds of granite, or flatrocks, are known to host assemblages of rare plant species in several piedmont locations. One of them is the **Gasburg Granite Flatrocks Preserve,** which lies south of Richmond near Gasburg and Lake Gaston, and west of where I-95 hits the North Carolina border. Rare plants such as the granite umbrella sedge and Small's purslane eke out desperate lives in shallow depressions and around the edges of this flatrock ecosystem. Whereas spring wildflowers adapt to the stresses of varying light conditions throughout the year by carefully timed, often quick blooming cycles, the wildflowers on the granite flatrocks live under even more difficult conditions, more reminiscent of the desert. Rather than surviving as underground storage bulbs, they propagate as seeds, sometimes nestled in gravel and organic material only a fraction of an inch deep.

In May, tiny forests of three-inch-tall Small's stonecrop are topped with delicate white flowers. The crimson coloring of their stems and leaves provides protection against the bright sunshine. Prickly pear cactus, red cedar, and post oaks live around the edges of this very dry habitat. Due to the sensitive nature of the area, it is closed to the public.

THE COASTAL PLAIN

East along Route 58 the North Carolina border parallels the rolling hills of the piedmont, which flatten into coastal plain as the highway crosses the

fall line at Emporia. To the east and north stretch vast wet forests and swamps cut by the slow-flowing waters of rivers such as the Nottoway and Blackwater. These flooded lowland forests escaped widespread farming and logging and represent some of the least-changed ecosystems on the coastal plain. Wet, rich soils support an abundance of plants and insects that bolster the top end of the food chain—birds and mammals. Along the water's edge, bald cypress and water tupelo, also known as black gum, thrive. Vines such as the smooth-barked supplejack snake their way up anything that grows vertically, including other supplejack vines. Twisting and squeezing, they sometimes kill their hosts and still remain hanging from the canopy. Wild grape, peppervine, Virginia creeper, climbing hydrangea,

ABOVE: *A common summertime pleasure, beauty berry produces striking magenta fruit. Growing here in the Great Dismal Swamp National Wildlife Refuge, this shrub thrives in moist woodlands and clearings.*

RIGHT: *Smooth-barked supplejack vine exerts a slow but deadly stranglehold on its victim in the Dismal Swamp.*

and trumpet creeper also hang onto trunks and branches, contributing to the primordial ambience of the swamp. Even poison ivy seems monstrous and unreal, its vines sometimes growing as thick as a man's arm.

Canoeing the Nottoway or Blackwater is the best way to penetrate the swampland. The Nottoway is known as a brown-water river because it is enriched by runoff from the rich soils of the piedmont. One short river trip

Some 16 warbler species reside in the Great Dismal Swamp: Unlike other warblers, the blue-winged warbler (left) keeps its plumage all year; the magnolia warbler (above) is characterized by a black-streaked breast and bright yellow rump.

runs from the bridge at Route 653 a half dozen miles or so to Courtland. Along the Blackwater it's hard not to get a glimpse of the brown water snake, which sometimes suns itself on branches above the water. Every so often, these nonpoisonous snakes are known to fall without warning into a boat from an overhanging branch. The brown water snake resembles a much less common but very poisonous cousin, the cottonmouth. The tell-tale difference is the milk-white interior of a cottonmouth's mouth, shocking against the dark scales of its body. After nightfall on either of the rivers, the inhuman screams and hoots of the barred owl can chill the blood.

East of the Blackwater River along Route 58, then south on Route 32 at Suffolk, is Virginia's renowned Great Dismal Swamp. In the natural world, where those things most feared by humans are often destroyed by them with the greatest vigor, few places have sparked the human imagination as much as deep swamps, with their dark waters and deep shadows. Over the years the Great Dismal Swamp has been reduced to a small fraction of its original size. At one point it nearly ceased to exist altogether; only the last-minute and concerted efforts of private and public groups in Virginia and North Carolina managed to preserve 106,000 acres of what's

Rare in the nineteenth century, the chestnut-sided warbler (left) now thrives in abandoned farm fields. The black-throated green warbler (above) broadcasts its song from high in the forest canopy.

now known as the **Great Dismal Swamp National Wildlife Refuge❖.**

Even here, ditches, dikes, and fires have destroyed the vast stands of cypress and white cedar that once seemed endless. The red maple is quite common, along with shrubs such as the swamp azalea, sumac, inkberry, and sweet pepperbush. Paradoxically, human influence has created a wider variety of habitats than were originally found here: brier thickets, canebrakes, loblolly pine barrens, evergreen shrub bogs, tupelo and cypress swamps, and mixed forests.

Fanning out from Lake Drummond, a 3,100-acre lake in the middle of the refuge, are five drainage ditches, including one built by George Washington and his slaves. A four-and-a-half-mile walk or bike ride along Washington Ditch Road ends at the lakeshore, which is lined with gnarly bald cypress trees cloaked in Spanish moss. The dark shallow waters of Lake Drummond, one of only two natural lakes in Virginia, reach only six feet at their deepest point. Scientists have dated the age of the lake at 4,000 years; the swamp itself formed some 9,000 years ago, perhaps when rivers running through the area were blocked, encouraging the accumulation of partially decayed organic matter, or peat. How the lake was created re-

125

mains a mystery. A possible explanation is that a fire burned the peat, thus creating the depression, though there is no evidence of such a fire.

The swamp's interior hosts such animals as black bears and bobcat and as many as 16 breeding species of warblers. For bird-watchers, the elusive Swainson's warbler and Wayne's warbler are prized sightings. Even a member of the blindfish family (fish that are mostly found in caves) swims here, oblivious to the heavy concentrations of tannic acid that make the swamp's dark waters poisonous to other fish. At night, the faint and ghostly glow in the woods might come from foxfire, luminescence given off by fungi in decayed wood.

A drive along Route 17, which follows the Dismal Swamp Canal along the eastern edge of the swamp, gives a brief look into the wonders of the swamp world. Typical plants of the swamp are visible: sweet bay, red bay, titi, sweet pepperbush, and switch cane. The devil's walking stick grows along the canal and in open places, a dangerous-looking and sometimes clothes-ripping tree or small shrub that has sharp spines all over its trunk, branches, and even the midribs of its leaves.

THE VIRGINIA COAST

Just 25 miles due east of the Great Dismal Swamp, Virginia's coastline and the wetlands around Back Bay offer a stark contrast. Gulls and terns fill the wide-open, often blue sky under which stretch great expanses of sand, dune, and marsh. Although close as the crow flies, the coastline is best reached from the north via Virginia Beach. (Proceed south along the city's General Booth Boulevard and Princess Anne Road, then east to Sandbridge Beach, and south from there.)

In less than an hour, it's possible to escape the urbanization of Virginia Beach and the nearby military bases and visit the secluded shores of Back Bay, a large, shallow body of water 12.5 miles long by 5 miles wide. It pushes up into the southeastern edge of Virginia like a wedge, separating the mainland from a long, thin spit that points south and extends some 70 miles, well into North Carolina. Driving on the low-lying, narrow spit south from the town of Sandbridge to **Back Bay National Wildlife Refuge❖**, it's easy to see how winter storms often overwash the spit, pouring salt water into the shallow bay, which averages only four to five feet in depth. Hurricanes sometimes make the road impassable and whip up the waters of the bay until choppy waves rip across the water's surface.

The refuge includes the eastern spit, a number of marshy islands at the northern end of the bay, as well as lands on the western shore. Between

November and March the area is filled with thousands of greater snow geese, fretting and honking among the salt grass and three-square. A free afternoon, a warm parka, and a pair of binoculars are all that's necessary to enjoy these active birds as they bicker, eat, and rise together in flight, their stunning white feathers accentuated by black wing tips. The geese come from breeding grounds on arctic tundra far to the north on Baffin Island and the northwest coast of Greenland. Their large numbers and their habit of pulling marsh plants up by the roots often cause eat-outs, bare areas devoid of grasses.

The road peters out into a parking area; further travel south is limited to bike and foot traffic. Along the long stretches of uninterrupted beach each summer, female loggerhead turtles pull their ungainly weight across the sand to lay their eggs above the high-tide mark, leaving tracks that look as if a small dory had been dragged across the sand. Once hatched, the baby turtles head immediately back to the ocean. Back Bay is the northernmost regular nesting spot of these turtles, a species once far more common. Although precious little time of their lives is spent on land, this is when they are most vulnerable to their primary predators, raccoons and humans. Scientists have found that baby turtles determine their course to the sea by reading the differences in light density on the horizon at night. Where sea meets sky is more sharply defined and brighter than where the land meets sky. Unfortunately, civilization has often disrupted the navigational system of these hatchlings, which become confused by car headlights and other artificial illumination.

Farther south along the spit is **False Cape State Park❖**, accessible by a 5.9-mile hike or bike ride and by boat. False Cape is so named because sea captains often mistook it for Cape Henry and the entrance to the Chesapeake Bay to the north. As at the Back Bay NWR, the northern impoundment here was created to encourage visits by migratory waterfowl. Planting grasses and mowing are two other techniques used to create ideal conditions for birds. The **Barbour Hill Nature Trail** runs 2.4 miles through a variety of habitats in this sandy world dominated by loblolly pines and live oaks. This is about as far north as one can find live oaks, so named because of their evergreen leaves. With its wide crown and broad branches, the live oak appears to spread more horizontally than vertically, making the large tree an ideal umbrella under which to escape the heat of the summer sun.

To the south and west of False Cape, the tip of **Mackay Island National Wildlife Refuge❖** spills just over the North Carolina border into Virginia. Remnants of an old barrier island, Mackay and Knotts islands are crossed by

ABOVE: *Northern pintail (left) feed from the surface, bobbing underwater for wigeon grass; traveling in large flocks, lesser snow geese (right) forage marsh grasses, bulrushes, and pasture gleanings.*

canals, ideal for canoeing and for a glimpse of the elusive king rail. Tundra (formerly called whistling) swans are common during the winter. Access is from the western side of the bay via Route 615 or from North Carolina.

Running parallel to Back Bay just to the west, North Landing River empties into Currituck Sound, the name given the bay once it spills over into North Carolina. Many plant species travel up the sound from the south, reaching the northernmost extremes of their range here. One example is saw grass, a tall freshwater species with small but sharp teeth on its lower stem, which is common in Florida's Everglades. Like Back Bay, the North Landing River feels the tug of wind tides. South-blowing winds leave expanses of mudflats, while north-blowing gales flood water into its many tiny guts and upper creeks. Along this slow-flowing river is one of Virginia's rarest communities, the pocosin, a peatland shrub bog. The pocosin is characterized by a tangle of evergreen shrubs, such as inkberry, fetterbrush, and wax myrtle. The thorny vine called greenbrier and scattered trees further contribute to a dense, nearly impenetrable confusion of vegetation. Before more was known about the pocosin, local wisdom held that it sheltered

LEFT: *With flexible leaves and deep roots, American beachgrass is ideally suited to the windblown dunes at the Back Bay National Wildlife Refuge.*
OVERLEAF: *Gray-green Spanish moss shrouds bald cypress trees in the primordial swampscape of the Seashore State Park and Natural Area.*

129

large colonies of poisonous snakes. The state-run **North Landing River Natural Area Preserve❖,** which has no public facilities, can be reached via Pungo Ferry Road or by boat or canoe, still the best way to see this scenic river. Between June and August, milkweed flowers color the marsh with flashes of bright orange, while the hum of insects fills the air.

Completing the rich coastal region of southeastern Virginia is **Seashore State Park and Natural Area❖,** tucked between high-rise condominiums and hotels north of Virginia Beach on Route 60 at Cape Henry. It is surrounded by water on three sides—the Atlantic, Chesapeake Bay, and Broad Bay. Nineteen miles of trails run through a surprising diversity of ecosystems. Cordgrass salt marshes, flooded twice daily, line the shores of Long Creek and Broad Bay. Loblolly pine and live oak flourish atop the ridgelines of ancient dunes rising 50 feet above the sea, and freshwater bald-cypress swamps lined with peat occupy the low areas between the dunes. The stagnant waters are colored brown from tannin, a natural acid found in leaves and wood. The acidity prevents bacteria from growing in the water, which was why ship captains added tannin to their water barrels for long voyages.

As with the other refuges and parks in this narrow corridor, Seashore State Park contains quite a number of southern-dwelling plants and animals at the northernmost extreme of their ranges. These same species cannot survive in south-central or southwestern Virginia, where the climate is too cold. The shore is warmer, mostly because the Gulf Stream, an ocean current, flows north from the Gulf of Mexico up the East Coast. At Seashore, the chicken turtle is just one example of a southern species moving north. It is readily identifiable by its unusual neck, which extends longer than the length of its shell. Other southern species include Spanish moss, live oak, sea oats, the short-billed dowitcher, and the southern cricket frog.

The short **Bald Cypress Nature Trail** leads through stands of the trees, their branches often laden with Spanish moss. Although it resembles a moss or a lichen, Spanish moss is actually a flowering plant; it blooms in early July with a delicate green flower. Beware of chiggers, tiny red insects often found crawling through the moss, which can inflict small but itchy bites. Collecting moisture and nutrients from the air, Spanish moss is an epiphyte, as is the resurrection fern, which also adorns the cypress and live oak. Withering away to a bundle of dead-looking brown material in dry weather, it springs back to life as a green, rich plant with the first shower.

In the vicinity of Newport News, the James River meets Chesapeake Bay. Small islands of loblolly pine and wax myrtle surrounded by brackish water form much of the **Ragged Island Wildlife Management**

Area❖, at the southeast corner of the James River Bridge on Routes 258 and 17. Black ducks, mallard, scaup, gadwalls, ruddy ducks, buffleheads, and goldeneyes are visible from the vantage of the boardwalk and hiking trails. As prime duck-watching occurs during hunting season in the fall, when the marsh grasses turn a beautiful shade of gold and yellow, it's best to visit on Sundays, when hunting is prohibited.

Captain James Smith founded Virginia's first European colony at Jamestown, two dozen miles up the James, just upstream from a peninsula that juts deeply into the river. **Hog Island Wildlife Management Area❖** occupies the tip of the peninsula today, reached off Route 10 on either Route 617 or 650. In the 1970s, sportfishing was prohibited on the James because of high levels of an industrial chemical known as kepone. Levels are safe now, and the western side of the peninsula attracts anglers for the big channel catfish that swim in the outflow from the Virginia Power Company's Surry Nuclear Power Plant. An ambitious system of water control structures is used to manipulate water levels to encourage visitation by waterfowl. A strange sight sometimes occurs between April and June when archers point their bows down into Hog Island's pond waters and shoot carp.

THE TIDEWATER

On a map, the James, York, and Rappahannock rivers appear stacked one atop the other, reaching north to the Potomac. Actually, the James east of Richmond, the entire length of the York, and the eastern half of the Rappahannock are not strictly rivers at all, but estuaries. Whereas rivers continually move freshwater downstream, an estuary feels the tidal pulse of the ocean, mixing fresh and salt water in a back-and-forth motion. The rivers bring fertile topsoil to the estuaries, while the ocean brings mineral salts and the surrounding marshes provide decaying organic material—all working together to produce one of the richest ecosystems in the country. This largely explains the abundance of waterfowl in these estuaries and of course in Chesapeake Bay, the world's largest estuary.

Where these estuaries cut deeply through the coastal-plain sediments, bluffs are formed, sometimes revealing ancient strata. On the south shore of the York in **York River State Park❖** off Route 607 from I-64, the river and its tributaries create a landscape in sharp relief, covered with deep ravines, dense hardwood forests, ridges, bluffs, and marshes. Along the river are fossil clues to the area's ancient past. Seas covered the area about five and nine million years ago. Huge whales once swam here, leaving their virtually indestructible vertebrae, some seven inches long

LEFT: *The redhead, a diving duck with a distinctive black-tipped blue bill, prefers shallow lakes and marshes, where it submerges completely in search of aquatic plants to eat.*

RIGHT: *Taskinas Creek, a tidal stream favored by canoeists, takes a sinuous route as it meanders through York River State Park.*

OVERLEAF: *A mosaic of fall colors paints the mixed hardwood forest of Westmoreland State Park, a thick woodland populated with red and silver maples, American beech, oak, and tulip trees.*

and weighing up to 12 pounds, as well as their more delicate ear bones, each several inches in length and shaped like the crest of a wave. Fossilized coral, other invertebrates, and the fierce-looking teeth of an ancient shark known as *Isurus* can also be found.

A short canoe trip up the York from the state park's visitor center leads to the mouth of Taskinas Creek, a tidal stream well worth exploring. From its entrance, where salt-marsh cordgrass dominates, the water grows gradually less salty and the plant life changes to less salt-resistant species, such as buttonbush and cattail, then finally to freshwater species such as arrow arum and pickerelweed. The park offers guided canoe trips, or visitors can rent their own canoes from sporting goods shops in Richmond.

Some of the best beachside fossil hunting in the area is located about a dozen miles downriver from the park around the mouth of Indian Field Creek, which the Colonial National Memorial Parkway crosses, nearly four miles west of its intersection with Route 17 at Yorktown. Riprap, jumbled piles of boulders placed to help stop erosion, make fossil combing difficult except during low tide.

Continue north up Route 17, across the York River. At Gloucester, Route 14 heads east to Mathews County, which occupies a peninsula that juts into the Chesapeake Bay. Off Route 609 in Onemo, **Bethel Beach Natural Area Preserve❖** occupies a stretch of sandy beach, dune, and salt marsh. In the winter, the mournful cry of the common loon hangs in the cool, still air. The loons are often joined by pied-billed and horned grebes and sea ducks, including black and surf scoters, in large numbers. In the spring, eagles and peregrine falcons hunt the marshes, while oystercatchers, black skimmers, terns, and gulls cruise the beach.

A sand spit reaching into the bay is closed off between April and September to protect breeding birds such as the rare least tern, which lays its

eggs in a shallow pit in the open sand. The least tern's flight resembles that of a swallow, with lithe movement and shallow wingbeat. Humans and other predators make good use of the least tern's practice of breeding on open beach—stuffed least terns were once such the rage as decoration for women's hats that the species all but died out. Another rare denizen of Bethel's sandy shore is the northeastern beach tiger beetle, an insect with an evil-looking set of mandibles and a strikingly colored black and yellow body.

The Northern Neck, the peninsula north of Mathews County, is sandwiched between the Potomac and the Rappahannock rivers. It is most easily reached from the south via Route 17 north to Tappahannock and then east on Route 360. At the northern end of the peninsula off Route 3 on Route 347 near the town of Montross, **Westmoreland State Park**❖ encompasses Horsehead Cliffs, which overlook the Potomac on eroding bluffs that soar 150 feet above the water. Here, too, erosion has revealed the remains of ancient sea creatures whose bodies settled into a soft, protective layer of sand and silt, only to emerge millions of years later as the Potomac's waters ate away at the coastal sediments. Fossils can be collected on the beach that connects the cliffs and marsh, but digging in the cliffs themselves is both prohibited and dangerous. The red layer in the cliffs is a soil layer containing hematite, an iron-rich mineral dissolved out of the top-lying sediments by rainwater.

Steep ravines and a forest of mixed hardwoods cover the rest of Westmoreland. One trail leads to Big Meadows, which is not a meadow at all but a marsh often uniformly covered with cattails. It was created about 50 years ago when beavers dammed a stream.

Upriver from Westmoreland, where the Potomac begins its great U-shaped curve to the north and heads toward Washington, D.C., is **Caledon Natural Area**❖. Five miles west of Dahlgren on Route 218, this is a well-known summering spot for bald eagles and home to other raptors. One-and-a-half-hour ranger-led tours are the best way to see the magnificent eagles, which are making a strong comeback in this region after the pesticide DDT nearly wiped them out. Aside from their main diet of fish, which they sometimes steal from the talons of an osprey, the eagles feed on waterfowl, grebes, coots, gulls, foxes, and muskrats. Parts of Caledon are regularly closed to the public to protect the eagles and migratory birds.

LEFT: *The bolete family (top left and bottom right) claims the most edible mushrooms in North America, although various species, especially those with orange and red spores, may be toxic. Members of the genus* **Amanita** *(top right and bottom left) have caused 90 percent of all fatal human poisonings; they have symbiotic relationships with trees.*

139

CHAPTER FOUR

VIRGINIA'S HIGHLANDS

O ne weekend sometime in October, as the scent of autumn fills the air, thousands of Washingtonians make a pilgrimage west across Interstate 66 to the mountains of Virginia. The gentle flanks of the Blue Ridge, rising up from the rolling piedmont, are suffused with electric golds, reds, yellows, and greens—a stunning sight even to the most neon-struck city dweller. Above the fall pageantry, a broad-winged or red-tailed hawk sweeps effortlessly across the bright blue sky, playing the air currents with nary a flap of its wings.

The Blue Ridge Mountains are the easternmost ramparts of the Appalachian Mountains, the long chain of ridges that, in the United States, stretches from Maine to Alabama. In Virginia, this chain, which also includes the Allegheny Mountains to the west, forms a series of low-lying mountain ridges, often capped by deeply weathered granite rocks and separated from one another by fertile valleys. The Virginia Appalachians, a relatively narrow corridor of mountainous terrain, run southwest from western Maryland, paralleling the West Virginia border all the way down to North Carolina.

The driving route in this chapter forms a long, thin loop that starts near Front Royal and follows Skyline Drive and the Blue Ridge Parkway south to the border with North Carolina, along the Blue Ridge Mountains. It then turns north on Interstate 77 to Wytheville, where it picks up Interstate 81 south, heading into the Appalachian Plateau and Virginia's

LEFT: *Late winter hoarfrost turns a stunted red spruce sparkling white with frozen dew atop Virginia's 5,344-foot-tall White Top. This Blue Ridge peak is one of the northernmost examples of a southern bald mountain.*

westernmost counties. The route then swings north through Norton on Route 23, looping back to I-81 at Abingdon and continuing northeast up I-81 through Virginia's Great Valley, before heading back to Front Royal. Much of the time the route travels in or near Virginia's George Washington and Jefferson National Forest, which represents more than a million and a half acres of protected public land—a seemingly endless trove of natural spots, trails, and hidden places.

Another awe-inspiring annual spectacle in the Virginia mountains is the fall hawk migration, which peaks in the middle of September when the days are still warm but the evenings bring a chill. Several thousand broad-winged hawks may pass overhead during a single day at places such as Rockfish Gap, at the northern end of the Blue Ridge Parkway where I-64 cuts through the mountains. Other raptors, such as ospreys, American kestrels, and more rarely, bald eagles, also pass along the thin mountain ridge during September, on their way south for the winter.

These airborne predators ease the physical task of their long journeys by riding the updrafts created when wind from the piedmont hits the steep mountain ridge and is forced upward. Another sight common in the fall is a kettle, a column of warm air rising up into the sky that attracts a number of hawks who ride the current like an elevator up into the sky, circling in tight spirals. Once they reach the top of the column, nearly out of sight, they break off, continuing on their way south.

Fast-running streams have eroded the topography of the northern Blue Ridge to such an extent that the entire section is a long, narrow series of sharp ridges, little more than four miles wide. Beginning at Front Royal, Skyline Drive hugs the crest of this thin ridgeline for 104 miles southward, weaving through the mixed deciduous forest and around the high peaks of Shenandoah National Park for frequent panoramic views of the patchwork fields to the east in the piedmont and Virginia's Great Valley to the west.

Continuing where Skyline Drive leaves off near Waynesboro, the Blue Ridge Parkway heads south 215 miles to the North Carolina border. This highway must be driven slowly, not only because of its distracting scenery but because of its constant dips and turns. The Appalachian Trail shares the ridges with Skyline Drive and the Blue Ridge Parkway; the trail is recognizable where it crosses the road by the characteristic white blazes on

OVERLEAF: *Panoramic vistas unfold beside the Blue Ridge Parkway as it weaves its course along the spine of the southern Appalachians, stretching 215 miles from Waynesboro, Virginia, to North Carolina.*

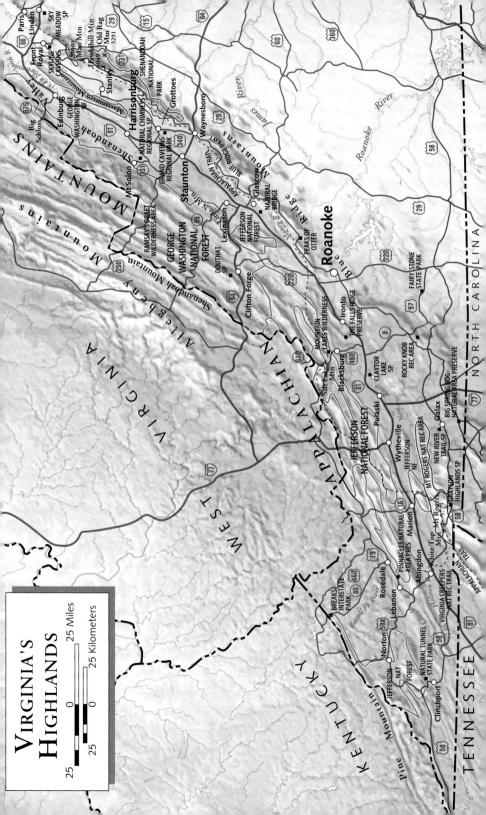

nearby trees. By Roanoke Gap (mile 114), the Blue Ridge, drained now by more leisurely flowing streams, spreads out into a plateau that grows higher and widens up to 40 miles across at points. The southern part of the Blue Ridge in Virginia, near the border with North Carolina, has the two highest points in the state, 5,729-foot Mount Rogers and 5,344-foot Whitetop. Whitetop is the first of the "southern balds," gently rounded mountains more commonly found in North Carolina and Georgia.

Fall is not the only time when color washes through the mountains.

ABOVE: *A thriving and protected population of white-tailed deer inhabits Shenandoah National Park, often congregating around Great Meadows at dawn and dusk.*

RIGHT: *The brilliant white flower bracts of the eastern dogwood bring the understory of Shenandoah National Park alive with color each spring.*

Spring brings waves of varying hues to the slopes of the Blue Ridge. The earliest indications of new life are the wildflowers that push through a year's accumulation of dull brown leaf and detritus to unfurl delicate drops of color. After the first bloom of wildflowers, flowering shrubs, including azaleas, rhododendrons, and mountain laurel, erupt into bloom in the understory. The buzz of bees fills the air, each insect intent on plundering the sweet nectar inside the pink and white clusters of mountain laurel flowers. The purple and white rhododendrons grow so high, thick, and tangled that paths through them are like tunnels through a primeval grove. Above the shrubs, the dogwood, black cherry, locust, tulip poplar, and mountain magnolia trees produce colorful blooms.

At the end of the Blue Ridge Parkway in Virginia, the driving route heads northwest on I-77, then southwest on I-81 into the physiographic province of the Appalachian Plateau, rugged mountain country cut with small, deep valleys that form veinlike networks. Far western Virginia boasts a large diversity of tree species, including American beech, sugar maple, white basswood, tulip poplar, ash, hickory, and magnolia. Pockets of this mixed forest are found in the Blue Ridge and Allegheny mountains in the dark and moist confines of narrow valleys known as cove forests.

North from the Appalachian Plateau, I-81 parallels the Blue Ridge in

Each spring some 18 million trilliums bloom at the G. R. Thompson Wildlife Management Area.

ABOVE LEFT: *Sessile trillium, or toadshade, sports wide mottled leaves and a tightly packed red flower.*

ABOVE RIGHT: *Trillium erectum's deep maroon color and rancid smell mimics carrion, attracting flies that pollinate the plant.*

RIGHT: *Painted trillium bears pink-accented wavy-edged flowers.*

BOTTOM: *At two feet, yellow-flowered Trillium erectum eclipses the diminutive white phacelia below.*

the Great Valley that separates those mountains from the ridge and valley province of the Allegheny Mountains to the west. From locale to locale, the Great Valley bears the names of nearby rivers: the New River, Roanoke, James, and Shenandoah valleys.

Running near the border and into West Virginia, the Alleghenies are a series of high and narrow mountains topped by erosion-resistant sandstone. The land is cut by deep water gaps and marked by deep valleys. More easily eroded limestone, dolomite, and shale underlie much of the lowlands. In places, slightly acidic groundwater containing organic matter has eroded these carbonate rocks into curious landforms. Otherworldly caverns have chambers the size of convention halls, decorated with geologic ornaments of large, tooth-shaped stalactites and stalagmites and other formations never seen above the surface. Communities of rare bats and amphibians live in these subterranean passages.

Sinkholes, tunnels, a gravity-defying natural bridge, and large pillars are other examples of the weathered limestone formations that are a type of karst topography. These features seem alien to the rugged green mountains of western Virginia, yet they are tangible examples of some of the grand geologic forces that have inexorably shaped this land over millions of years.

THE BLUE RIDGE: NORTH TO SOUTH

About an hour's drive west of Washington, D.C., the horse pastures and orchards of Virginia's rolling piedmont begin to yield to the first ripples of the Blue Ridge Mountains. Just west of Upperville on Route 50 the ridges grow higher and more pronounced. Near the small town of Paris, a short drive south on Route 17 leads to the Mount Bleak Visitor Center at **Sky Meadow State Park❖**. Trails wind up the ridge to high pastures, revealing wide-open views of the surrounding piedmont and a taste of the taller mountains of the Blue Ridge to the south.

Just over the ridgetops to the southwest—off I-66 just north of the town of Linden—lies the **G. R. Thompson Wildlife Management Area❖** on the eastern slope of the Blue Ridge. Although primarily a hunting area, spring wildflowers are the main attractions for many visitors, and May brings a truly explosive growth of large-flowered trilliums: One biologist conservatively estimates that 18 million trilliums bloom in this two-square-mile area, an endless feast of white and pink flowers. Also littering the area's forest floor are huge white mayapple blossoms, skunk cabbage, yellow lady's slippers, green violets, yellow violets, Dutchman's-breeches,

149

ABOVE: *A regal and fierce raptor, the red-tailed hawk surveys the open countryside for such prey as rabbits, rodents, birds, snakes, and lizards.*

RIGHT: *In Shenandoah National Park, Dark Hollows Falls drops 70 feet over the greenstone of an ancient lava flow.*

bloodroot, and golden alexanders.

The Appalachian Trail, on its long, sinuous path along the Appalachian Mountains, crosses the Thompson WMA, winding south for several dozen miles to **Shenandoah National Park❖**, a slender strip that runs north-south along the ridgeline and is arguably the prettiest stretch of mountains in the Blue Ridge. Beginning at Front Royal, Skyline Drive traverses the narrow ridgetop for the next 105 miles, dipping into gaps, crossing near waterfalls, and skirting rocky peaks ranging from 2,000 to more than 4,000 feet high. Frequent overlooks offer stunning views of the piedmont to the east and the Shenandoah Valley and Allegheny Mountains to the west. White-tailed deer often nibble on the grass alongside the road at dusk. As night falls, cool breezes pick up and lights in the valley below sparkle, gently mirroring the stars in the sky above.

Because of the narrow ridgeline, most of the park's 491 miles of trails head either up summits or down precipitous gorges with waterfalls. South on the drive, off milepost 19.4, the trail at Little Devil Stairs drops precipitously through a gorge into deep shadows and repeatedly crosses a stream. Whiteoak Canyon, located off milepost 42.6, features a series of six dramatic waterfalls that drop from 35 to 86 feet. Nearby, at milepost 43, the 1.2-mile Limberlost Trail passes into a majestic grove of old hemlocks, some of which are more than 300 years old, and white oaks that may be more than 400 years old. The area was never logged, thanks to the efforts of George Freeman Pollock, who founded the nearby Skyland Resort in 1894.

Although not the highest peak in the park, 3,291-foot **Old Rag Mountain** offers some of the most spectacular views. It is accessible from Skyline Drive directly as well as by footpath. One of the most popular hikes up Old Rag Mountain begins from outside the eastern perimeter of the park, off Route 231 south of Sperryville. Views from numerous rock

ABOVE: *Classified as a carnivore, the primarily nocturnal black bear generally maintains a vegetarian diet of twigs, berries, bark, roots, and nuts.*

outcrops and huge boulders along the upper parts of this strenuous, 7.2-mile round-trip route make the effort worthwhile. The trail passes between narrow rock walls, a channel through which molten lava flowed 600 million years ago. In the granite outcrops near the summit are "buzzard baths," large, often water-filled holes that defy explanation. It is known, however, that the granite near the top may be some of the oldest exposed rock in the entire Appalachian range—some 1.1 billion years old.

Farther south on Skyline Drive, a short trail starting at milepost 46.7 leads to the summit of the park's highest peak, 4,049-foot **Hawksbill Mountain,** a spot high enough to find a patch of sweet-smelling Fraser fir (also called balsam), the only fir species native to the southeast. An observation tower on top offers panoramic views of the town of Stanley and of Nakedtop, Stony Man, and Old Rag mountains in the distance. This is one of the best spots in Shenandoah National Park to watch the annual hawk migration. Those who bushwhack off the trail may find signs of old logging trails or even gasoline cans rusting underneath piles of leaves, the only remaining signs (aside from the absence of large trees) that logging operations ravaged this area earlier in the twentieth century.

At milepost 51 the forest suddenly recedes, revealing 150 acres of open

ABOVE: *Not only its sweet fruit but also the twigs and leaves of the high-bush blueberry serve as food for bears, birds, deer, and rabbits.*

land known as **Big Meadows.** Today, the park service maintains the meadows and boggy wetland, which were probably first created centuries ago by fire lit by either Native Americans or lightning. Tiny, sweet blueberries abound during the summer and make a nice addition to morning cereal. The blooms of black-eyed susans, milkweed, daisies, and columbines fill the meadows with delicate patches of color.

At milepost 54.7, a short but rugged scramble over rocks leads to the summit of 3,620-foot-high **Bearfence Mountain,** one of the few spots in the park with a 360-degree view. The fencelike aspect of the rocks surrounding the summit may have prompted the name. Although Shenandoah has the highest density of black bears of any national park—one per square mile— it's rather rare to see these shy creatures. More evident than the bears themselves is their scat, often stained purple by berries in the summer months.

The **South River Falls,** reachable from the South River Picnic Area at milepost 62.9, is a good spot to watch breeding birds. For a mile the trail descends past flowering spurge, a wildflower that bears small white flowers in midsummer, to a platform near the head of a deep, rocky gorge and the precipitous drop of South River Falls. The steepness of the slope provides good views of the forest canopy; a large number of breeding birds can be

153

sighted, including Louisiana waterthrushes, ovenbirds, wood thrushes, vireos, scarlet tanagers, and American redstarts, and many other warblers.

As Skyline Drive winds south to its terminus at Rockfish Gap, near Waynesboro, the vegetation gradually grows more southern, the land noticeably drier. Rhododendrons, with their unmistakable large, shiny evergreen leaves, now make their appearance in the understory. Skyline Drive becomes the **Blue Ridge Parkway❖,** which continues south for another 469 miles, connecting Shenandoah park with Great Smoky Mountains park in North Carolina. More than 32 trails branch off the 217-mile Virginia section of the parkway into neighboring George Washington and Jefferson National Forest.

The most dramatic section of the parkway in Virginia is the first 114 miles, between Waynesboro and the booming city of Roanoke, a place to find dinner and a bed after a day in the mountains. Numerous overlooks offer ample opportunities to pull over; it's possible to watch a turkey buzzard soar on thermals, find a trail up to a nearby peak, or simply study the curious spur ridges that spill off the main ridge like long, hairy fingers.

Springtime brings waterfalls swollen with snowmelt and the breathtaking sight of white and pink rhododendron blossoms blanketing the hillsides. Many of the parkway's trails wind through cool tunnels of the shrubs. At milepost 34.4 on the parkway, the **Yankee Horse Overlook Trail❖** leads across a narrow-gauge railway, used in the 1920s to remove logs from the area, through second-growth forest to Wigwam Falls, a sheet of water pouring 30 feet over a monolithic rock face in a shaded grotto.

Although most of the interpretative centers are closed during the winter, traveling the parkway at that time of year brings its own pleasures. With the foliage gone, views open up at almost every turn. Light green lichens cover the bark of many of the oaks, and, thus clad, the trees resemble skeletons on the march. White-tailed deer are easy to spot; luck might bring a glimpse of a buck and a doe locked in an embrace.

At mile 63.6, the **Trail of Trees** curves along the bluffs of the James River, the lowest point on the parkway. Several dozen trees are identified, including some exotics from Asia. Along the trail is the lonely reminder of a once-common tree in the eastern United States: the original American chestnut. A fungal disease known as the chestnut blight was accidentally introduced to this country from Asia in 1904, and it eventually all but eliminated the tree, a species coveted for its tasty nuts and durable wood. Although the living roots and stumps of blight-stricken chestnuts sometimes still push up sprouts, they too will die by the time the saplings reach several inches in diameter. Below the trail, the James River continues its silent but steady course, eroding a channel into the Blue Ridge so deep that volcanic and sedimentary rock 500 million years old are exposed.

Perhaps the most visited section of the parkway in Virginia centers around the **Peaks of Otter❖** at mile 86, actually three rocky peaks named Sharp Top, Flat Top, and Harkening Hill. Since colonial times, people have sweated up the steep but relatively short (1.5-mile) trail to the summit of 3,875-foot Sharp Top, which seems to push right up into the Virginia sky like a knife. Atop its rocky summit, stunning views of the surrounding mountains make it easy to understand why Virginians believed this to be their state's highest point for many years. Handrails and steps are installed on the steepest sections.

A nice way to end the hike is with a cup of coffee at the Peaks of Otter Lodge, its large glass windows overlooking Abbott Lake and the sharp rise of the mountains, blanketed with a lush forest of oak, maple, hickory, and birch.

Southwestern Virginia

South from Roanoke on the parkway, the sharp ridges flatten and grow broad, turning into a high plateau of rolling pastures and fields of tobacco and corn where pleasant hiking and 360-degree views are plentiful. At mile 169, **Rocky Knob Recreation Area❖** lies on the edge of the plateau and includes 1,500-foot-deep **Rock Castle Gorge,** named for its turretlike outcrops of crystalline quartz. A strenuous 10.8-mile loop trail, the **Rock Castle Gorge National Recreation Trail,** follows the rim, then descends into the gorge. In early March, the 2,000-foot difference in elevation between Rocky Knob and the bottom of the gorge keeps winter's snow and ice on the summit while spring has begun below.

About 20 miles off the parkway, south from Rocky Knob on Route 8, then northeast on Route 57, is **Fairy Stone State Park❖,** an area once covered with iron ore mines. Today, the park is known for the curious crystals, or fairy stones, from which it takes its name. Actually, they are made of a mineral known as staurolite, found in some types of metamorphic schists and gneisses. These crystals, often twinned with others to form cross shapes, erode out of the surrounding rock.

Just before the Blue Ridge Parkway crosses the border into North Carolina, south of the town of Galax, the **Big Spring Bog Natural Area Preserve** protects a rare cranberry glade, found near a small creek that flows among rolling hills into Chestnut Creek, a tributary of the New River. Sometimes called southern muskegs, bogs such as Big Spring contain carpets of sphagnum moss that serve to insulate the water table located just beneath the surface. The moisture keeps the air temperature cool, enabling subarctic plants to survive as relics of the last ice age. Because these life-forms live in a precarious balance, the Virginia Department of Conservation and Recreation restricts visits by the public.

In the town of Galax, a short drive northwest from the parkway on Route 97, the New River flows as it winds north from its headwaters in North Carolina. The name is misleading—the river is probably North America's oldest, first cutting its course in the Paleozoic era, before the Appalachian Mountains themselves began to rise under geologic pressures. Its origin explains why the New is the only river to cut across the grain of the Appalachians, and perhaps, too, why it's one of the few rivers to run south to north. Later, as it reaches West Virginia, the New crashes through boulder-strewn rapids and offers some of the best early-spring white-water rafting in the Mid-Atlantic region.

The 57-mile-long **New River Trail State Park**❖ travels from Galax north to Pulaski—29 miles of it along the river—following an abandoned railroad right-of-way. It is representative of a new breed of park known as a greenway—a narrow, linear preserve protecting a corridor of land and river. Spectacular cliffs, where the ancient river has cut through rock, are visible from along the graded cinder roadbed, suitable for walking and mountain biking.

Before the point where it cuts northwest across the mountains, the New River has been dammed and broadens out into 5,000-acre Claytor Lake. Ten miles of trails run through **Claytor Lake State Park**❖, which sits on the lake's northern shore northeast of Pulaski, just south of I-81.

Heading down I-81 just south of Wytheville, the roar of 18-wheelers hurtling along downhill grades and laboring uphill gives little indication of the remote wilderness just ahead. The speed of life immediately slows off the highway by virtue of the curving roads and the silent, constant presence of the mountains to the south. Much of the rugged land that fits in the wedge formed by I-81, I-77, and the North Carolina border has been set aside as **Mount Rogers National Recreation Area**❖, part of George Washington and Jefferson National Forest, which contains Virginia's two tallest peaks, 5,729-foot Mount Rogers and 5,344-foot White Top. These

---

OVERLEAF: *From White Top Mountain's wintry peak, the Blue Ridge range of southern Virginia stretches to the horizon. Until the mid-morning sun burns it off, shimmering hoarfrost coats White Top's conifers.*

A brilliant parade of butterflies brings color to the mountains of the Blue Ridge.

ABOVE: *The buckeye, recognizable by the dark eyespots on its brown hind wings, feeds on the nectar of a butterfly weed.*

TOP RIGHT: *The strikingly patterned atlantis, a fritillary butterfly, frequents streams and moist meadows all over the United States.*

MIDDLE RIGHT: *The dark wings of the female eastern tiger swallowtail evolved to mimic the distasteful pipevine swallowtail.*

BOTTOM RIGHT: *The silvery crescentspot earns its name from spots on its hind wings.*

mountains rise like giant ocean swells, without sharp peaks.

Adjacent to both mountains is **Grayson Highlands State Park❖,** one of Virginia's best-kept secrets. It lies on the southern edge of the recreation area, accessible from I-81 by way of Route 16 south from Marion. A short hike might disrupt several dozen wild turkeys, who will jet away with the loud flapping of their stocky wings. Panoramic 360-degree views are within a short walking distance, atop the bare igneous rocks of Little and Big Pinnacle on **Haw Orchard Mountain,** so named for the hawthorne trees, with their long, prickly thorns, that cover the mountain. Gone are most of the red spruce trees that once covered these peaks, lost to logging operations many years ago, and the resulting open highlands are more reminiscent of Maine or the Rockies than Virginia. Visible on the ridges are a number of shaggy wild ponies, descendants of a herd released years ago by the Wilburn Ridge Pony Association to graze the highlands year-round. Each spring and fall, the herd of approximately 150 ponies is rounded up and checked for disease. Some are auctioned to keep the population level under control.

At Massie Gap, the Appalachian Trail climbs up to **Mount Rogers** via Wilburn Ridge, an open ridge with good views and, in June, breathtaking displays of acre upon acre of blooming rhododendrons. Mount Rogers is clearly visible, capped with a dark green covering of Virginia's only mixed spruce and fir forest. Mosses and ferns thrive in this environment, kept moist by almost constant fog conditions, creating a magical realm that seems to belong to a tale written by the Brothers Grimm. No views, however, await the hiker who makes the 4.5-mile climb to the heavily forested summit. The way to Mount Rogers passes over an orange-blazed trail, one of several horse paths at Grayson Highlands, the only state park in Virginia with facilities for horse camping. One of the trails leads to the **Virginia Highlands Horse Trail❖** just outside the park's boundaries. It stretches 75 miles from Pine Mountain in the north to Elk Garden in the south.

White Top, Mount Rogers's neighboring peak, can be reached outside the park by heading west from Grayson Highlands on Route 58 toward Abingdon. The rounded peak looms above the road, its high meadows like a bald pate surrounded by the stands of red spruce. Route 58, Virginia's highest road, switchbacks up the flank of White Top through cool groves of evergreens high above the surrounding countryside, to meadows littered with dark brown rocks colored with metallic ore. On a clear day on this Appalachian bald, the northernmost of its kind, miles and miles of rugged Tennessee and North Carolina mountains form a horizon of blue and purple hues of almost infinite variety. On certain winter days, after the fog has lifted but before the sun has warmed the morning air, hoarfrost clings to the scattered red spruce on the summit, delicately painting the trees with a white coating of sparkling ice.

Back off the mountain heading west toward Abingdon, Route 58 passes near the **Virginia Creepers National Recreation Trail❖,** a rails-to-trails path (a railroad bed converted to a walking path) that winds along the forested banks of Whitetop Laurel Creek. The 18-mile trail crosses and recrosses the creek, providing many opportunities for trout fishing in pools and cascades, including several sections for fly-fishing. At Damascus, the trail connects to the **Abingdon to Damascus Trail❖,** extending the path to 35 miles, a leisurely day trip on a mountain bike.

South from Abingdon, I-81 crosses briefly into North Carolina before meeting Route 23 (I-181), which heads back into western Virginia. This route passes over the North Fork of the Holston River, Copper Creek, and the Clinch River, which run parallel southwesterly courses separated by mountain ridges. In these streams are found some of Virginia's rarest freshwater fish, most of the 33 species of freshwater mussels, and the spiny river snail.

The Stock Creek Valley near Clinchport is home to **Natural Tunnel State Park❖,** which contains an immense natural tunnel through the limestone bedrock. The southern entrance of this 850-foot-long tunnel is a gaping natural amphitheater, a 100-foot-tall and 150-foot-wide hole in the mountainside large enough to accommodate Stock Creek and a pair of train tracks. Geologists believe that it was created when Stock Creek ran into a cavern that had formed along a fracture in the earth's crust. The railway was added after rich deposits of coal were discovered in the area during the late 1800s.

Route 23 swings north to Norton, a coal town built on the Norton formation of rocks. Coal seams run through this formation, laid down more than 300 million years ago. The only flat area in this rugged land is probably the result of strip mining—road cuts east of the town reveal seams of low-grade coal. (Local driveways are often made from this type of coal.) Much of the surrounding area is part of George Washington and Jefferson National Forest, including **Big Stone Gap,** one of the two major breaks in the long, steep ridges. The other, **Cumberland Gap,** is 50 miles west at the very western tip of the state. Daniel Boone blazed the Wilderness Trail through

---

OVERLEAF: *Spectacular star-shaped flowers mark the spring-blooming serviceberry. This native tree is also known as the shadbush or shadblow because it flowers when the shad ascend nearby rivers to spawn.*

161

LEFT: *The Carolina chickadee sounds a higher and more rapid call than its northern cousin the black-capped chickadee.*

RIGHT: *The Russell Fork River has gouged a deep canyon around the Towers, a rocky pinnacle dominating Breaks Interstate Park.*

here in 1796, a route soon followed by pioneers as they moved westward.

Some of the area's most spectacular scenery is found at the **Pinnacle Natural Area Preserve❖,** east of Norton on Alternate Route 58, then north on Route 19 to Lebanon. A 600-foot dolomite pinnacle rises above the Clinch River at its confluence with Big Cedar Creek. A well-developed trail system leads up to Copper Ridge, for views of the pinnacle and the water below. The natural area also includes cove woodlands, limestone cliffs, ridgetop glades, and other unusual animal and plant communities. On the dolomite and limestone ledges live uncommon calcium-loving plants, such as glade spurge, Carey's saxifrage, and smooth cliff brake fern.

North on Route 19, just beyond Rosedale, Route 80 heads northwest to the Kentucky border and **Breaks Interstate Park❖,** in the George Washington and Jefferson National Forest. Some say that the canyon cut by the Russell Fork River is the deepest east of the Mississippi, a claim hard to dispute while peeking over the edge of the Towers Overlook, watching white water boil over the rocks some 1,600 feet below but not hearing a sound. The river curves around the Towers, a pyramid of rocks that stretches along a half-mile section of the five-mile-long canyon. These craggy, difficult mountains are near where the McCoy-Hatfield feud erupted.

VIRGINIA'S GREAT VALLEY: BLACKSBURG TO FRONT ROYAL

Back into the ridge and valley country, Route 460 heads toward the college town of Blacksburg. Northwest of Blacksburg on Route 700 spreads a remote area known as the **Mountain Lake Wilderness❖,** more than 10,000 acres of high ridges, red spruce bogs, low stream valleys, and sandstone ledges. The ridges are covered in red spruce, hemlock, and yellow birch, and the area is often dry, windy, and susceptible to brief summer storms

that blow in quickly. In the steep ravines, slicing into the mountains, are pockets of 300-year-old white oaks and hemlocks that escaped logging. Blackberry and raspberry bushes abound in the lower stream valleys, as do numerous species of mushrooms, which peak from late July to August.

Mountain Lake, located on private property, is one of Virginia's two natural lakes (the other is Lake Drummond in the Great Dismal Swamp). Geologists still puzzle over the origin of the lake, which sits atop a mountain that certainly is not volcanic. Current belief holds that the lake was formed in the late nineteenth century when an earthquake along the Palaski fault caused a small rockslide to block the outlet. Large blocks of sandstone—remnants of stone structures and fences—now lie on the bottom of the lake, testifying to the populated valley that once flourished here.

South on Route 613 beyond the Mountain Lake Hotel, which overlooks the lake, are the Mountain Lake Biological Station and a trail leading up to the crest of Salt Lake Mountain, Bear Cliff, and Bald Knob. Ask permission from the caretaker for passage on the private lands—the hike is well worth it. Just across the broad crest of Salt Lake Mountain on Bear Cliff the mountainside falls away abruptly, revealing views to the south and east: On good days, the sharp-pointed Peaks of Otter, off the Blue Ridge Parkway, are visible. Bear Cliff consists of several descending tiers of Tuscarora sandstone blocks, the erosion-resistant sedimentary rock that

165

ABOVE: *Once owned by Thomas Jefferson, Natural Bridge was considered an icon of the sublime. David Johnson painted this panorama in 1860.*

caps many of the area peaks. Each of these immense blocks, broken off from one another during the freezing and thawing cycles of the last ice age, is separated from the next by passages, some 10 to 15 feet wide. Stunted yellow birches cling to the nutrient-poor ridgetops, where timber rattlesnakes often lie on the rock, warmed by the sun.

A path follows the base of Bear Cliff's highest tier to the southwest, by the crest of South Pond Mountain, before passing through thickets of mountain laurel and, a mile and a half later, to the top of Bald Knob, also home to a microwave relay center. It's the highest point in the immediate area, with commanding views of the surrounding countryside.

Southeast of Blacksburg, near the town of Ironto, lies the **Falls Ridge Preserve❖,** a Nature Conservancy property; visitors must get advance permission. It occupies a heavily wooded, steep ridge that rises up from the valley created by the North Fork of the Roanoke River. Running directly across the manager's property and the preserve itself is the Salem Fault, a geologic split separating rock made of Cambrian limestone from

RIGHT: *Erosion hewed the monumental form of the Natural Bridge, a magnificent limestone arch that soars more than 200 feet above Cedar Creek.*

that of shale and sandstone. The impact of geology on plant life is dramatically illustrated here: The soil created by the shales and sandstone nourishes acid-loving hemlocks, rhododendrons, azaleas, and mountain laurels. These plants end at the fault, giving way to the ferns and other calcium-loving plants that thrive on limestone-based soils. Down the road from the manager's house is a spring-fed travertine waterfall about 80 feet high; the water flows over a formation of mineral and lime buildup, deposited by the springwater over the course of thousands of years. Large sinkholes on the preserve suggest that unexplored limestone drip caverns lie below the surface.

About 60 miles up the fertile Shenandoah Valley near the town of Glascow on I-81, it's hard to miss the signs for **Natural Bridge❖,** a big tourist spot and a dramatic example of the effect of water on carbonate rock. In a scene reminiscent of mesa country out west, a massive arch of limestone spans a deep, wooded gorge 200 feet over Cedar Creek. It's all that's left of a huge cavern that was carved out by the slightly acidic waters of Cedar Creek and subsequently collapsed, leaving only the bridge.

ABOVE: *During spring breeding season, the male American toad issues a sweet trilling sound from its vocal sacs. Generally nocturnal, this large toad is a champion insect eater.*

LEFT: *With its heavy rains, springtime quickly swells the volume of water tumbling over Lacy Falls, near Natural Bridge.*

To escape from the crowds at Lexington, head west on I-64 toward Clifton Forge. At the intersection of I-64 and I-81, the road cuts expose dark gray limestone fractured with white veins of calcite. Ten miles west on I-64 at Clifton Forge head north on Route 220 to **Douthat State Park❖** for a taste of the windswept ridges and dense forests of the Allegheny Mountains. Forty miles of interconnecting trails include Buck Hollow Trail, which overlooks Buck Lick Trail, an interpretive trail built by the Civilian Conservation Corps in the 1930s. The park surrounds a 50-acre lake stocked with rainbow trout.

A more scenic passage west into the Alleghenies from I-81 is Route 39, one of Virginia's most beautiful roads, northwest of Lexington. This passes through Goshen Pass, a water gap carved over the centuries by the Maury River. At the pass, a 150-foot-long suspension footbridge traverses the dizzying Maury River Gorge, which drops precipitously 1,000 feet. On the other side of the bridge is Round Mountain, where there are spectacular views of the limestone cliffs exposed by the river. **Goshen**

Pass Natural Area borders the gorge on the southwestern edge of Little North Mountain, which stretches south for 20 miles in a single sharp ridge until it hits Goshen Pass. This natural area, the pass, and Little North Mountain combined include some 35,000 acres of state-owned preserve. For those not wishing to hike the area's 40 miles of trails, frequent pull-offs on Route 39 offer countless views of the rugged mountain scenery.

About 20 miles northwest of Staunton on Route 250 (accessible from either I-81 or Route 220) is **Ramsey's Draft Wilderness Area❖,** one of the more remote and rugged stretches of the George Washington and Jefferson National Forest. Here as many as 6,000 acres of virgin forest—hemlocks, white pines, oaks, and yellow poplars—escaped logging because of the steep terrain. Ramsey's Draft, a sprightly mountain stream, drains the inside of a small U-shaped valley formed by Shenandoah Mountain to the west, Bald Ridge to the east, and a small connector ridge. The Ramsey's Draft Trail leads seven miles along the stream, often fording it, to a forest of large hemlocks on the northern prong. Walking the steep slopes surrounded by large hemlocks inspires a peacefulness well worth wet feet from crossing and recrossing the stream.

Not far to the northeast, off Route 731 near Mount Solon, is **Natural Chimneys Regional Park❖.** Although more crowded than Ramsey's Draft, it includes seven tall limestone towers ranging from 65 to 120 feet high. At first glance they seem to rise out of the woods like a North American Stonehenge, ancient remnants of a long-lost civilization. The explanation for their existence, detailed on signs along an easy three-mile overlook trail, seems almost as miraculous. Some 500 million years ago, these towers were one vast block of limestone. Layers of protective chert prevented the remaining seven chimneys from the erosion that destroyed the rest of the block over the last one million to 10,000 years.

From here to the north and east begin to appear the large, commercial cavern operations that draw nearly a million visitors each year. These profit by exploiting the drip caverns with enormous stalactites and stalagmites that continue to grow and form, though the changes are too gradual to be noticeable from one year to the next. Colored lights, ridiculously named features, even an organ that operates by striking stalactites and stalagmites of various sizes—all detract from the otherworldly mystery of these subterranean passages. Yet even with these human intrusions, the sense of time and magnitude is so tangible that it's worth braving the crowds and concession stands to explore at least one thoroughly.

The area's oldest commercial cavern operation is **Grand Caverns Regional Park❖** near the town of Grottoes (off I-81 at exit 235, then east on Route 256). It was once visited by Thomas Jefferson, who rode his horse here from Monticello. Cathedral Hall, 280 feet long by 70 feet high, is one of the largest rooms of any known cavern in the East. Also impressive are the massive columns that form when stalagmites and stalactites join. Head up I-81 to I-66 east; in Front Royal Route 340 south leads to an underground site with a different atmosphere, **Skyline Caverns❖.** Coursing water has smoothed passageway walls free of any formations—except at the ends of certain tunnels, where delicate calcite flowers, known as anthodites, sprout sea urchin–like spines. How they formed remains a mystery. The region's largest and most dramatic caverns are **Luray Caverns,** on Route 211 near Luray. A one-mile-long brick path leads through dizzying passages, past such geologic curiosities as Saracen's Tent, a translucent stalactite many yards high, which grows at the rate of a square inch every 300 years.

The **Massanutten Mountains❖,** a thin ridge of Massanutten sandstone, split the Shenandoah Valley in half for about 50 miles from Harrisonburg north to Front Royal, running between the South and North forks of the Shenandoah River. Like a long tuning fork, the Massanutten range consists

171

ABOVE: *A common member of the sunflower family, the splashy yellow flowers of coreopsis flourish beside the Blue Ridge Parkway. They also favor old fields, roadsides, and other habitats disturbed by humans.*

of three main ridges, all part of the George Washington and Jefferson National Forest: The base of the fork is Massanutten Mountain South, while the tines are Massanutten East and West. Trails lead all over the mountains; one for the visually impaired features explanations of the natural history of the area in braille. Much longer hikes lead up to craggy outcrops with excellent views. The 9-mile Signal Knob Trail on Massanutten Mountain West passes great views from Buzzard Rock Overlook, finally arriving at 2,106-foot Signal Knob, used as a lookout point by both Confederate and Union troops during the Civil War. One of the most spectacular sights occurs from Woodstock Tower, off Mill Road east from Woodstock. From the tower, a short walk from the road, are views of the Shenandoah River as it bends seven times in snakelike curls.

The premier hike in this area is along the **Big Blue❖,** a long trail that rivals the Appalachian Trail in beauty, passing near cliff faces, through forest glades, and along waterfalls. Big Blue, so named for its blue blazes, serves as a big western loop to the Appalachian Trail. It spans 144 miles, 112 of which are in Virginia, and has the advantage of being much less

ABOVE: *Although logging decimated its slopes in the 1920s, Shenandoah National Park has undergone a handsome recovery. Unbroken vistas meet the eye gazing west from the park, toward the Massanuttens.*

traveled than its famous sister trail. From Hancock, Maryland, Big Blue crosses the Potomac and descends south through West Virginia until it reaches Virginia, then recrosses into West Virginia before heading east across the Shenandoah Valley, climbing the Massanutten Mountains, crossing into the northern end of Shenandoah National Park, and meeting the Appalachian Trail at Mathews Arm. The Potomac Appalachian Trail Club manages the trail and publishes a complete guide to it.

West from Edinburg, Route 675 cuts over to the West Virginia border near the Wolf Gap Campground and an area known as **Big Schloss❖,** where the Big Blue crosses east into Virginia. Part of the George Washington and Jefferson National Forest, these are rugged mountain ridges filled with large rock outcrops that offer spectacular views of the surrounding area. The largest outcrop is Big Schloss itself (*Schloss* is German for "castle"), on the crest of Mill Mountain. A six-mile trail leads from the Wolf Gap Campground up to the top of this massive rock outcrop. A small wooden footbridge leads over a crevice to spectacular 360-degree views of large tracts of forest—one of the best views of unbroken woodland in the state.

173

NORTH CAROLINA

NORTH CAROLINA'S COAST AND PIEDMONT

S kimming just above the wave tops, a line of eastern brown pelicans shoots across the edge of the sea, each bird flapping its wings and sailing in perfect rhythm with the others. The harmony among these large birds, each with a wingspan of nearly seven feet and a body of silvery brown feathers, is an unforgettable sight.

Only a generation ago, these magnificent birds were a rarity along the barrier islands of North Carolina, because of the use of the pesticide DDT. Pelicans ate fish contaminated by DDT, which caused thinning of the pelicans' eggshells and led to massive nesting failure. In a few short years, the population of a bird with lineage that can be traced back 100 million years to the age of dinosaurs was drastically reduced. After the pesticide was banned, the pelican rebounded and once again is a common denizen of the North Carolina shore and Outer Banks.

North Carolina's Outer Banks, a series of thin barrier islands far off the mainland, possess one of the most intriguing and enchanting ecosystems in the Mid-Atlantic area. This chapter covers these islands as well as the rest of the coastal plain, which stretches 100 to 140 miles west to the fall line. In addition, the chapter includes the piedmont, which stretches westward to the foot of the Blue Ridge Mountains.

The driving route heads south from Norfolk, Virginia, on Route 17 into

PRECEDING PAGES: *Near Oregon Inlet, willowy stalks of golden sea oats, a native grass, stabilize the shifting dunes of North Carolina's Outer Banks.*

LEFT: *Cape Hatteras Lighthouse, a noted landmark, once had 1,500 feet of beachfront. Today less than 200 feet remain because of ocean erosion.*

North Carolina's northeastern corner, passing the Great Dismal Swamp and crossing over to the Outer Banks at Point Harbor. From the Virginia border to Shackleford Banks, the Outer Banks run 140 miles along the coast, a thin spit of land separated from the mainland by large bodies of shallow, brackish water with sandy bottoms. On small islands sheltered behind the barrier islands are important nesting sites for brown pelicans and a variety of herons, ibis, gulls, and terns.

It is hard to imagine a spot where the forces of nature are more tangible than on these thin barrier islands: The wind constantly sculpts the dunes and beachfront, the sun burns relentlessly, ocean waves and tides pound the shore, and storms reshape the topography from one season to the next, washing over the islands, cutting new inlets, and filling old ones. These conditions conspire to create a complex, dynamic environment—one in which the land is actually retreating toward the mainland in a process by which oceanside erosion is balanced by the accretion of sand on the bay side. The remains of houses and buildings washed away by storms and the relentless shifting of the sand are ample proof of the fact that human beings are only visitors in this environment. This, along with their isolation and raw beauty, makes the Outer Banks a special natural place to explore.

A good portion of the banks are protected by two preserves: In the north, from Whalebone Junction to Ocracoke Inlet, is Cape Hatteras National Seashore; Cape Lookout National Seashore preserves the southern Outer Banks from Ocracoke Inlet to Beaufort Inlet. Route 12 runs south through Cape Hatteras National Seashore, ending at the ferry from Ocracoke to the mainland. At Cape Hatteras the banks broaden slightly and dogleg to the west. Just inland, the nine-square-mile expanse of Buxton Woods is an example of the pockets of maritime forest that live a precarious existence in areas behind the dunes. At Cape Hatteras, too, the warm Gulf Stream flows north and heads off to sea. That current helps moderate the climate and, consequently, many southern and subtropical plants such as Spanish moss, dwarf palmetto, and yaupon reach their northern limits here.

The ferry from Ocracoke goes to Swan Quarter, where the driving route follows Route 264 west, then Route 17 south to Wilmington. It passes through the extensive swamps and wetlands that characterize much of the low coastal plain, intercut with large estuaries in the northern half.

OVERLEAF: *Aquatic plants and bald cypress trees now grow in the artificial lake at Merchants Millpond State Park. This 760-acre pond served a thriving logging industry in the early nineteenth century.*

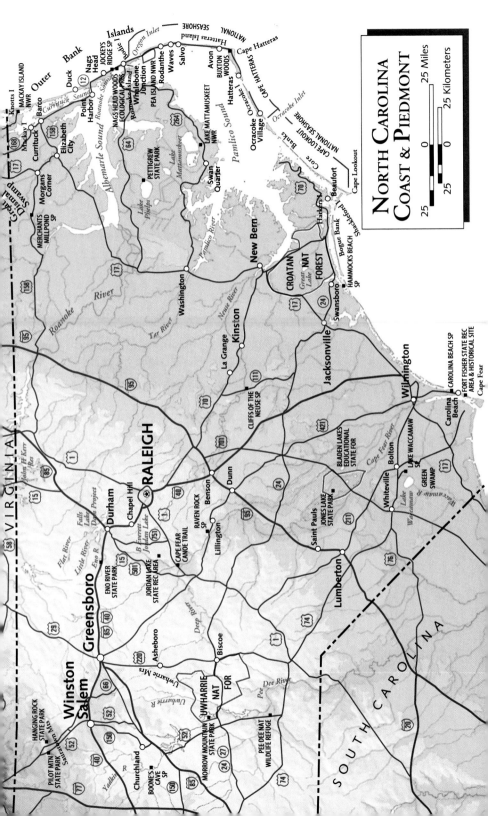

25 Miles

0

25

25 Kilometers

0

25

VIRGINIA

SOUTH CAROLINA

RALEIGH

Winston Salem

Greensboro

Durham

Chapel Hill

Wilmington

Jacksonville

New Bern

Kinston

Washington

Elizabeth City

Nags Head

Cape Hatteras

Cape Lookout

Beaufort

Lumberton

Whiteville

Asheboro

Biscoe

Dunn

Benson

Lillington

Saint Pauls

Bolton

Carolina Beach

Swansboro

La Grange

Currituck

Barco

Knotts I

MACKAY ISLAND NWR

Mackay I

Morgans Corner

Merchants Millpond SP

Great Dismal Swamp

Duck

Point Harbor

JOCKEYS RIDGE SP

NAGS HEAD WOODS ECOLOGICAL PRES.

Whalebone Junction

Rodanthe

Waves

Salvo

Avon

BUXTON WOODS

Hatteras

Hatteras Island

PEA ISLAND NWR

Roanoke Island

Roanoke Sound

Oregon Inlet

Bodie I.

Outer Bank

Islands

Currituck Sound

Albemarle Sound

Pamlico Sound

Core Banks

Ocracoke Island

Ocracoke Village

Ocracoke Inlet

CAPE HATTERAS NATIONAL SEASHORE

CAPE LOOKOUT NATIONAL SEASHORE

PETTIGREW STATE PARK

Lake Phelps

Lake Mattamuskeet

LAKE MATTAMUSKEET NWR

Swan Quarter

Pamlico River

Roanoke River

Tar River

Neuse River

Cape Fear River

Waccamaw R.

CROATAN NAT FOREST

Great Lake

Havelock

Bogue Bank

HAMMOCKS BEACH SP

Shackleford Banks

CLIFFS OF THE NEUSE SP

RAVEN ROCK SP

CAPE FEAR CANOE TRAIL

B. Everett Jordan Lake

JORDAN LAKE STATE REC AREA

ENO RIVER STATE PARK

Eno R.

Falls Lake Dam Project

Flat River

Little River

Johns H Kerr Res

BLADEN LAKES EDUCATIONAL STATE FOR

JONES LAKE STATE PARK

GREEN SWAMP

LAKE WACCAMAW SP

Lake Waccamaw

FORT FISHER STATE REC AREA & HISTORICAL SITE

CAROLINA BEACH SP

Cape Fear

PEE DEE NAT WILDLIFE REFUGE

MORROW MOUNTAIN STATE PARK

UWHARRIE NAT FOR

Uwharrie Mtns

Uwharrie R.

Deep River

Pee Dee River

HANGING ROCK STATE PARK

Sauratown Mts

PILOT MTN STATE PARK

BOONE'S CAVE SP

Churchland

Yadkin R.

58

17

168

158

158

64

264

70

24

17

17

17

421

211

76

74

1

1

1

15

85

95

95

95

40

40

401

40

74

85

85

85

220

66

52

52

52

150

150

27

24

20

29

12

55

501

700

111

Here are examples of dense shrub bogs, known as pocosins, visible at Croatan National Forest, and Carolina bays, shallow oval lakes of unknown origin that occur throughout the state. As the highway heads south, the coastal plain grows sandier. The large estuaries that divide the northern coastal plain are absent. The world's only native population of Venus's-flytraps grows in this area, thriving in the mineral-poor and acid-rich soils along with a host of other carnivorous plant species.

The route heads west from Wilmington on Route 74/76, then north on Interstates 95 and 40 to Raleigh and Greensboro. To the west is an area known as the Sandhills, about a million acres in the southwestern corner of the coastal plain covered with the sand, clay, and gravel sediments left by streams when the area was covered by inland seas millions of years ago. Vast, open forests of longleaf pine once carpeted this area, which contained a number of both wet and dry habitats where unusual amphibians, reptiles, and butterflies thrived. Now only a fraction of undisturbed forest remains, home to such rare species as Bachman's sparrow and the red-cockaded woodpecker.

From Greensboro, the driving route completes a large U-shape, following Route 220 south past the low-lying Uwharrie Mountain range, then west on Route 74 to Charlotte, and north on I-85 and through the piedmont on Route 52 to intersect the Blue Ridge Parkway over the border in Virginia. At one time or another during the past three centuries, almost all of the piedmont has been cultivated, logged, or developed, destroying large hardwood forests of oak, chestnut, hickory, tulip poplar, and beech. Today, more than half of the piedmont is abandoned farmland, gradually growing back its forest cover. Stands of pine forest are indications of the vegetation succession cycle, a step before the return of the deciduous hardwood forest. Much of the rich bottomland forest along riverbanks has also been lost to large dam projects that have drowned the floodplain and created huge lakes.

Toward the western end of the piedmont arise dramatic monadnocks, areas capped by erosion-resistant rock. While the rest of the piedmont weathered and eroded, these spots remained, eventually standing far above the rest of the piedmont plain. Hanging Rock and Pilot Rock are excellent examples of these large, round-shouldered blocks. Atop these rocks appear hardy pockets of vegetation, which cling precariously to thin pockets of soil sometimes no more than a few inches thick. These plants, ideally suited to their environment, appear to grow right out of the rock itself, affirming the tenaciousness of life at a very basic level.

NORTHEASTERN NORTH CAROLINA
AND THE OUTER BANKS

Heading south from Norfolk, Route 17 swings along the eastern edge of the Great Dismal Swamp and crosses over into North Carolina on its way to Elizabeth City. Although a good chunk of the Great Dismal is protected in North Carolina, exploration of this remarkable swamp is best undertaken in Virginia, where there are public facilities and canals crossing the area. Two nearby sites, however, offer ample opportunity to poke around the coastal wetlands of North Carolina's far northeastern corner.

Twenty miles west on Route 158 from Morgans Corner and Route 17, **Merchants Millpond State Park❖** encircles a 760-acre millpond and the nearby Lassiter Swamp. On first sight, it's hard to tell that the pond is human-made and was once the site of busy industry. Enormous cypress and gum trees, hung with Spanish moss, rise from its shallow waters, and yellow cow lily, duckweed, and other aquatic plants float on its surface. The northern parula, a warbler with a bluish body and yellow throat and breast, nests in the Spanish moss, adding its exuberant song to the air, while migratory ducks, such as greater scaup, canvasback, American wigeon, and northern pintail, swim the pond in season. More than 180 years ago, Bennetts Creek, which runs slowly through Lassiter Swamp, was dammed by early industrialists eager to harness water power for grinding corn and sawing wood. Today, little remains of this commerce but the pond itself and a number of tree stumps, their tops overgrown with shrubs and ferns. In time, the stumps themselves will disappear as the wood decays, forming small mounds, or hummocks, in the swamp.

Renting a canoe at the old tobacco barn is the best way to see the park, but second best is hiking the 6.7-mile-long Millpond Loop Trail, which passes through upland hardwoods, along the banks of the pond, and close to Lassiter Swamp, home to gargantuan cypress trees up to 8 feet in diameter and 117 feet in height. From the trail, a stand of curiously deformed water tupelo trees (also called tupelo gums) are visible in the swamp, their trunks and branches gnarled with knobby growths. Each disfigurement marks the site of a major battle between the tree and the American mistletoe, a parasitic plant with roots that dig below bark and suck important nutrients from its host. Far from passive, the tree mobilizes its defenses by surrounding the infected area with a woody growth. New invaders grow high up in the canopy and are identifiable by their leathery evergreen leaves and white berries.

On the eastern, opposite side of the Great Dismal Swamp and Route

183

ABOVE: *Barren and swept by strong winds, the massive dunes surrounding Kill Devil Hill provided ideal conditions for the Wright brothers' world-famous aviation experiments in October 1902.*

17 lies a different type of wetland, the **Mackay Island National Wildlife Refuge❖,** dominated by brackish marsh. A free car ferry leaves regularly from Currituck, reached by taking Route 158 northeast from Elizabeth City and then Route 168 north from Barco. Located in the far northern reaches of Currituck Sound, the refuge extends over two low-lying islands, Knotts and Mackay, which are separated by the Great Marsh, a favorite haunt of numerous geese, ducks, and swans. The refuge is closed during the late fall and winter to protect breeding populations of these birds, including some 50,000 snow geese and 4,000 tundra swans.

Between spring and fall, however, water and wading birds are easily seen from the .3-mile-long Great Marsh Trail, which leads through pines to a freshwater pond. Longer trails along Mackay Island Road and several dike trails are accessible by foot and bicycle. Traveling the canals themselves by canoe or small boat remains the best way to see birdlife up close. A quiet paddler might stumble on the thrilling sight of a great blue heron or an egret wresting its meal of fish or amphibian from the marsh.

Just a couple of miles east of Mackay Island at the Virginia–North Carolina border begins the long expanse of barrier islands known as the Outer Banks. For the first 30 miles or so, the thin spit of land encloses Currituck Sound, contained like a long thin cigar between the island and the mainland. From Barco, Route 158 travels south along the sound on

184

ABOVE: *Strong prevailing winds carve patterns into the sand at Jockey's Ridge State Park. Here the East's largest unstabilized dune, under constant assault from offshore winds, varies by as much as 30 feet.*

the mainland before cutting east and over to the Outer Banks at Point Harbor, where the waters of Currituck and Albermarle sounds mix.

The commercial establishments of a popular beach culture crowd the highway south from Route 158 and Route 12 until the beginning of Cape Hatteras National Seashore near the southern end of Bodie Island. The area between the town of Duck and the national seashore is not without its merit; the most notable and impressive sight is the largest unstabilized (devoid of vegetation or artificial structures) sand dune in the eastern United States at **Jockey's Ridge State Park❖,** off Route 158 Bypass near Nags Head, and visible from as far away as eight miles. Reputedly the dune gained its name when it served as a grandstand for locals who perched on its flanks while watching pony races. Seven other area dunes are also large enough to warrant their own names. Most famous of all, of course, is Kill Devil Hill, site of the Wright brothers' experiments with flight and now the location of the First Flight memorial and exhibit.

Whipped and shaped constantly by the offshore wind, Jockey's Ridge is known as a medano: a large, shifting, asymmetrical hill of sand, largely devoid of plant life. The dune ranges from 110 to 140 feet high, demonstrating the power of the prevailing wind to sculpt and form the sand. The views from atop the ridge are well worth the sandy scramble, although they may be shared with the many hang gliders who find the

185

ABOVE: *The white ibis sports a long, down-curved bill and travels in flocks, its long neck extended. The barrier islands along the Atlantic coast provide vital breeding habitat for this gregarious wading bird.*

height, soft landing surface, and constant 10- to 15-mile-an-hour winds ideal for their sport. To the east, the vast green Atlantic stretches off toward Europe. To the west is low-lying Roanoke Island, site of the first English settlement in the New World. Situated between barrier island and mainland, it marks the intersection of four large sounds: Currituck, Albemarle, Pamlico, and Roanoke.

More than 400 years ago, those hardy immigrants encountered coastal habitats similar to those found today in parts of the **Nags Head Woods,** a 1,600-acre expanse of hardwood forest, freshwater ponds, marsh, relict dunes, and pine hammocks adjacent to Jockey's Ridge and bordering Roanoke Sound. Largely untouched since Captains Philip Amadas and Arthur Barlowe first claimed the North American continent for England in 1584, the maritime forest is full of mature southern red oaks, loblolly pines, beeches, hickories, and hollies, some of which are 300 years old or more. More than 30 freshwater interdunal ponds are home to marbled and red-backed salamanders and eastern painted, snapping, and yellow-bellied slider turtles. Within the area is the **Nags Head Woods Ecological Preserve❖,** an area owned by the Nature Conservancy, which maintains a visitor center and three trails, including the 2.25-mile-long Sweetgum Swamp Trail and the 2-mile-long Blueberry Ridge Trail. The preserve is perhaps the best re-

186

Above: *Common denizens of North Carolina's coastal waterline include (clockwise from top left): an American oystercatcher, a ruddy turnstone, a spring pairing of laughing gulls, and a lesser yellowlegs.*

maining example of an undisturbed maritime forest on the East Coast.

From Roanoke Island, Route 64/264 cuts east over to the Outer Banks intersecting the north-south–running Routes 12 and 158 at Whalebone Junction. Just south of this crowded intersection begins one of the East Coast's premier coastal parks, **Cape Hatteras National Seashore❖.** It stretches 72 miles from Bodie Island to Ocracoke Inlet, encompassing several barrier islands, a national refuge, and miles of pristine beach, dunes, marsh, and maritime forest. A world-famous surf fishing and bird-watching spot, the seashore has numerous camping areas and hiking trails, including the unmarked 75-mile-long **Cape Hatteras Beach Trail,** which traverses the length of the preserve.

At the northern end of the park is a visitor center at Bodie Island light-house, unmistakable with its striped coat of black-and-white paint. The lighthouse was one of six (one to the north and four to the south) erected as warnings to wayward ships sailing too close to the dangerous shoals on the ocean side of the barrier islands. The .4-mile-long Bodie Island Nature Trail leads along boardwalks through marshes to an observation tower.

Just to the south, across Bonner Bridge over Oregon Inlet, is **Pea Island National Wildlife Refuge❖,** one the best spots in the Outer Banks for watching birdlife. It stretches south for 13 miles to Rodanthe and at-

tracts thousands of snow and Canada geese each winter, along with two dozen species of ducks and many tundra swans. During the spring and fall, least terns, willet, black skimmers, and oystercatchers nest along the beach and dune, while ibis, egrets, and herons raise their young in Pamlico Sound. In the impoundments originally created by the Civilian Conservation Corps, brown pelicans sometimes search for small fish before moving offshore.

Fall, winter, and spring are the best times to wander the four-mile-long trail around North Pond and to climb the two observation platforms to scan the pond and marshes for signs of migratory birds. In the summer, the abundance of biting flies and mosquitoes makes lingering uncomfortable. The refuge earned its name from the dune pea, a plant that grows wild on the sand. Locals cook the pods and eat them.

Route 12 continues down the narrow strip of barrier island passing the small towns of Waves, Salvo, and Avon before reaching Cape Hatteras itself, the seaward-pointed elbow of the Outer Banks, where the narrow, sandy barrier island abruptly cuts west, revealing a sharp, ocean-lashed point. Since 1870, the candy-striped lighthouse has warned ships' captains of the dangers of Diamond Shoals, the submerged tail of the cape that extends out to sea for several miles. Today, the lighthouse is in danger itself, for the same reasons that make any building on barrier islands precarious at best: the erosion, dune migration, and overwash of the is-

ABOVE: *Needing a protective cover for its soft body, the hermit crab appropriates and recycles the shell of a mollusk.*

LEFT: *Spindrift, surf foam tossed from the Atlantic by a stiff wind, lingers on a beach at the Pea Island National Wildlife Refuge.*

OVERLEAF: *After strict regulation of the pesticide DDT, North Carolina's population of brown pelicans recovered strongly. Here they nest in the dunes.*

land—all the things that enable a barrier island to survive the onslaught of the ocean. Once 1,500 feet of beach fronted the lighthouse; now less than 200 feet remain. Erosion threatens to topple the lighthouse soon and destroy one of the state's most recognizable symbols.

At the cape, the barrier island swells to its thickest point: 3.2 miles separate Pamlico Sound and the Atlantic. In this swell of beach is **Buxton Woods❖,** a nine-square-mile maritime forest, the largest on any North Carolina barrier is-

land. It is filled with steep relict dunes as tall as 55 feet, possibly the remains of ancient shorelines. On the crests of these ridges are stands of live oak, loblolly pine, and laurel oak, and the wet swales between the dunes are filled with swamp dogwood, southern bayberry, Carolina willow, and red bay as well as grasses, cattails, and woody vines. The thick and varied canopy provides many places of shelter for migratory birds, ranging from hawks to numerous warbler species, including worm-eating, prothonotary, and prairie warblers.

As in most maritime forests, many of the trees at Buxton have become dwarfed or deformed by the salt in the air—especially those closest to the sea or on high ridges. Although the salt air may stunt exposed live oaks to little more than shrubs, the trees may grow to normal height in a sheltered area nearby. The .6-mile-long Buxton Woods Nature Trail and others loop through a fairly diverse forest, its diversity due in part to the varied topography created by the relict sand dunes. Another contributing factor is the relatively moderate climate, tempered by the moist sea breeze and the movement of the Gulf Stream offshore. For this reason, Buxton Woods contains the most northern examples of palm trees on the East Coast, a grove of dwarf palmettos. The woods also contain several species of orchids.

Throughout the Outer Banks appear the almost prehistoric visages of brown pelicans, sweeping low across the wave tops. These large white-crowned birds will dive on a school of menhaden, mullet, or silversides, sometimes from a height of 60 or 70 feet, streamlining themselves to resemble aerial bombs. Special air sacs under their skin cushion the impact and help to carry them back to the surface, their pouches full of water and squirming fish. They then squeeze out as much as three gallons of water, swallow the fish, and fly off to continue their fishing.

The southernmost island of Cape Hatteras National Seashore is Ocracoke, a rather narrow island reached by a free ferry from the town of

Hatteras at the tip of Hatteras Island. Ocracoke is covered with low yaupon and myrtle shrubs. The park service manages a small herd of wild ponies, thought to be descendants of horses brought by English colonists in the late sixteenth century.

As on many of the barrier islands, surf fishing is excellent here. During the summer, anglers catch sea mullet, pompano, and small bluefish from either end of the island. One of the best spots for catching red drum is on Vera Cruz Shoal in the middle of Ocracoke Inlet, best reached with the help of a local guide. Strong winds and tides can make small boating around the inlets more than a little dangerous.

From Ocracoke Village, a two-and-a-half-hour-long ferry ride crosses Pamlico Sound to Swan Quarter on the mainland. (Ferries also cross to Cedar Island.) During the winter, the chance to view flocks of snow geese and other wintering waterfowl gives bird-watchers reason to make the cold and windy trip.

THE SOUTHERN COAST: SWAN QUARTER TO CAPE FEAR

Ten miles northeast of Swan Quarter on Route 264, and crossed by Route 94, is **Lake Mattamuskeet,** North Carolina's largest natural lake. About 18 miles long and 6 miles wide, it averages only 3 feet deep. Native

LEFT: *In the center of its delicate web, a female argiope spider, poisonous only to its prey, awaits flying insects near Lake Phelps.*
RIGHT: *The leaves of the native waterlily can measure a foot or more across; in summer, its large, fragrant flowers perfume the air.*

American legends tell of a raging fire that burned a huge hole in the peatland during a drought, creating a depression that filled with water. So far, scientists can't offer a better explanation for the so-called Carolina bay, one of many that exist in spots across the North Carolina coastal plain as well as in states to the north and south. These lakes derive their name from the sweet bay, loblolly bay, red bay, and other bay shrub and tree species often found growing around them. Edged by freshwater marsh and forest, this Carolina bay acts as a magnet for migrating tundra swans, Canada geese, snow geese, and ducks. As many as 45,000 tundra swans may winter on the lake. The lake, its small island, and the western shore are protected by the **Mattamuskeet National Wildlife Refuge❖.** The best way to see the birdlife is to pull over on the Route 94 causeway that crosses the lake. A large breeding population of ospreys has built their nests in the bald cypress trees along the water's edge.

Pettigrew State Park❖ sits on the northern shore of Lake Phelps, North Carolina's second largest natural lake and also a Carolina bay lake, about 20 miles northeast of Mattamuskeet as the crow flies and reachable by following Route 94 north, then heading west on Route 64. The park's wide and grassy Carriage Trail winds 2.7 miles through stands of bald cypress, sweet gum, tulip poplar, and black gum to an overlook of the lake. The deciduous forest on the lakeshore contains bald cypress trees, some as wide as ten feet in diameter, as well as the state's largest examples of sweetleaf, alder, papaw, black gum, red bay, and green ash. Anglers flock to the park for largemouth bass, yellow perch, and sunfish.

From Swan Quarter head west on Route 264 along the Pamlico River, then take Route 17 south at Washington to the Neuse River, a wide estuarine waterway that flows into Pamlico Sound, its sandy shores lined with marsh and cut with creeks. Far upstream, west past Kinston and La Grange on Route 70, then south on Route 111, is **Cliffs of the Neuse State Park❖.** Here the Neuse has carved 90-foot-tall cliffs, revealing the sedi-

195

mentary history of the coastal plain. Layers of sand, clay, shale, gravel, and marine fossils create an earth-colored tapestry, visible from an observation deck at the lower end of the cliffs. These deposits were left over millions of years by the rise and fall of the shallow seas that once covered the area.

Back where the Neuse becomes a wide, slow-flowing estuarine river near New Bern on Route 70 is **Croatan National Forest❖**. With more than 150,000 acres of shrub bogs, lakes, and pine forest, it is a largely wet world inhabited by alligators, poisonous water moccasins and copperheads, black bears, and countless birds. Here are some of the state's best and most extensive pocosins. To the casual observer, a pocosin (from a Native American word for "raised bog") is an impenetrable mass of evergreen shrubs tangled with vines, growing on accumulated beds of peat. At Croatan, four roadless wilderness areas within the forest protect 30,000 acres of this rare and little understood habitat.

In the midst of these pocosins are large shallow lakes, probably the results of fires burning out the peat. The only trail of its kind, the 3.5-mile-long **Sheeps Ridge Trail** leads to Great Lake entirely through a pocosin. The trail winds over wet sphagnum moss, where two species of insectivorous pitcher plants, red-leaved parrot and green-leaved trumpet, grow along with cotton grass and other wetland plant species. Both pitchers lure their prey into their slippery maws with the promise of sweet nectar. The one-way ride ends in a digestive soup that eventually turns the insect into a nutrient-rich gruel. Other carnivorous plants, such as sundew and Venus's-flytrap, grow in more open areas.

On the sea side of Croatan is Bogue Banks, a thin barrier island that protects the mainland from the Atlantic. Shackleford Island, the barrier island just to the east, is one of three islands that make up **Cape Lookout National Seashore❖**. Forming a big check mark, the seashore runs 56 miles from Shackleford to Ocracoke Inlet, with Cape Lookout forming the crook in the check. Here no roads bisect the island, and no bridges connect it to the mainland—and the dunes have not been artificially stabilized. As a result, North and South Core Banks and Shackleford Banks offer some of the wildest and most isolated beaches and marshes on the Outer Banks. A ferry from Harkers Island, just across the North River from Beaufort, transports passengers and four-wheel-drive vehicles to a spot near the cape, which is the site of the Cape Lookout Lighthouse, and to Shackleford Banks. The two islands to the north are low-lying, marked by shrubs and grass, and often overwashed by the sea, which permits little substantial vegetation growth. Loggerhead turtles visit the beaches on their annual egg-laying run each summer.

Quite different from its neighbors, Shackleford Banks runs generally east-west, at right angles to the prevailing winds and ocean currents, featuring the buildup of a protective dune that, in turn, has helped promote the growth of a maritime forest. Hurricanes during the past century have killed sections of this maritime forest, creating eerie ghost woods. Snags of dead cedar and oak trees lie awash in sand.

West and south of Bogue Banks is Bear Island, a 3.5-mile-long undeveloped barrier island that is home to **Hammocks Beach State Park❖.** During the spring and summer, a passengers-only ferry leaves from docks southwest of Swansboro, reached by taking Route 24 east from Route 17 at Jacksonville. The ferry passes through a salt marsh often filled with large wading birds, such as herons and egrets, and numerous seagulls and terns. No roads cross the island. Solitary beach and sky are all that's visible; rarely does the ocean overwash Bear Island, and so tall, moving dunes have risen. Some dunes rise as high as 60 feet, encroaching on the small maritime forest of loblolly pine, live oak, and red oak. Camping on the island is restricted during certain summer periods when loggerhead sea turtles lay eggs on the beach.

From Jacksonville, Route 17 continues south to Wilmington, where it picks up Route 421 south toward Cape Fear. Just before the town of Carolina Beach is **Carolina Beach State Park❖,** adjacent to the Cape Fear River. Coastal habitats are well represented here, from longleaf pine, live oak, and turkey oak forests on relict sand dunes and swales filled with shrub bogs to shallow ponds and dry, open savannas. A dwarf cypress forest grows in Cypress Pond, one of three unusual lime sink ponds found in the park. Lime sink ponds arise in depressions created in the earth by faults in the underlying limestone strata.

The half-mile **Fly-Trap Trail** passes over boardwalks and along pocosins where a fascinating variety of plants grow, including a number of native orchids, such as grass pink and white ladies' tress, which grow in June, and the August-blooming white-fringed orchid. However, the most interesting is Venus's-flytrap, an insectivorous species that is native only within a 70-mile radius of Wilmington. Charles Darwin described the mysterious flytrap as the most wonderful plant in the world. Little is

---

OVERLEAF: *An aerial view of Core Banks on the Cape Lookout National Seashore reveals a classic barrier island: a thin strip of sand that absorbs the ocean's pounding winds and surf and protects a rich back bay.*

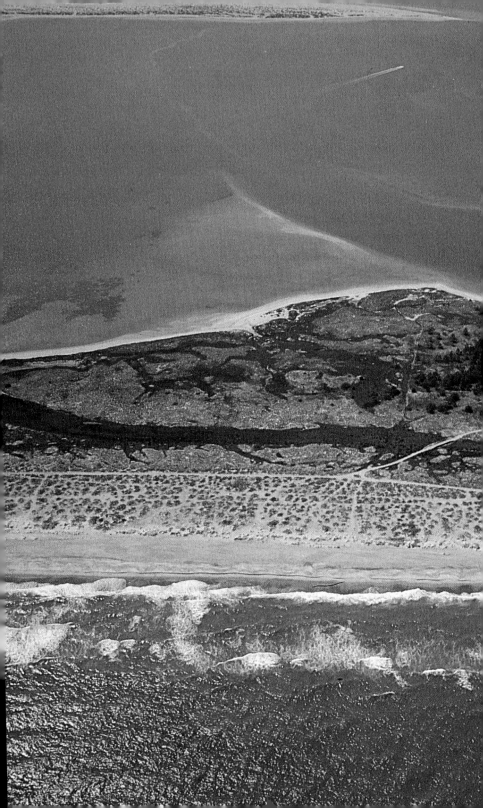

known about the mechanism that enables the flytrap to clamp its hinged leaf on unsuspecting insects so swiftly. Once ensnared, the insect is slowly dissolved by the plant's digestive juices. The trap usually opens again within three to five days, and each trap dies after opening and closing three times. A perennial herb, the flytrap blooms with small white flowers in May. The park's mineral-poor and acid-rich soils are ideally suited for carnivorous plants: In addition to the flytrap, pitcher plants, sundews, bladderworts, and butterworts grow here. Visitors must avoid handling these plants, to prevent further reduction in their shrinking numbers. Poachers of rare plants have severely reduced these remarkable communities.

Continuing south on Route 421, the road runs down a peninsula sandwiched by the Cape Fear River to the west and the Atlantic to the east. Route 421 crosses near the site of Fort Fisher, a pivotal Civil War fort, dead-ending at a ferry dock on the Cape Fear River side. Not far away, a tangled rock jetty known as the Rocks stretches west and south to Zekes Island and then continues on to the marshes of Bald Head Island. Built in 1881, the jetty created a shallow estuarine bay, known as the Basin, between it and the barrier island to the east. A low-tide scramble on the Rocks is an excellent way to see pelicans and herons in the Basin and to explore the marshy expanse of Zekes Island. These low-lying islands and marshlands are protected from the sea by a thin barrier island. More than three miles of undeveloped beach are protected in **Fort Fisher State Recreation Area❖**. Also worth examining is the unusual beachfront at the **Fort Fisher State Historical Site❖**, the state's only naturally occurring rock outcrop on the Atlantic. Visible at low tide, the rocks are made of shells and remnants of Pleistocene fossils fused together by calcite into a matrix known as coquina. In the tidal pools left by the departing sea live a number of small marine invertebrates.

THE COASTAL PLAIN:
WILMINGTON TO RALEIGH

From Wilmington, Route 74/76 cuts west through the low-lying wetlands of North Carolina's coastal plain, crossing just north of Lake Waccamaw after 38 miles. On the southeastern end of this sandy, tree-lined, Carolina bay lake is **Lake Waccamaw State Park❖**, reached by Routes 214, 1757,

---

LEFT: *The world's only naturally occurring population of Venus's-flytrap grows within a 70-mile radius of Wilmington, North Carolina. The small white flowers of this rare native carnivorous plant appear in May.*

and 1947. The park itself includes sandy beach, second-growth longleaf pine forest on sandy ridges, pocosin, cypress-gum swamp, and the headwaters of the black-water Waccamaw River. The lake's most impressive features are its beautiful sandy shores and clear waters. Unlike most Carolina bay lakes, Waccamaw has clear, nonacidic waters, which support an unusual number of fish and mollusk species, some endemic only to this area, such as the Waccamaw killifish, darter, spike mussel, and lance. Such diversity in a lake only five miles wide is difficult to explain. Part of the reason lies in the limestone beds that neutralize the highly acidic stream waters that feed into the lake.

Just east, Route 211 heads south from Bolton through the Green Swamp, a rich area of swamp, pocosin, and longleaf pine savanna that once encompassed some 200,000 acres. The swamp shrank during the eighteenth and nineteenth centuries, when much of the longleaf pine was cut down for use in the shipbuilding industry and for making turpentine. Later, parts of the swamp were drained, then developed, further shrinking the wetland. The Nature Conservancy operates the **Green Swamp Nature Preserve**❖ five miles north of Supply on Route 211, where a boardwalk crosses some of the nation's finest wetland savanna: wide-open areas devoid of shrubs and hardwoods where grasses, wildflowers, and herbs grow beneath tall longleaf pines. These savannas occur on slight ridges within the dense pocosin habitats. Ten species of orchids and a number of other wildflowers thrive in this easily disturbed environment. Because of the fragility of the habitat, visitors must contact the Nature Conservancy before entering.

Additional examples of typical Carolina bay lakes exist north of Route 74/76, off Route 701 north from Whiteville at **Jones Lake State Park**❖, adjacent to the **Turnbull Creek Educational State Forest**❖.

West of north-south–running I-95, which intersects Route 74/76 near

Lumberton, is an area known as the Sandhills, almost a million acres of sandy ground on the far southwestern corner of North Carolina's coastal plain. The region was once a vast pine barren where longleaf pines dominated the higher ground, loblolly pines grew along stream floodplains, and pond pines inhabited the wetter bog areas. More than 250 years of logging and development decimated most of this large forest.

One pocket of old-growth longleaf pine remains, located at the **Weymouth Woods/Sandhills Nature Preserve❖,** near Fort Bragg Military Reservation and Southern Pines, northwest on Routes 20, 211, and 1 from the Saint Pauls exit on I-95. From the visitor center, the mile-long Pine Barrens Trail loops among longleaf pines that are hundreds of years old. Their ramrod-straight trunks shoot high in the air, making it clear why the British navy used them for masts. These pines have the longest needles (up to 18 inches) and cones (up to 10 inches) of any eastern pine tree. On the ground beneath these trees are savannas of wire grass, where fox squirrels often scamper. This rodent is larger than its cousin, the gray squirrel, and sports telltale black patches on its head, paws, and tail.

Especially of note in the preserve are colonies of the endangered red-cockaded woodpecker, a small, elegant bird with a zebra-striped back, black cap, and white cheeks. These woodpeckers need living, mature pine trees of at least 85 years of age in which to bore nesting cavities. Located between 20 and 50 feet up the trunk, below the lowest living branch, these nests often take years to finish. The woodpecker begins by pecking a hole upward so the pine resin drips out, and digs down to form the nesting chamber only once the tree's heartwood is reached. Other woodpecker species, bluejays, and flying squirrels compete for red-cockaded woodpecker nests once they are complete.

A good place in North Carolina to view the fall zone, the demarcation line between the geologies of the coastal plain and piedmont, is **Raven Rock State Park❖,** reached by taking Route 421 north at Dunn on I-95 and driving beyond Lillington to Route 1314 north. The park straddles the Cape Fear River and features stark 150-foot-tall quartzite bluffs, laid bare and sculpted over eons by the relentless undercutting force of the water. These are the tallest cliffs in North Carolina's fall zone. From the 2.1-mile-long Raven Rock Loop Trail, which leads down wooden stairs to an observation area, it's possible to peer back more than 400 million years: The oldest layer is Precambrian quartzite, a hard rock probably derived from ancient beach sands. Above this is younger, metamorphic slate, topped in turn with assorted gravels left by great inland seas, probably during the interglacial periods of the Pleistocene.

The rapids on the Cape Fear River are also characteristic of the fall zone, where the water tumbles from the generally hard rocks of the piedmont to the more easily eroded sediments of the coastal plain. In the park, the **Cape Fear Canoe Trail** traverses Lanier's Falls and the Fish Traps, where Native Americans once fished the rapids with trap baskets. The 56-mile-long canoe trail begins where Route 1 crosses over the Deep River. A buoy marks the spot in the park set aside for canoe camping.

THE PIEDMONT: RALEIGH TO THE BLUE RIDGE

I-40 crosses I-95 beyond Benson on its way north to Raleigh. In the piedmont around and north of the Raleigh-Durham area, feats of human engineering have significantly altered the environment. The Army Corps of Engineers built massive dams to protect downstream areas from flooding, and these impoundments have perhaps changed the landscape more dramatically than any other human alteration in the piedmont region. Three of the largest of these impounded lakes are found around and to the north of the Raleigh-Durham area: Kerr Dam and Reservoir, off I-85 out of Durham and straddling the border with Virginia; Falls Lake Dam Project, off I-85 just to the northeast of Durham; and Jordan Lake, to the south of Durham and Chapel Hill off Routes 15 and 64. All have state recreation areas and small natural areas that feature hiking trails and boat launches.

Damming rivers to create these lakes obliterated the rich alluvial and swamp bottomland forests on the rivers' upstream floodplains and created in their place long, narrow lakes with many thin fingers. Changing the habitat and topography drove some wildlife away, including several species of warblers, pileated woodpeckers, and the red-shouldered hawks that once thrived in these forests. Replacing these species are a number of waterbirds, especially during the fall and spring migration.

Cutting off the natural flow of water affected many fish species, specifically those known as anadromous species (marine fish that swim into freshwater streams to spawn), such as shad and herring. Curiously, at Kerr Lake the damming process locked in a population of striped bass, an anadromous fish, which eventually reproduced. Supplemented each year by an infusion of fingerlings from state fisheries, the landlocked fish thrives here and is a favorite of anglers.

Jordan Lake State Recreation Area❖ is the largest summertime home of the bald eagle in the eastern United States. Most congregate at the north end of the lake and are often visible between May and August

ABOVE: *The flowers of the native Atamasco lily (left) quickly change from pure white to pink as they age. Now rare, the insectivorous hooded pitcher plant or flytrap (right) produces an odorless flower in spring.*

from an observation platform located off Routes 751, 1733, and 64. Early in the morning or early in the evening is the best time to view this magnificent bird, which finds the lakeshore ideal for hunting fish and the mature forest perfect for roosting.

Amid the urban sprawl in the northwestern outskirts of Durham runs a small jewel of a river protected by a narrow corridor of parkland. Four noncontiguous areas define the **Eno River State Park❖** as it protects the Eno on its way east to meet the Little and Flat rivers; all three of these rivers eventually flow together to become the Neuse. Steep second-growth forests descend to the Neuse, which rates class II rapids during the winter and early spring. In the Pump Station Access Area, off Cole Mill Road from I-85, the 2.25-mile-long Pump Station Trail loops close to the river into the rich alluvial floodplain, littered with ferns, herbaceous plants, and a profusion of wildflowers in April and May. The spring hiker will find the uncommon yellow lady's slipper, the pink-petaled wild geranium, and the white foamflower growing in abundance. Wood thrushes, with their mellifluous, flutelike call are common among the sycamore, river birch, and sweet gum trees of the bottomland forest.

Also off Cole Mill Road, the 2.5-mile-long Bobbit Hole Trail follows the river as it hits rocky bluffs, makes an about-face, and widens into a

ABOVE: *Its distinctively shaped leaves earned the bird-foot violet (left) its name. An introduced plant, the annual morning glory (right) now thrives throughout North Carolina's coastal plain and piedmont.*

swirling pool about an acre in size before continuing downstream through a rocky, boulder-strewn bed. Far more reminiscent of the mountains than of the piedmont, especially with the presence of mountain laurel and catawba rhododendron on the steep, wet banks, this area is probably a relict from glacial times. In the water swims the Roanoke redeye, a small, feisty bass endemic only to the Roanoke, Tar, and Neuse river basins.

Out of Durham, Interstate 40/85 presses west to Greensboro, the western piedmont, and the first signs of mountainous country. The low-lying hills south of Greensboro and Asheboro are the Uwharrie Mountains. The passage of time, along with the erosional forces of wind and water, have softened and rounded these once-mighty mountains, which now average less than 1,000 feet. To the west of Route 220, as it runs south from Asheboro, is **Uwharrie National Forest❖,** a nearly 50,000-acre patchwork of private and public lands, intercut by rural roads and dotted with small hamlets. Atop the ridges are chestnut and scarlet oak forests, turning to oak and hickory forests on the slopes and becoming beech, tulip poplar, ash, oak, and hickory woods in the small ravines and stream floodplains. The westernmost extensive stand of longleaf pine in the piedmont grows on the dry slopes of Gold Mine Branch, above the Uwharrie River. The area also has some unusual wetlands known as hillside seepage bogs.

Perhaps the best place to experience the muted but beautiful Uwharrie Mountains is across the Pee Dee River from the national forest at **Morrow Mountain State Park❖,** reached by crossing the forest on Route 24/27 west from Biscoe to Route 740 north. The park is dominated by 936-foot-tall Morrow Mountain and several other monadnocks, small ridges capped by erosion-resistant areas of rhyolite, a volcanic rock much like granite in mineral composition. In addition to a number of trails that scale the monadnocks and rock outcrops for views of the area, the .6-mile-long Quarry Trail leads through an artificial gorge, created when rock was quarried to construct buildings. These exposed, folded rocks are made of slate, the remains of volcanic ash spewed forth from ancient volcanoes. These lava eruptions formed the Uwharrie Mountains long ago.

ABOVE: *Often remaining motionless high in the forest canopy, the male scarlet tanager can be difficult to spot, even with its brilliantly hued spring plumage.*

RIGHT: *The wet and shady bottomlands of North Carolina's piedmont support a variety of lacy ferns and harbor many different types of native mushrooms.*

From Blowing Rock, just off the Blue Ridge Parkway deep in the Blue Ridge Mountains, the Yadkin River flows 203 miles west then south near Winston-Salem to the western perimeter of Uwharrie National Forest, where it picks up the Uwharrie River and becomes the Pee Dee River. The Pee Dee continues south for 230 miles into South Carolina, feeding into the Atlantic near Georgetown. Just south of the national forest, on the western banks of the Pee Dee, is **Pee Dee National Wildlife Refuge❖,** reached by taking Route 220 south, Route 74 west, and Route 52 north. The hills of the piedmont gently roll down to the river's floodplain, where impoundments and dikes have created habitat for migratory birds. A 2.5-mile-long interpretative nature drive passes along narrow dike tops and through a hardwood bottomland forest, providing views of waterfowl and songbirds. The spring migration of raptors brings northern harriers, American kestrels, red-shouldered hawks, and the occasional bald eagle. The area has one of the largest white-tailed deer populations in the state.

Route 74 continues west through Charlotte, and runs north of two spectacular monadnock mountains, both included in **Crowders Mountain**

State Park❖, reached by taking Route 1125 south from the junction of Route 74 and I-85. Once taller than the Alps, the sheer rock cliffs and quartzite peaks of 1,705-foot-tall King's Pinnacle and 1,625-foot-tall Crowders Mountain are all that's left after more than 500 million years of weathering. Trails up the ridge pass very dry soils in which stunted Virginia pines and other trees often grow no taller than three to six feet. Down below are wet woodlands along streambeds filled with a rich assortment of ferns, including southern lady, cinnamon, and netted chain ferns. Many such ferns are visible on the .9-mile-long Fern Nature Trail, as is a groundcover plant known as running cedar, which snakes along the ground.

On clear days, one of the best walks is a five-mile trip up to the top of Crowders Peak along Rocktop, Tower, and Crowders trails for views of Charlotte, some 30 miles distant. The trail offers good vantages of rock climbers challenging the numerous rock walls and of the roosting spots of black vultures and turkey vultures. It also passes Table Rock, a half-acre flat rock pitted with indentations from water erosion over the eons.

Because the Blue Ridge Mountains angle to the southwest, the southern piedmont extends quite far west. One of the most interesting western piedmont sites is the remote **South Mountains State Park❖,** a series of rugged mountain knobs, outliers of the Blue Ridge Mountains, which begin in earnest 20 miles to the west. The park is reached by taking Routes 226, 10, 1545, 1905, 1901, and 1904 north from Shelby at Route 74. Pines dominate the highest ridges, with a heath understory of rhododendron, holly, and mountain laurel. Over time the erosive powers of Jacob's Fork River, Shinny Creek, and their tributaries have carved deep ravines. The major attraction of the park is High Shoal Falls on Jacob's Fork, where water plunges over a cliff face into a deep pool some 80 feet below. The half-mile-long Lower Falls Trail is a steep and rocky scramble to the base of the falls, a damp world of ferns and mosses where rosebay rhododendrons cling to the steep slopes. Many trails crisscross the area, including 29 miles of horse trails and a strenuous 18-mile-loop trail for mountain bikers.

From Charlotte, I-85 heads northeast on its way to Winston-Salem, crossing the Yadkin River. The exit after the river crossing leads west to **Boone's Cave State Park❖,** on Route 150 toward Churchland. This 110-acre area is the smallest of the state parks; it gets its name from the story that Daniel Boone explored and possibly lived or hid from Native Americans on the high bluffs that overlook the Yadkin River here. Down a steep wooden stairway with handrails, a path descends toward the banks of the river, where there are granite outcrops and the entrance to a short and narrow cave. Floodwaters from the river carved this hole in the rock, which stretches for 80 feet but is never more than 5 feet tall.

The park also serves as a stop-off on the 165-mile-long **Yadkin River Canoe Trail,** a mostly flat-water float along the curling river, stretching from Ferguson at the W. Kerr Scott Reservoir not far from the Blue Ridge to the river's confluence with the Pee Dee adjacent to the Uwharrie National Forest. Overseen by the Yadkin River Trail Association, the trail offers 38 access points and crosses 5 reservoirs.

One of the most spectacular places the Yadkin flows by is **Pilot Mountain State Park❖,** off Routes 52 and 2053, 24 miles north of Winston-Salem. From the gentle hills of the piedmont rises the rounded face of Pilot Mountain, a monadnock with sheer rocky sides and a cap of chestnut oak, table mountain pine, mountain laurel, and rhododendron. The park is divided into two sections: The northern area includes the Big and Small Pinnacles of Pilot Mountain, and the southern contains two miles of the Yadkin River and a floodplain pond. They are connected by a forested corridor 5 miles long and 300 feet wide, which is accessible to hikers and equestrians.

The .75-mile-long Jomeokee Trail loops around the base of the Big Pinnacle, its often vertical walls rising 200 feet above the talus-strewn base. A common raven might soar high above, emitting its hoarse cry before heading back to its nest in the sheer cliff face. Larger than its relative the crow, the raven prefers the isolated and protected perches of cliff walls for its nest, so the species is usually found only in the mountains.

Rock climbing up Big Pinnacle is prohibited, but hikers can enjoy great views from atop Little Pinnacle, a shorter peak connected to the larger one by a narrow saddle. From Pilot Rock, the Sauratown Trail leads 30 miles east across the crest of the ancient Sauratown Mountain range, connecting the park with **Hanging Rock State Park❖,** another excellent example of a weathered monadnock. Hanging Rock is located on the other side of Route 52, off Routes 66 and 1001. The northwestern face of Moore's Wall, one of the park's sheer rock faces, challenges the mettle of even expert climbers. Atop any of the several peaks at Hanging Rock, the views are of a kind usually seen only by birds on the wing. Below and spreading far off in the distance is a breathtaking patchwork quilt of agricultural fields.

OVERLEAF: *A craggy monadnock towers above the gentle contours of North Carolina's western piedmont. Pilot Rock's sheer cliff face shelters the easternmost nesting population of the common raven.*

NORTH CAROLINA'S MOUNTAINS

E very June, nature creates a remarkable spectacle on the high, open balds of the southern Appalachians. On the flanks of the Roan Mountain Massif, the Great Craggies, and elsewhere in the mountains of western North Carolina, the catawba rhododendrons dotting the open heath fields (called slicks) explode into a thunderous display of pink and lavender bloom. Just months earlier, these sinewy bushes endured the bitter winter winds that sweep relentlessly across these mountains, their glossy green leaves tightly curled against the cold.

Yet each spring the shrubs again blaze with color, and thousands of North Carolinians and others make an annual trek to witness their pageantry. Often the only reminders of the brutal winters are the blow-downs and frost cracks that mar the bark of nearby red spruce trees. No theory fully accounts for the existence of the open heath slicks and grass meadows that appear throughout a land otherwise covered by a thick carpet of forest. This mystery adds a deeper allure to the great beauty of these open realms—regions that have come to typify the magic of the southern Appalachians.

This chapter focuses on the montane region of North Carolina, which spreads southwest from Virginia to South Carolina and Georgia, and west to the border with Tennessee. It makes up the largest section of the region known as the southern Appalachians, the lower end of the 2,000-mile-long mountain range that runs from Newfoundland to Georgia. Two

LEFT: *In one of nature's grandest spectacles, each June a vivid sea of catawba rhododendron lights up the exposed ridges of Roan Mountain, which straddles the border between North Carolina and Tennessee.*

vast national forests—Pisgah and Nantahala—occupy this region, as does one of the most popular national parks, Great Smoky Mountains. It's here that the Appalachian Mountains are at their highest, most rugged, and bulkiest: 43 peaks rise above 6,000 feet, and 82 top 5,000 feet. Great changes in elevation along with high precipitation and a moist climate create a series of habitats that harbor North America's most diverse array of tree species—some 130 species grow in the Great Smokies alone. Never covered by glaciers or drowned by inland seas, the vegetation has developed relatively undisturbed for millions of years. The result is an unusually wide array of forest communities, which in turn support a diverse host of life-forms, ranging from slime molds and salamanders to peregrine falcons and black bears.

The driving route proceeds south, beginning at the Virginia border and ending at the South Carolina border. It starts by following the National Park Service's Blue Ridge Parkway as it snakes along the crest of the Blue Ridge Mountains. As the route moves southward, the vegetation becomes more northern in character, due mostly to the rise in altitude. South of Blowing Rock, the parkway enters one of the four ranger districts of the Pisgah National Forest, nearly half a million acres of forestland that protects much of the central region of montane North Carolina. From Blowing Rock to just north of Asheville, the Pisgah encompasses the Blue Ridge's eastern escarpment, a sharply defined ridgeline that soars dramatically above the rolling farmland of the piedmont stretching to the east. The views along the escarpment are often spectacular.

To the west of the escarpment, an increasingly complicated jumble of mountains fills the horizon southward along the parkway. One observer has compared these mountains to a ladder. The two sides of the ladder constitute the north-south running mountain ranges—the Blue Ridge to the east and the Unakas to the west. The Blue Ridge Mountains occupy the edge of the montane province abutting the piedmont, whereas the Unakas define North Carolina's border with Tennessee and include the Iron, Unicoi, and Great Smoky mountains.

The rungs in the ladder analogy are represented by the numerous cross-ranges, a tangle of ridges, balds, and peaks that connect the Blue Ridge and the Unakas. In between are broad valleys and isolated upland

---

OVERLEAF: *From the top of Roan Mountain, a wintry panorama stretches forth across North Carolina's Blue Ridge range. The open grass and heath balds at the summit are rare in the thickly forested Appalachians.*

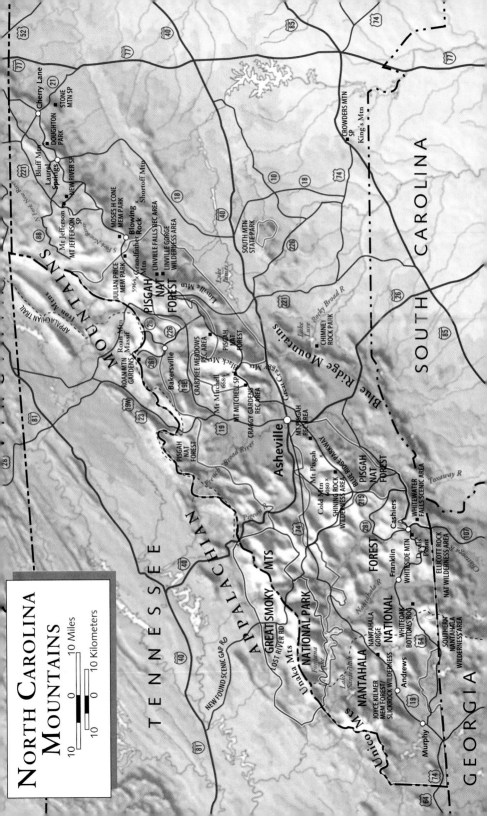

coves and ravines along the flanks of the mountain ridges.

The most prominent of the cross-ranges are the Black Mountains, so named for the dark green forests of spruce and fir trees that cover their tall peaks and ridges. At 6,684 feet, Mount Mitchell not only crowns this high-altitude range but soars higher than any other peak in the East. From atop the observation tower is a clear vista of mountains stretching for miles, a breathtaking sight tempered only by the graveyard of dead spruce and fir trees around the summit. Upwards of 90 percent of this high-altitude forest in the southern Appalachians has been killed by the double plague of insect pests and airborne pollution.

Trails in western North Carolina are usually strenuous, dipping precipitously into cove forests or climbing lofty ridges where the forested summits often frustrate clear views. Though the trails may not furnish vistas, they do provide much to see. On a carefully selected hike it's possible to walk in several short hours through nearly every type of forest habitat found in the Appalachian Mountains, from Georgia to Newfoundland: Stands of interlocking spruce and fir, trees common 1,000 miles to the north, dominate peaks and ridges above 4,500 feet. There are also pine-edged dry ridges, grassy and heath balds, patches (called orchards) of stunted northern red oaks, mixed oak forests, and eastern hemlock forests along wet stream corridors.

Perhaps most fascinating are the wet hardwood cove forests, sheltered from the elements as well as the logger's ax in deep valleys where 25 to 30 tree species grow amid a confusion of moss-covered rocks, lichens, shelf fungi, mushrooms, slime molds, and ferns. Here, certain trees achieve enormous dimensions: Hemlocks swell to 20 feet in circumference, yellow poplars to 30 feet.

South of Asheville, the parkway continues through another ranger district of the Pisgah, the peak for which the area was named. Fifteen miles or so south of Mount Pisgah, the parkway abruptly cuts to the northwest, toward the Great Smokies. As the Appalachians hit the South Carolina border, they, too, change orientation, heading west instead of southwest. In this area, included mostly in the Nantahala National Forest, moist warm air from the south hits the tall, cool mountains and drops its moisture, creating a verdant landscape of fierce white-water rivers, plunging waterfalls, deep gorges, and miles of dense vegetation that frustrate even the most persistent attempts at bushwhacking. Walking through these forests, one sees how this wetness fuels the process of death and decay as well as the arrival of new life.

The parkway ends close to Cherokee, near the entrance to Great Smoky Mountains National Park, one of the last true wildernesses in the East and the jewel of the southern Appalachians. Only two roads cross its half-million-acre expanse. Those wishing to glean more than a cursory look at this rugged mosaic of forested mountains must meet nature on its own terms by hiking or horseback riding into the interior on the hundreds of miles of trails.

The rewards can be as dramatic as catching a glimpse of a black bear bounding through the woods on a quiet early morning, or as tranquil as discovering a fragile but colorful lady's slipper in the damp woods near a bubbling mountain stream. Whatever the visitor may find, it's a rare privilege today to look on nature in its wild and natural form.

ALONG THE BLUE RIDGE

The Blue Ridge Parkway enters North Carolina near the town of Galax, Virginia, named for a striking ground-cover plant that grows throughout the southern Appalachians. The galax is marked by large, round evergreen leaves and was once gathered by North Carolinian mountain families who sold it to florists for decoration in the days before refrigeration made a wider variety of greenery available. During the fall, when the deciduous trees have lost their leaves and a cool crispness has descended over the southern Appalachians, beds of rich green or red galax provide a refreshing contrast to the brown leaf litter.

The first spectacular view on the parkway in North Carolina is the massive granite dome of Stone Mountain, which rises several miles to the southeast of the overlook at milepost 232. In the afternoons, the sheer, 600-foot-tall, oval northern face reflects the sun's glow, a stunning sight against the backdrop of the piedmont and waves of green forest. From the parkway, **Stone Mountain State Park❖** can be reached by taking Route 21 south at the town of Cherry Lane, then following routes 1002 and 1784 to the entrance.

The rocks that make up Stone Mountain were formed some 300 million years ago when molten magma from deep within the earth flowed into the bedrock, creating a pluton, a large plug of igneous rock some 25 square miles in size. Complex geologic processes in conjunction with the erosion of softer overlying rock eventually exposed parts of the pluton, including the rocky outcrops of Stone Mountain.

Atop the dome are weather pits or pan holes, evidence of the continuing weathering process known as exfoliation, the peeling away of surface layers through freezing and thawing, rain and wind. The process gradually produces a thin layer of topsoil, on the order of one inch every 500 years. Despite this paltry growing medium, tenacious groups of chestnut oaks and shrubs cling to the rocky dome, anchored by a shallow layer of soil. Lichens,

Like some great beached whale, the massive gray form of Stone Mountain lies exposed just off the Blue Ridge Parkway (above). Erosion has smoothed the 600-foot, sheer northern face (right) of the mountain.

mosses, and ferns grow on the rock face along the edges of the vegetation, also contributing to the erosion of the rock surface. On top of the rock, the soft, rounded shoulders of rock beckon the hiker to advance closer and closer until the face falls dangerously away to the forested floor far below.

Stone Mountain Trail leads to the south face, where rock climbers ascend long, smooth granite walls on climbing routes with such names as Taken for Granite and Fantastic. Occasionally, wild goats are visible high above, picking their way gracefully on the steep upper slopes. Across a stream valley are Wolf Rock and Cedar Rock, smaller rock exposures with views of the piedmont and the Blue Ridge as stunning as those from Stone Mountain. Cedar Rock not only offers exceptional views of Stone Mountain but also carries a diverse granite outcrop plant community, including eight rare moss species.

Back on the parkway, the route heads south to **Doughton Park❖** at milepost 238. Here, open meadows and windfalls offer good views of the tangle of mountains to the south. Ridges shoot eastward, descend to the piedmont, and form two cove forests. Some 30 miles of trails offer an opportunity that's rare along the rest of the parkway: the chance to hike from

Above: *A thrilling, unmistakable sight, the Eastern bluebird with its reddish chest and bright blue plumage frequents woods and farmland. It is often spotted along North Carolina's northern Blue Ridge Parkway.*

the ridgeline all the way down to the piedmont, a strenuous but exhilarating way to experience a rich cross-section of the region's forest communities.

The one-mile, round-trip Fodder Stack Trail begins on **Bluff Mountain** near 3,790-foot-tall Wildcat Rocks, named for the bobcat dens found there, and leads to 3,615-foot-tall Fodder Stack, also on Bluff Mountain. Views from the quartzite outcrops are excellent, particularly out over Basin Creek Cove and the piedmont beyond, where black vultures, turkey vultures, and other raptors can be seen winging across a bright blue sky. The trail passes Carolina hemlocks, table mountain pine trees, and bigtooth aspens at the far southern end of their range. The bigtooth aspens are recognizable by—and named for—the curved teeth along the edges of their broad ovate leaves. Trails in the park pass by a number of rare wildflowers and plants, including the spreading avens.

Along the parkway south from Doughton is one of the better spots to glimpse wild turkeys, which sometimes cross the road between mileposts 243.5 and 246 in the early mornings or late afternoons. The chestnut color at the tips of their tail feathers and a slighter build distinguish them from the domestic turkey. Hunting and the chestnut blight, which knocked out a major food source, have decimated their once-abundant ranks, but populations of wild turkeys are growing again, thanks in part to restocking efforts.

ABOVE: *A clumsy flyer, the skittish wild turkey runs from danger and feeds on nuts, fruits and insects. Overhunting and the blight of the native chestnut tree have reduced the ranks of this once-populous species.*

As the parkway cuts southwest from the Virginia border to Blowing Rock, some 70 miles distant, it isolates the far northwestern corner of North Carolina, a triangular section bounded by Virginia to the north and Tennessee to the west. Within this section run the South and North forks of the northeast-flowing New River, which join together several miles shy of the Virginia border. Twenty-two miles of the South Fork and 4.5 miles of the main stem are encompassed in an unusual preserve known as the **New River State Park❖,** a narrow corridor that rolls through remote second- and third-growth forests and past small farms, grassy meadows, ridges, and rocky outcrops high above the river where red-tailed hawks nest. Belying its name, the New is actually one of the oldest rivers in North America, its meandering northeastern course set long before the Appalachians themselves were created by geological upthrusting.

The area is best explored in a leisurely way by canoe, taking advantage of any one of the three places set up for canoe camping. The park's southernmost put-in is **Wagoner Road Access Area,** reached by taking Route 18 north from the parkway to Laurel Springs, then Route 88 west to Route 1590. The slow-moving waters, fed by tributaries and punctuated by small riffles, are ideal for beginners, and the scenery makes even a short trip worthwhile. The wet, low forests along the river are home to rhododen-

Billion-year-old quartzite rock ledges characterize the top of 5,964-foot Grandfather Mountain (above). A brilliant fall display of wild sumac (left) frames a sweeping view of the Pisgah National Forest.

drons and mountain laurels that burst with blossoms every spring. Numerous wildflowers and other plants also grow here, many of which are rare and unusual, such as the purple sedge, spreading avens, and Carolina saxifrage. Floating silently around a bend in the river at dusk, one may surprise a white-tailed deer, its front legs spread while it thirstily laps the river's waters. Or luck may bring a sighting of a startled black bear, often no bigger than a large dog, crashing back into the woods.

On clear days, the New River and its surrounding countryside unfold like a huge map from the overlooks on nearby 4,683-foot-tall Mount Jefferson. Despite its small size, **Mount Jefferson State Park❖**, reached by heading north on Route 163 from Horse Gap on the parkway, then up Route 221 to Route 1152, offers spectacular views for minimal effort. The easy, 1.2-mile round-trip Rhododendron Trail leads to Luther Rock and a 360-degree panorama that in clear weather takes in mountains of three states: Toward the east and the piedmont is North Carolina's Pilot Mountain; to the north is Virginia's Mount Rogers; to the west are Tennessee's Iron Mountains; to the south is North Carolina's Grandfather Mountain. On the north side of the summit, the northern red oaks are stunted and often damaged from the snow, ice, and wind that batters the

ABOVE: *Joining the rhododendron on the grassy heaths of North Carolina's southern bald mountains, flame azaleas burst into bloom during May and June, with flowers ranging from yellow to scarlet.*

peak in winter. Underneath the rocky ledges on the second overlook on Route 1152 are fissures, narrow cavelike openings extending 15 feet into the rock, created by the separation of rock faces over time.

HEART OF THE BLUE RIDGE

Just south of milepost 290, near Blowing Rock, the tablelands of the Blue Ridge Plateau end, giving way to the ladderlike web of mountain ranges and cross-ranges. The first of four ranger districts of the **Pisgah National Forest❖** begins to spread out to the east, south, and west. The first of North Carolina's national forests, the Pisgah occupies much of the central part of the montane region, straddling the Blue Ridge as well as the Unicoi Mountains along the border with Tennessee.

Just north of Blowing Rock, the park service operates the **Moses H. Cone Memorial Park❖,** an area once owned by a textile tycoon who built a residence here in the late nineteenth century. His legacy is 25 miles of carriage trails that wander gently through meadows and forests of white pine, hemlock, sugar maple, and rhododendron. It's easy to spend the day roaming these broad, interconnected trails without retracing a route. The

Above: *Mountain laurel brightens heath balds and the understory of mountain slopes with pink or white blooms in the spring. A shrub or small tree, its bark is a dark reddish brown and shreds easily.*

one-mile loop trail through the cove hemlock forest around Trout Lake is a good spot to look for nesting songbirds in the spring, especially the Blackburnian and Canada warblers, as well as the yellow-bellied sapsucker, veery, and rose-breasted grosbeak. Wildflowers greet the hiker around every curve of the Watkins Carriage Road during the spring; they include white trilliums, louseworts, violets, wild geraniums, and cinquefoils.

Between Cone Park and Grandfather Mountain is **Julian Price Memorial Park❖,** an area with many camping facilities and three fine trails, including the 4.9-mile Boone Fork Trail. Blackberry bushes in the area are full of sweet fruit for hungry hikers in the summer. Less than a mile after the trail passes through a beautiful grove of birches—a surprise to those who associate these trees with New England—it meets the **Tanawha Trail❖.** One of the state's most scenic trails, it leads 13.3 miles from Price Park south to 5,964-foot-tall Grandfather Mountain. The word

---

Overleaf: *Sunlight glints off the ancient rocks of Linville Gorge, one of the deepest canyons in the East. The steep walls cut by the Linville River helped to preserve mature stands of hemlock from extensive logging.*

Tanawha comes from the Cherokee and translates as "fabulous hawk [or eagle]." Anyone who has witnessed the eagle-eye views of the surrounding countryside from the open rock fields, heath balds, and outcrops on this mountain or has watched the fall migration of broad-winged hawks from one of the mountain's tall pinnacles will find this an apt description.

Engineers building the Tanawha Trail used wooden steps around rock outcrops, high bridges over streams, boardwalks through rock fields, and other design techniques to allow hikers to cross fragile habitats with minimal damage. Nearly half the trail climbs the southeastern flank of Grandfather Mountain. South from the Rough Ridge Parking Area at milepost 302.9, the Tanawha Trail pushes through hardwood forest and spruce until it dramatically opens into an area of catawba rhododendron and mountain laurel, known as a heath slick. The trail crosses a wooden boardwalk, installed to protect the fragile heath environment, for part of its journey up Rough Ridge to 4,690-foot-tall Ship Rock, an outcrop with spectacular views of the towering, craggy ridgeline of Grandfather Mountain above and the flat expanse of the piedmont and Linville Gorge below. Ship Rock is an excellent place to watch for broad-winged hawks during the fall migration.

Much of **Grandfather Mountain** is privately owned but open to the public. The rewards are often well worth the admission fee. The highest point in the Blue Ridge and one of the world's oldest peaks, its unusual quartzite ridges and peaks contain rocks that are estimated to be more than 1.1 billion years old. Time has fractured the high rock, creating a rugged topography of craggy outcrops, cliffs, and boulders. Perched on the edge of the piedmont, the mountain forms some of the Blue Ridge's most severe relief, immediately rising 4,000 feet above the rolling hills.

Variations in altitude and the composition of minerals in the rocks have spawned a wide variety of plant communities, most of which can be explored along the area's many trails. Atop the summit are spruce and fir, stunted by the tempestuous winter weather conditions. Heath areas of blueberry thickets and tangles of rhododendron punctuate the mountain's flanks, while birch forests occupy the wet lower altitudes, and hardwood forests carpet the rest. Streams spill down the steep sides. Among these rich habitats are some 20 rare plant species, including pink-shelled azalea, Heller's gayfeather, Gray's lily, and balsam groundsel.

After a full day of hiking at Grandfather or on the Tanawha Trail, a stop at the **Lost Cove Overlook** (mile 310) for a breath of cool evening breeze brings the day to a nice close. The strange phenomenon known as the brown mountain lights, mysterious pale orange lights that dance above the dark hillside, may even appear. For years, these strange lights have defied all explanation, and they remain a lively ingredient in local mountain myth and a source of much conjecture.

From the flanks of Grandfather Mountain flows a tributary of the Linville River, which cuts south through the Blue Ridge, drops over Linville Falls, and enters Linville Gorge, one of the East's deepest canyons, before emptying into Lake James. From the parking lot at the **Linville Falls Recreation Area❖**, off milepost 316.4, the 2.1-mile round-trip Linville Falls Trail traverses the river on a steel and concrete footbridge and leads through a stand of unlogged Carolina and eastern hemlock, emerging at three overlooks. The falls first drop 12 feet into a pool, then flow over a ledge before plunging 60 feet into the gorge. Peregrine falcons and red crossbills are known to nest here, and rhododendrons and mountain laurels cling to the steep sides of the gorge, seeming to defy gravity.

The erosive action of the river has exposed a glimpse of the massive forces that have formed these rugged mountains. At the upper falls overlook, a large thrust fault is visible. This cleavage formed deep within the earth during the mountain-building process that occurred with the collision of the continents, when billion-year-old rock, cranberry gneiss, was thrust on top of 600-million-year-old rock, a greenish quartzite. Upthrust and erosion brought this rock to the surface, signs of the titanic might of geologic processes that have created this rugged region.

On its 12-mile course south from Linville Falls to Lake James, the gorge at times grows to 1,600 feet in depth. Backpackers and rock climbers alike flock to this V-shaped canyon for the same reasons loggers shunned it: its extreme contours and remote access. On the taller, jagged eastern ridge are the dominating peaks and ridges of Jonas Ridge, Hawksbill, Table Rock, the Chimneys, and Shortoff Mountain. A dirt road leading to Wiseman's View runs along Linville Mountain, the gorge's less rugged western ridge, for spectacular views of the river far below.

Some 25 miles of trails are managed by the U.S. Forest Service in the area known as the **Linville Gorge Wilderness Area❖**, including the 11.5-mile Linville Gorge Trail, which shadows the river along the western side. Pieces of quartzite have fallen down the steep sides, creating a talus-strewn river-

OVERLEAF: *The only rhododendron species to thrive in high, exposed locations, the catawba (here on Roan Mountain) fends off bitter temperatures with curled leaves and welcomes spring with opulent blossoms.*

bank. From the river, it's possible to discern the changes in vegetative zones from the hardy table mountain and pitch pines on the dry ridges and the hemlocks and white pines on the valley walls to the wetter cove and hardwood forests closer to the water.

One spot not to miss in early summer is the **Roan Mountain Massif❖** in the Pisgah National Forest, 15 miles to the northwest of Linville Falls on the North Carolina–Tennessee border, between the Unaka and Blue Ridge mountains. Take Route 226 north from the parkway to Route 261. There the wide-open heath balds, filled with thousands of catawba rhododendrons, burst into bloom, making the mountainsides look as though they are on fire with a gentle lavender flame. This is one of the most spectacular areas in the southern Appalachians: Grass and heath balds frequently interrupt the hardwood and spruce and fir forests, offering vast open areas and unlimited views from a number of ridgetops that surpass 6,000 feet.

The Appalachian Trail travels for 10 miles along the ridge, in a section many agree is the prettiest in its entire 2,100-mile length. Nowhere else are shrub balds and grass-herb balds more extensive than here, partially because of the high rainfall and cool climate, although these conditions cannot fully explain the phenomenon. Whatever the cause, emerging into an open bald and looking south for an unblocked view of the Black Mountains is one of North Carolina's most inspiring natural experiences.

Roan Mountain Gardens❖, located on the flanks of 6,267-foot-tall Roan High Knob, offers a triple-loop trail through the famous 600-acre natural garden of catawba rhododendron and flame azalea. The trail is reached by taking Route 226 north from the parkway near milepost 330,

then Route 261 north from Bakersville. Catawba thrives in open sun, unlike other rhododendron species common to the southern Appalachians that prefer the shade below the thick tree canopies found on steep mountain slopes. The white undersides of its thick evergreen leaves identify the catawba. Despite the paved trail and the June crowds, the abundance of bloom makes a short trip worthwhile.

Back on the parkway heading south toward Mount Mitchell, the ridgetop narrows, enclosed by the Catawba River Valley to the south and the Toe River Valley to the north. At milepost 339, one of the Toe River system's many tributaries, Crabtree Creek, crashes down a 60-foot-tall waterfall in the **Crabtree Meadows Recreation Area**❖. Most visitors come to this small area for a glimpse of the cascading falls. Equally impressive, however, is the abundance of wildflowers and songbirds along the 2.5-mile round-trip Crabtree Falls Trail, which descends sharply from the campground through an oak forest into a moist cove forest of hemlock and rhododendron. White trillium and jack-in-the-pulpit are common. The eye-catching yellow lady's slipper may be less so but is instantly recognizable with its bright yellow sacklike flower and green leaves. Also visible are dwarf iris, mayapple, and buttercup. A number of warblers haunt the forest, adding their mellifluous songs to that of the waterfall. They include the northern parula and the Blackburnian, black-and-white, chestnut-

sided, and hooded warblers, to name just a few.

Southward on the parkway, the horizon off to the right is filled with a jumble of tall green peaks—the Black Mountains, so named for their dark mantle of Fraser fir and red spruce. Seventeen of the Black Mountain peaks top 6,000 feet, including 6,684-foot-high Mount Mitchell, the tallest mountain east of South Dakota's Black Hills. It and five other lofty peaks are encompassed by **Mount Mitchell State Park❖,** which occupies the eastern limb of the U-shaped range formed by the Black Mountains. Mount Mitchell and the park can be reached by taking Route 128 north at milepost 355.4.

For the purist, Mount Mitchell will seem too crowded and built-up— with a restaurant along the road that leads close to the summit. An observation tower crowns the peak, offering spectacular views of the Blue Ridge, the Blacks, and the Craggies to the west. A disturbing sight also greets visitors to the peak: Dead and dying Fraser fir and red spruce form an eerie graveyard around the observation tower and summit trails. Forestry experts believe airborne pollution to be one of the main culprits. The deposit of such pollution on the branches of the trees and in the soil may weaken the trees against insect attack and the relentless assault of extreme temperatures, gale-force winds, and heavy snow. Earlier logging efforts and wildfires have also contributed to the decimation of what was once a pristine high-altitude spruce-fir forest.

The crowds on Mount Mitchell can be left behind in minutes by hiking out on one of the numerous trails. Deep Gap Trail leads a little more than a mile north through more sickly forest to the windy rock summit of Mount Craig and stunning views of Mitchell and the rest of the Blacks. The old adage "spiny spruce and friendly fir" helps distinguish between the two evergreen species, red spruce and Fraser fir, as spruce needles are sharp and pointed, whereas the fir's are soft and rounded. Locally known as balsam, Fraser fir is endemic only to the southern Appalachians, which makes the die-off even more tragic.

These spruce-fir forests are the farthest southern extension of the great spruce-fir forests that cover vast areas of the Canadian subarctic and continue south with a number of interruptions. The spruce-fir forests of the

CLOCKWISE FROM TOP LEFT: *Denizens of the mountain forests include the tireless, charming eastern chipmunk, which chatters "chip-chip-chip"; the yellow lady's slipper with its Latin name meaning "a little shoe"; the common yellowthroat, a warbler that thrives in brushy habitats; and colorful native columbine, with its delicate drooping flowers.*

southern Appalachians are probably relict communities pushed south by advancing glaciers during the last ice age. Although the modern spruce-fir species found here differ from their northern cousins, this southern community attracts a similar animal biota, including many species at the southern extremes of their normal range. Northern bird species that nest in the spruce-fir forest include the red-breasted nuthatch, brown creeper, winter wren, and golden-crowned kinglet—all more common in northern climes. Patient hikers might hear the whistling "too-too-too" call of the northern saw-whet owl, a tiny brown bird with a blackish face near the southern limit of its nesting range. The northern flying squirrel and the New England cottontail rabbit are examples of northern mammals that can be found in these high-altitude evergreen forests.

South of the Blacks begin the Great Craggy Mountains, perhaps the most famous cross-range in the southern Appalachians because of their accessibility. The **Craggy Gardens Recreation Area❖,** between mileposts 364.1 and 367.6 on the parkway, straddles the main crest of the Craggies between Craggy Dome and Craggy Knob. It includes a 700-acre natural garden of catawba rhododendron, which can be explored from the .8-mile-long Craggy Gardens Self-Guiding Trail. Spring offers the most spectacular colors, but mountain ash, wild crabapple, and a myriad assortment of wildflowers keep the area in bloom throughout the summer as well.

There's probably no better way to observe the diversity of the forest habitats of the southern Appalachians than by hiking the trails of the Craggies—including a stretch of the Mountains-to-Sea Trail. High-altitude vegetation ranges from the heath and grass balds and the spruce-fir forests to old beech and yellow birch trees, dwarfed and twisted by strong winds. Down the flanks of the range are hardwood forests and areas of virgin eastern hemlocks, some individuals reaching heights of more than 100 feet. A rich assortment of rare plants survives on the rocky cliffs and in the lower watersheds, including the one-flowered rush, endemic only to this area.

Off on the eastern edge of the Appalachians, southeast from milepost 384.7 near Asheville and south from the parkway on Route 74, the privately owned and run **Chimney Rock Park❖** occupies a dramatic cliff face above Hickory Nut Gorge, a canyon cut over the eons by the Rocky Broad River. Hewn through the core of a solid granite monolith known as Chimney Rock, an elevator rises more than 250 feet, depositing visitors near the top for commanding views of Lake Lure, the piedmont, and the deep gorge. On clear days, King's Mountain is visible, some 75 miles to the east. A trail from the top leads back to the parking lot via the Rock Pile, a good

ABOVE: *E. T. H. Foster's 1877 nostalgic landscape* **Evening on the French Broad, N.C.** *romanticizes a ruggedly scenic area of North Carolina's Blue Ridge, once dotted with summer homes of antebellum planters.*

place to catch a glimpse of a nesting pair of peregrine falcons, reintroduced into the wild by the state of North Carolina in the 1980s. The best times to see these magnificent predators are from late March to mid-May and again in early summer to midsummer, when the young have hatched.

Weathering along joints and shear zones in the rock created the dramatic ledges and rock formations along the southern edge of the gorge, as well as fissure caves. A small cave is found near the parking lot at Chimney Rock Park. Not far away is **Bat Cave,** North America's largest fissure cave. More than two miles of passageways penetrate the rock face on several different levels. The granitic cave, which harbors some rare salamander species, is located on private property, and access is controlled by the Nature Conservancy.

THE WESTERN FORESTS: ASHEVILLE TO SOUTH CAROLINA

South of Asheville is the Pisgah Ranger District of the Pisgah National Forest, contiguous with the Nantahala National Forest, which stretches off to the west. The high-altitude Pisgah Ridge runs for 25 miles southwest from Asheville to Tanasee Bald and is dominated by 5,749-foot-tall **Mount Pisgah❖,** rising off to the west of the parkway at mile 408.6. Local legend has it that an adventurous minister climbed the peak in the late eighteenth century and was so awestruck by the view that he named

243

it for the peak from which Moses first saw the promised land. An observation platform now affords even better views of the rugged mountains and the Pigeon River, but the rocky hike, especially near the top, is strenuous. Industrialist George Vanderbilt once owned much of the area and built a horse trail from the French Broad River to his hunting lodge on the side of the mountain. Part of that pathway has been restored as the 16.4-mile **Shut-In Trail❖,** a national recreation trail probably named for its passage through tunnel-like corridors of rhododendron and mountain laurel. Elsewhere the trail mounts steep knobs to old forests of ancient oaks. The trail's overall altitude change of 3,611 feet makes it a tough, though rewarding, outing.

Near Beech Gap on the parkway, the road makes an abrupt turn from its southwesterly path to the northwest. Inside the area framed by the road's right angles is the **Shining Rock Wilderness Area,** part of the **Pisgah National Forest❖.** It includes most of the Shining Rock Ledge, a high-altitude ridge running from Cold Mountain ten miles south to Black Balsam Knob. Prior to 1913, this rugged area contained one of the largest stands of spruce-fir forests in the southern Appalachians, but extensive logging and subsequent fires have created an area filled with heath balds, second growth, and animal life usually found at lower elevations. The railroad grades that the loggers left behind do provide a benefit, however—many good avenues for penetrating this rugged and remote preserve. A backpacker's dream, the 30-mile-long **Art Loeb Trail❖** runs along the crest, passing the stunning white quartz cliffs of Shining Rock itself to excellent views of the Great Balsam Mountains to the west and the Pisgah Ridge to the east. This national recreation trail crosses the parkway at milepost 421.2; the closest parking is half a mile to the south.

Spreading to the south and west of the parkway as it heads to the Great Smokies is **Nantahala National Forest❖,** more than a half-million acres of rugged wilderness area that fills most of the state's southwestern corner. The area's name, from the Cherokee for "land of the noonday sun," no doubt refers to the countless deep gorges that feel the direct sun only when it's overhead at midday. The trails are steep, rugged, and deeply forested, and hikers often pass for miles without a clear view, ensconced in a large, green tunnel.

At North Carolina's border with South Carolina and Georgia, the Appalachians suddenly change course, switching from a northeast-southwest to an east-west orientation. The sharp, eastern escarpment of the Blue Ridge, dividing the North Carolina mountains from the state's piedmont region, swings around until it faces south. Warm, moist air blowing up from the Caribbean and the Gulf of Mexico hits this ridge crest and drops heavy precipitation when it rises and meets the cool air of the mountains. This area consequently records some of the heaviest rainfall in the East. A handful of southeast-flowing rivers, such as the Horsepasture, Chattooga, Toxaway, and Whitewater, flow fast and furiously, eroding deep gorges in the escarpment and creating spectacular waterfalls.

South from the parkway on Route 215, then west on 64 and south on Route 281, the highway crosses the Whitewater River above the most dramatic falls in the southern Appalachians. A short, paved trail from the parking lot at the **Whitewater Falls Scenic Area❖** brings a view of the 411-foot Upper Falls, which drop precipitously off the Blue Ridge Escarpment in two steps. Across the border in South Carolina, the river plunges another 400 feet at the Lower Falls. Stay on the pathway—a number of people who have underestimated the slipperiness of the rock and the severity of the drop have been killed here.

One of the most beautiful of these so-called escarpment rivers is the Chattooga, which in parts is designated a national wild and scenic river. A section of the river passes through **Ellicott Rock Wilderness Area❖**, located at the meeting point of North Carolina, Georgia, and South Carolina. Although the river drops more gently than many others nearby, it still has a steep descent, plunging more than 50 feet per mile. Farther south in South Carolina and Georgia, the Chattooga becomes one of the premier white-water rafting rivers in the East. The wilderness area is reachable by taking Route 107 south from Route 64 at Cashiers, then going right on Bull Pen Road (Forest Road 1178) and driving until it crosses the river. Trails from this point include the 2.2-mile round-trip Chattooga River Trail, which passes through a thick forest to the rock-filled river.

One of the best vantages of this rugged region occurs to the north, near the headwaters of the Chattooga, on top of the vertical cliffs of **Whiteside Mountain❖.** Past Cashiers, Route 64 heads west and Wildcat Road bears off toward Whiteside Mountain, an immediately recognizable mass of tree-capped granite rising 2,100 feet above the Chattooga River valley. Sheer rock cliffs soar between 400 and 750 feet, their faces so smooth they look as if they were cleaved by some supernatural force. A patient observer armed with a spotting scope will discover that the cliffs are home to ravens and peregrine falcons, the latter reintroduced here during the 1980s. To protect these magnificent raptors, climbers are prohibited access to the rock face during nesting season.

The south-facing walls bear white streaks where the granite is colored with light-colored feldspar and quartz. They are generally vegetation-free, due to the weathering effects of wind and sunlight. In contrast, the north cliffs, known as Devil's Courthouse, are moister and better protected from the elements. These cliff faces are dark in color because of the growth of lichens and mosses. The two-mile Whiteside Mountain Trail ascends to the 4,930-foot-high summit known as Devils Point and winds along the cliff edge for spectacular views.

ABOVE: *Large and broad-winged, red-tailed hawks are often visible only above as majestic silhouettes migrating to their breeding grounds in the north.*

RIGHT: *In the Nantahala National Forest, the upper portion of spectacular Whitewater Falls plunges 411 feet over the Blue Ridge Escarpment.*

Cutting across the midsection of the Nantahala National Forest, the Nantahala Mountains stretch north for 25 miles from the Georgia line to Fontana Lake on the border of Great Smoky Mountains National Park. This is the last of the major transverse mountain ranges of the Appalachians. The Appalachian Trail runs along the crest of the range, topping many summits more than 5,000 feet high, including Wayah Bald, where on clear days views of the Great Smokies and the rolling hills of Georgia are visible from the fire tower. The bald can also be reached by car up a steep gravel road by taking Route 64 to Route 1310, and Forest Road 69 to the top. The orange color of rocks visible along the trailside has resulted from the weathering of iron oxides in the rock.

The northeast-flowing Nantahala, a popular white-water rafting river, drains the area to the west, while the Little Tennessee drains the range's eastern slopes. Near the Georgia border, a U-shaped ridge of mountains encloses the headwaters of the Nantahala, forming Standing Indian Basin. The richest mountain wetlands in the southern Appalachians are on the upper stretches of this river. The **Whiteoak Bottoms Bog❖** is one of the better examples of the bogs, swamps, marshes, and seepages that support a wide variety of salamanders, frogs, turtles, and unusual plant species. The area, located downstream from the Standing Indian campground, reached from Route 64 west of Franklin and Forest Road 67-1 south, has no trails.

ABOVE: *Common in this region, the eastern cottontail can leap 15 feet when challenged. Prodigious breeders, the female produces three to four litters annually, often mating within hours of giving birth.*

The wetlands and basin are in the shadow of 5,498-foot-tall **Standing Indian Mountain.** The dominant peak in this area, it is worth climbing both for the views and for exploring a number of vegetation types, which range from the stunted trees and narrow heath bald plants on the summit to white oak and hardwood forests lower down. Forest Road 71, off Route 64, leads nearly to the summit. More ambitious visitors can hike the Appalachian Trail as it traverses the high crest of the U-shaped ridge for 21 miles from Deep Gap to Wallace Gap. Much of the ridge, including Standing Indian and the area to the south, is contained in the **Southern Nantahala Wilderness Area❖.** This high backcountry offers numerous opportunities for backpacking adventures. It also provides a home to native black bears, turkeys, grouse, and deer, as well as European wild boars, an alien species that escaped from a game reserve in the 1920s. These boars, also called wild hogs, have black hair, long legs, and tusks. Rooting for tubers and roots, the boars tear up rhododendron thickets and dig up the earth on balds, causing destructive erosion in many areas. In addition, this aggressive species competes with native animals for berries, acorns, and nuts. One boar alone can consume some 1,300 pounds of acorns and nuts in a year. Luckily, there are not many of them.

ABOVE: *A sun lover, good climber, and fine swimmer, the woodchuck, when alarmed, emits a loud whistle before retreating to its underground burrow. During hibernation breathing slows to once every six minutes.*

Route 64 continues west to Murphy, where Route 19 heads northeast (past Andrews and Route 129), crossing the **Nantahala Gorge❖,** a spectacularly deep and narrow gorge with steep walls that rise as high as 1,100 feet. Route 129, farther south, heads northwest from Route 19, passing Lake Santeetlah and the **Joyce Kilmer Memorial Forest❖,** which occupies the northwestern corner of the Nantahala National Forest. Remote and rugged, this area contains tracts of old-growth forest, spared from the ax when the local logging company went bankrupt in 1890. The area was closed to logging before other companies could begin cutting. Specimens of hemlocks, tulip poplars, and oaks grow as large as six feet in diameter. Excellent views of old-growth forest appear on the 1.2-mile **Joyce Kilmer National Recreation Trail,** which begins in the parking lot at the picnic area at the end of Forest Road 416, reached off Route 129 at the northern end of Lake Santeetlah. Along the trail is a memorial to soldier and poet Joyce Kilmer, who wrote the poem "Trees." The area contains two basins, the Little Santeetlah Creek watershed and the Slickrock Creek watershed, separated by a ridge. The Slickrock Creek and Hangover Lead trails, among others, provide backpackers with a chance to walk through some of the most remote areas in the national forest.

ABOVE: *The Smokies harbor more salamander species than anywhere else in the world; here a red eft, an immature newt, pauses on green moss.*

THE GREAT SMOKIES

No national park is more popular or more diverse in its variety of species than the **Great Smoky Mountains National Park❖,** which beckons like a gleaming pot of gold at the very southern end of the Blue Ridge Parkway. At more than half a million acres, it's one of the largest wilderness areas in the East and a place where superlatives apply. More than 1,500 species of flowering plants grow here; 130 tree species are represented, more than are found in all of northern Europe; about 74 percent of the Southeast's spruce-fir forest lies within the park; 27 species of salamanders live here, more than anywhere else in the world; in addition, its 125,000 to 200,000 acres of old-growth forest include one of the largest uncut tracts of temperate deciduous forest in North America.

Much of the richness of the vegetation and associated animal and plant life has to do with the range of altitudes, the wet weather, and the relatively moderate climate found here. As the area was neither scraped clean by massive glaciers nor inundated by inland seas, its indigenous plants have had millions of years to establish footholds in this realm. The 300 rare vascular plants include wildflowers such as the mountain catchfly orchid, Virginia spiraea, and the Appalachian avens, a delicate flower that grows on cliff faces,

LEFT: *Fall brings a rainbow of bright colors to the ridges of Great Smoky Mountains National Park, which is home to more than 130 tree species.*

requiring botanists to rappel over cliffs in order to monitor it.

A ridge of northeast-southwest–running mountains divides the blimp-shaped park, serving as a boundary line between North Carolina and Tennessee and a home to 68.6 miles of the Appalachian Trail. For 36 miles of the 71-mile-long ridge, the altitude remains above 5,000 feet and crosses such notable balds and summits as Thunderhead and Clingmans Dome. Smaller ridges shoot off the main ridge, creating deep ravines and coves, often graced by streams and creeks.

Remarkably, only two roads cross the park: Little River Road, west from the visitor center, and Newfoundland Gap Scenic Road, which runs from Cherokee in North Carolina to Gatlinburg in Tennessee, with a spur road leading to Clingmans Dome. From Newfoundland Gap Scenic Road the majesty of the Smokies is inescapable, mountains stretching off to the horizon in every direction. At times, it appears that fluffy cumulus clouds have floated down from the sky and filled the valleys and coves, leaving the ridgetops and summits to peek out like deep green islands. Created by transpiration (the passage of water from plant leaves to the atmosphere) and the wet climate, this smokelike haze is the signature of the area as well as the reason for its name.

The best way to experience the richness of Great Smoky park is to wander any of the multiple trails that run some 900 miles through the park—leaving behind the crowds that walk or drive the well-trodden and obvious routes. Follow a trail into one of the ravines and the light grows dim as the canopy of large hemlock, beech, sugar maple, and yellow birch trees blocks out the sun. Just as the thick vegetation becomes claustrophobic, the clear music of a mountain stream cuts through the muffled sounds of the forest and the rich earthy smell of dampness, ferns, and decay fills the nostrils. Around dusk in spring and early summer, a short walk off the seven-mile Clingmans Dome Road into the spruce-fir forest will be met by the haunting song of a veery, filling the air with its downward spiraling call. As darkness falls, the barred and northern saw-whet owls sound their calls.

During these moments, which occur more often in the Great Smokies than just about anywhere in the Mid-Atlantic region, an echo of the deep, untamed primeval forest fills the senses—and hints at the character of the wild forests that covered this continent before the coming of the Europeans.

RIGHT: *For centuries delicate clouds of white mist have draped the low-lying valleys of the Great Smokies. Water passing into the atmosphere from dense, moist forests creates this famous smokelike haze.*

GLOSSARY

alluvial fan deposit of alluvium, gravel, sand, and smaller materials that has formed a fan shape, usually at the base of mountains; created by water rushing down a mountain

anadromous describing those fish that ascend rivers from the sea in order to breed and can live in both salt and fresh water; includes salmon, trout, and shad

aquifer underground layer of porous, water-bearing rock, sand, or gravel

barrier island narrow island made of sediment—sand, silt, and gravel—that protects the coast from direct battering by storm waves and winds

biotic pertaining to plants and animals

bog wetland formed in glacial kettle holes; common to cool climates of northern North America, Europe, and Asia; its acidic nature produces large quantities of peat moss

boreal relating to the northern biotic area characterized especially by the dominance of coniferous forests

brackish referring to salty or briny water, particularly a mixture of fresh and salt water found in estuaries

coastal plain large area of low, flat land lying next to an ocean; wetlands may develop in such low-lying areas

coniferous describing the cone-bearing trees of the pine family; usually evergreen

continental drift theory that the continental land masses drift across the earth as the earth's plates move and interact in a process known as plate tectonics

deciduous referring to plants that shed their leaves seasonally and are leafless for part of the year

dike a wall or barrier; a natural dike is a vertical sheet of rock formed when molten rock cools on its way to the earth's surface and is exposed by erosion

endemic having originated in and being restricted to one particular environment

escarpment cliff or steep rock face that separates two comparatively level land surfaces; formed by faulting or fracturing of the earth's crust

estuary region of interaction between ocean water and the end of a river, where tidal action and river flow mix fresh and salt water

geothermal energy heat generated within the earth; intense heat causes rocks to melt and form magma; heated rocks also create hot springs when heated water rises to the earth's surface

grotto a cave, or artificial structure made to resemble a natural cave

igneous referring to rock formed by cooled and hardened lava

karst area of land lying over limestone and dotted with sinkholes, underground streams, and caves formed as rainwater erodes the soft limestone

mesophyte plant that grows under medium moisture conditions

metamorphic referring to rocks that have been changed into their present state after being subjected to heat, pressure, or chemical alteration

monadnock height of land containing more erosion-resistant rock than the surrounding area

montane relating to the biogeographic zone of relatively moist, cool upland slopes below timberline; dominated by evergreen trees

peat partially decayed, spongy plant matter that makes up much of the substance of bogs; considered the first stage in the transformation of plant material into coal

piedmont area at the base of a mountain or range; in the eastern United States, the piedmont area stretches from the base of the Appalachian Mountains to the Atlantic coastal plain

pluton formation of lava that cooled before reaching the earth's surface

pocosin dense, swampy evergreen community that forms on elevated areas between streams; thorny shrubs and vines make it nearly impenetrable

rapids broken, fast-flowing water that tumbles around boulders; classified from I to VI according to increasing difficulty of watercraft navigation

savanna tropical grassland with clumps of grasses and widely scattered tree growth; occurs in areas where a prolonged dry season alternates with a rainy season

schist metamorphic rock with a layered appearance; composed of often flaky parallel layers of minerals

sedge family of grasslike plants found in brackish swamps and marshes along the Atlantic coastal plain

sedimentary referring to rocks formed from deposits of small eroded debris such as gravel, sand, mud, silt, or peat

sinkhole funnel-shaped hole formed where water has collected in the cracks of limestone and carried the stone away; also formed when cave roofs collapse

sphagnum moss that grows in wet, acidic areas; decomposes and compacts to form peat

talus rock debris that accumulates at the base of a cliff

tundra cold region characterized by low level of vegetation; exists as alpine zones of mountain ranges in lower latitudes, or arctic zones of polar areas in the far north

watershed entire river system, or an area drained by a river and all its tributaries

wetland area of land covered or saturated with groundwater; includes swamps, marshes, and bogs

FURTHER READING: DELAWARE, MARYLAND, NORTH CAROLINA, VIRGINIA, AND WASHINGTON, D.C.

BARTH, JOHN. *The Sotweed Factor.* Garden City, NY: Doubleday, 1967. A large and wonderful fictional account of colonial Maryland by one of America's most respected writers.

BERNHARD, VIRGINIA. *A Durable Fire.* New York: Morrow, 1990. Captain John Smith and Pocahontas come alive in this historical novel about Jamestown, England's early colony in Virginia.

BURNS, JASPER. *Fossil Collecting in the Mid-Atlantic States.* Baltimore, MD: Johns Hopkins University Press, 1991. A straightforward and handsome presentation of the fossil sites in the area.

DENNIS, JOHN V. *The Great Cypress Swamps.* Baton Rouge, LA: Louisiana State University Press, 1988. This large-format volume offers interesting details on the life and ecology of cypress swamps, including Carolina bays.

DUNCAN, WILBUR H., AND MARION B. DUNCAN. *The Smithsonian Guide to Seaside Plants of the Gulf and Atlantic Coasts.* Washington, D.C.: Smithsonian Institution, 1987. A comprehensive illustrated guide to flora along the coast.

FRYE, KEITH. *Roadside Geology of Virginia.* Missoula, MT: Mountain Press, 1986. An accessible, detailed look at the geology of the Old Dominion.

HEDEEN, ROBERT A. *Naturalist on the Nanticoke.* Centreville, MD: Tidewater Publishers, 1982. A biologist's richly detailed observations of life on one of Delmarva's least disturbed rivers.

LAMBERT, DARWIN. *The Undying Past of Shenandoah National Park.* Boulder, CO: Roberts Rinehart, 1989. The park's first employee takes an in-depth look at these recycled park lands and their history, which unfolds over centuries.

MICHENER, JAMES A. *Chesapeake.* New York: Random House, 1978. An anecdote-laden, larger-than-life romp through the history of the Chesapeake Bay.

WARNER, WILLIAM W. *Beautiful Swimmers: Watermen, Crabs and the Chesapeake Bay.* Boston: Little, Brown, 1976. A brilliant, deftly written natural history of the Atlantic blue crab and the watermen who collect them.

WEIDENSAUL, SCOTT. *Seasonal Guide to the Natural Year: Mid-Atlantic.* Golden, CO: Fulcrum Publishing, 1992. In an unusual presentation, this guidebook tracks the area's natural happenings by time of year.

WILDS, CLAUDIA. *Finding Birds in the National Capital Area.* Washington, D.C.: Smithsonian Institution, 1992. An excellent guide to the region's birds.

WILLIAMS, JOHN PAGE, JR. *Exploring the Chesapeake in Small Boats.* Centreville, MD: Tidewater Publishers, 1992. An indispensible guide for those planning to paddle or motor around the creeks, guts, and rivers of the Chesapeake.

LAND MANAGEMENT RESOURCES

The following public and private organizations are among the important administrators of the preserved and protected areas described in this volume. Brief explanations of the various legal and legislative designations of these areas follow.

LAND MANAGEMENT AGENCIES

Delaware Division of Fish and Wildlife
Maintains 43,000 acres of state wildlife area. Issues state hunting, fishing, and boating licenses. Part of the state's Department of Natural Resources and Environmental Control.

Delaware Division of Parks and Recreation
Manages approximately 16,500 acres of land including 13 state parks, preserves, and seashore areas. Part of the state's Department of Natural Resources and Environmental Control.

Delaware Forest Service
Manages and protects all state forest lands for natural resources, timber production, recreation, and conservation education. Division of the state's Department of Agriculture.

Maryland National Capital Park and Planning Commission
Bicounty land management agency for Prince George and Montgomery counties. Manages and maintains stream-valley parks, regional parks, and natural-area parks for recreation and conservation.

Maryland State Forest and Park Service
Manages and maintains all 35 state forests and parks totalling 242,514 acres. Part of the state's Department of Natural Resources.

Maryland Wildlife Division
Manages all 68 state wildlife management areas and cooperative management areas totalling 124,780 acres. Part of the state's Department of Natural Resources.

National Biological Survey Department of the Interior
Administers and conducts environmental research in centers located on federally owned land throughout the country. Areas of research include environmental contaminants, migratory birds, and endangered species.

National Park Service (NPS) Department of the Interior
Regulates the use of national parks, monuments, and preserves. Resources are managed to preserve and protect landscape, natural and historic artifacts, and wildlife; also administers historic and national landmarks, national seashores, wild and scenic rivers, and the national trail system.

The Nature Conservancy (TNC) Private Organization
International nonprofit organization that owns the largest private system of nature sanctuaries in the world, some 1,300 preserves. Aims to preserve significant and diverse plants, animals and natural communities. Some areas are managed by other private or public conservation groups, some by the Conservancy itself.

North Carolina Division of Forest Resources

Manages state parks for recreation, conservation, and educational purposes. Division of the state's Department of Environmental, Health, and Natural Resources.

North Carolina Division of Parks and Recreation

Maintains 29 state parks and all state recreation areas, lakes, rivers, trails, and natural heritage areas. Part of state's Department of Environment, Health, and Natural Resources.

U.S. Fish and Wildlife Service (USFWS) Department of the Interior

Principal federal agency responsible for conserving, protecting, and enhancing the country's fish and wildlife and their habitats. Manages national wildlife refuges, fish hatcheries, and programs for migratory birds and endangered species.

U.S. Forest Service (USFS) Department of Agriculture

Administers more than 190 million acres in the national forests and national grasslands and is responsible for the management of their resources. Determines how best to combine commercial uses such as grazing, mining, and logging with conservation needs.

Virginia Department of Conservation and Recreation

Responsible for management of all state parks, natural areas, preserves and trails totalling approximately 70,000 acres. Oversees the departments of state parks, natural heritage, planning and recreation resources, and soil and water conservation.

Virginia Department of Forestry

Responsible for forest management, research, and education in all state forests, totalling approximately 40,000 acres. Also responsible for fire control on all state and privately owned land.

Virginia Wildlife Division

Manage 33 wildlife management areas totalling 180,597 acres for the conservation of wildlife habitat, hunting, and recreation. Part of Virginia Department of Game and Inland Fisheries

Wildfowl Trust of North America Private Organization

Nonprofit organization that manages 310 acres of Maryland wetlands for the preservation of wildfowl and their habitat.

LAND DESIGNATIONS

Demonstration Forest

Forest land set aside for research on forest management and multiple-use practices, and for public education. Managed by individual states.

National Forest

Large acreage managed for the use of forests, watersheds, wildlife, and recreation by both the public and private industry and individuals. Managed by the USFS.

National Historical Park
Extensive acreage designated to preserve an area of national historical significance. Managed by the NPS.

National Park
Spacious primitive or wilderness land area that contains scenery or natural wonders so outstanding that it has been preserved by the federal government. Managed by the NPS.

National Recreation Area
Site established to conserve and develop for recreational purposes an area of national scenic, natural, or historic interest. Power boats, dirt and mountain bikes, and ORVs allowed with restrictions. Managed by the NPS.

National Recreation Trail
Created by the National Trails System Act of 1968 to provide outdoor recreation trails for public use, in or accessible to urban areas. Managed by the NPS.

National Scenic Area
Land protected and enhanced under the National Scenic Area Act of 1986 for its natural beauty or its cultural and recreational resources. Managed by the USFS.

National Scenic Trail
Created by the National Trails System Act of 1968 to provide long-distance public recreational trails through nationally significant scenic, historic, natural, or cultural areas. Managed by the NPS.

National Seashore
Area of pristine, undeveloped seashore designated to protect its natural state and provide public recreation in a natural setting. Camping and ORVs allowed with restrictions. Managed by the NPS.

National Wildlife Refuge
Public land set aside for wild animals; protects migratory waterfowl, endangered and threatened species, and native plants. Managed by the USFWS.

Natural Area
Area designated and preserved in its natural state for its exceptional value as an example of the natural history of the United States. Managed by individual states.

Wilderness Area
Area with particular ecological, geological, or scientific, scenic, or historic value that has been set aside in its natural condition to be preserved as wild land; limited recreational use is permitted. Managed by the BLM.

Wildlife Management Area
Land managed or owned by the state to protect wildlife. Aside from seasonal restrictions, hunting, fishing, and public access are allowed. Managed by individual states.

The Atlantic Coast and Blue Ridge

NATURE TRAVEL

The following is a selection of national and local organizations that sponsor nature-related travel activities from extended tours to day trips and ecology workshops.

NATIONAL

National Audubon Society
700 Broadway
New York, NY 10003
(212) 979-3000
Offers a wide range of ecological field studies, tours, and cruises throughout the United States

National Wildlife Federation
1400 16th St. NW
Washington, D.C. 20036
(703) 790-4363
Offers training in environmental education for all ages, wildlife camp and teen adventures, conservation summits involving nature walks, field trips, and classes

The Nature Conservancy
1815 North Lynn St.
Arlington, VA 22209
(703) 841-5300
Offers a variety of excursions from regional and state offices. May include hiking, backpacking, canoeing, horseback riding. Contact above number to locate state offices

Sierra Club Outings
730 Polk St.
San Francisco, CA 94109
(415) 923-5630
Offers tours of different lengths for all ages throughout the United States. Outings may include backpacking, hiking, biking, skiing, and water excursions

Smithsonian Study Tours and Seminars
1100 Jefferson Dr. SW
MRC 702
Washington, D.C. 20560
(202) 357-4700
Offers extended tours, cruises, research expeditions, and seminars throughout the United States

REGIONAL

Appalachian Trail Conference
PO Box 807
Harper's Ferry, WV 25425
(304) 535-6331
Nonprofit organization that coordinates the preservation and management of the 2,100-mile trail running through Maryland, Virginia, and North Carolina

Delaware Department of Tourism
99 Kings Highway
PO Box 1401
Dover, DE 19903
(800) 441-8846
Provides specific traveler information as well as general tourism brochures for out-of-state visitors

Maryland Department of Tourism and Promotion
217 East Redwood Street
Baltimore, MD 21202
(410) 333-6611
Travelers may call or write for specific information, or to order a general vacation planning kit

North Carolina Travel and Tourism Division
430 Salisbury Street
Raleigh, NC 27611
(919) 733-4171
(800) VISIT NC (to order general tourism guide)
Provides informational brochures and answers specific travel inquiries

Virginia Division of Tourism
901 E. Byrd Street
Richmond, VA 23219
(804) 786-4484
(800) VISIT VA (to order vacation planning guide)
Call or write with specific travel questions, or to order travel guides

260

HOW TO USE THIS SITE GUIDE

The following site information guide will assist you in planning your tour of the natural areas of Delaware, the District of Columbia, Maryland, North Carolina, and Virginia. Sites set in **boldface** and followed by the symbol ❖ in the text are here organized alphabetically by state. Each entry is followed by the mailing address (sometimes different from the street address) and phone number of the immediate managing office, plus brief notes and a list of facilities and activities available. (A key appears on each page.)

Information on hours of operation, seasonal closings, and fees is not usually listed, as these vary from season to season and year to year. Please also bear in mind that responsibility for the management of some sites may change. Call well in advance to obtain maps, brochures, and pertinent, up-to-date information that will help plan your adventures in the Atlantic Coast and Blue Ridge areas.

Each site entry in the guide includes the address and phone number of its immediate managing agency. Many of these sites are under the stewardship of a forest or park ranger or supervised from a small nearby office. Hence, in many cases, those sites will be difficult to contact directly, and it is preferable to call the managing agency.

The following umbrella organizations can provide general information for individual natural sites, as well as the area as a whole:

DELAWARE

Delaware Division of Fish and Wildlife
89 Kings Highway
PO Box 1401
Dover, DE 19903
(302) 739-5297

Delaware Division of Parks and Recreation
89 Kings Highway
PO Box 1401
Dover, DE 19903
(302) 739-4401

Delaware Forest Service
2320 S. DuPont Highway
Dover, DE 19901
(302) 739-4811

MARYLAND

Maryland State Forest and Park Service
580 Taylor Ave., E-3
Annapolis, MD 21401
(410) 974-3771

Maryland Wildlife Division
580 Taylor Ave., E-1
Annapolis, MD 21401
(410) 974-3195

NORTH CAROLINA

North Carolina Department of Cultural Resources
109 E. Jones St.
Raleigh, NC 27601
(919) 733-7862

North Carolina Division of Parks and Recreation
PO Box 27687
Raleigh, NC 27611
(919) 733-4181

VIRGINIA

Virginia Department of Conservation and Recreation
203 Governor St., Ste. 302
Richmond, VA 23219
(804) 786-7951

Virginia Division of State Parks
203 Governor St., Ste. 306
Richmond, VA 23219
(804) 786-1712

Virginia Wildlife Division
4010 W. Broad St.
Richmond, VA 23230
(804) 376-9588

DELAWARE

ASSAWOMAN WILDLIFE AREA
Delaware Div. of Fish and Wildlife
PO Box 1401, Dover, DE 19903
(302) 739-5297; (302) 834-8433
BW, F, H, MT, PA, T

BEACH PLUM ISLAND NATURE PRESERVE
Delaware Div. of Parks and Recreation
c/o Cape Henlopen State Park
42 Henlopen Dr., Lewes, DE 19958
(302) 645-8983 **BW, F, H, T**

BLACKBIRD STATE FOREST
Delaware Forest Service
502 Blackbird Forest Rd.
Smyrna, DE 19977
(302) 653-6505
Primitive camping **BW, F, H, PA, XC**

BOMBAY HOOK NATIONAL WILDLIFE REFUGE
U.S. Fish and Wildlife Service
RD 1, Box 147, Smyrna, DE 19977
(302) 653-9345; (302) 653-6872
Day-use area; 12-mile auto tour route; 3
observation towers
BW, GS, H, I, MT, T, TG

BRANDYWINE CREEK STATE PARK
Delaware Div. of Parks and Recreation
PO Box 3782, Greenville, DE 19807
(302) 577-3534; (302) 655-5740
**BT, BW, CK, F, GS, H,
HR, I, MT, PA, RA, T, TG, XC**

C & D CANAL WILDLIFE MANAGEMENT AREA
Delaware Div. of Fish and Wildlife
PO Box 1401, Dover, DE 19903
(302) 739-5297 **BW, F, H, HR**

CAPE HENLOPEN STATE PARK
Delaware Div. of Parks and Recreation
42 Cape Henlopen Dr.
Lewes, DE 19958
(302) 645-8983; (302) 645-6852
Includes the Seaside Nature Center
BW, C, F, GS, I, MT, PA, RA, S, T, TG

CHINCOTEAGUE NATIONAL WILDLIFE REFUGE
U.S. Fish and Wildlife Service
PO Box 62, Chincoteague, VA 23336
(804) 336-6122

Day-use area; no pets allowed
**BT, BW, F, GS, H, HR,
I, MB, MT, PA, RA, S, T, TG**

DELAWARE SEASHORE STATE PARK
Delaware Div. of Parks and Recreation
Inlet 850, Rehoboth Beach, DE 19971
(302) 227-2800; (302) 539-7202
**BT, BW, C, F, GS, H, I,
MT, PA, RA, S, T, TG**

FENWICK ISLAND STATE PARK
Delaware Div. of Parks and Recreation
PO Box 76, Millville, DE 19970
(302)539-9060; (302) 539-1055 (summer)
BW, F, GS, H, PA, S, T

FORT DELAWARE STATE PARK
Delaware Div. of Parks and Recreation
PO Box 170, Delaware City, DE 19706
(302) 834-7941
BW, F, GS, H, I, MT, PA, RA, T, TG

IRON HILL PARK
New Castle County Parks Div.
187-A Old Churchmans Rd.
New Castle, DE 19720
(302) 323-6450 **BW, H, PA**

KILLENS POND STATE PARK
Delaware Div. of Parks and Recreation
RR 1, Box 858
Felton, DE 19943
(302) 284-4526; (302) 284-3412 (summer)
Summer entrance fee
**BT, BW, C, CK, F, GS, H,
I, L, MT, PA, S, T, TG, XC**

LITTLE CREEK WILDLIFE AREA
Delaware Div. of Fish and Wildlife
PO Box 1401, Dover, DE 19903
(302) 739-5297 **BW, F, H**

LUMS POND STATE PARK
Delaware Div. of Parks and Recreation
1068 Howell School Rd.
Bear, DE 19701
(302) 368-6989 **BT, BW, C, CK, F, H,
I, MT, PA, RA, S, T, XC**

NANTICOKE WILDLIFE AREA
Delaware Div. of Fish and Wildlife
PO Box 1401
Dover, DE 19903
(302) 739-5297; (302) 875-9997
BW, F, H, HR, PA, T

BT Bike Trails	**CK** Canoeing, Kayaking	**F** Fishing	**HR** Horseback Riding
BW Bird-watching		**GS** Gift Shop	
C Camping	**DS** Downhill Skiing	**H** Hiking	**I** Information Center

NORMAN G. WILDER WILDLIFE AREA
Delaware Div. of Fish and Wildlife
PO Box 1401, Dover, DE 19903
(302) 739-5297; (302) 284-3114
BW, C, H, HR

PORT MAHON PRESERVE
The Nature Conservancy of Delaware
321 So. State St., Dover, DE 19903
(302) 674-3550
Stay in car; do not disturb birds **BW**

PRIME HOOK NATIONAL WILDLIFE REFUGE
U.S. Fish and Wildlife Service
RD 3, Box 195, Milton, DE 19968
(302) 684-8419
Day-use area
BW, CK, F, H, I, MT, PA, T, XC

REDDEN STATE FOREST
Delaware Forest Service
Rte. 4, Box 354, Georgetown, DE 19947
(302) 856-2893 **BW, F, H, HR, I, PA**

TRAP POND STATE PARK
Delaware Div. of Parks and Recreation
Rte. 2, Box 331, Laurel, DE 19956
(302) 875-5153; (302) 875-2392
BW, C, CK, F, GS, H, HR, I, MT, PA, RA, S, T, TG

WHITE CLAY CREEK STATE PARK
Delaware Div. of Parks and Recreation
425 Wedgewood Rd., Newark, DE 19711
(302) 368-6900
Includes White Clay Creek Preserve and portion of the Mason-Dixon Trail; camping for youth groups only
BW, F, H, HR, MT, PA, RA, T, XC

WOODLAND BEACH WILDLIFE AREA
Delaware Div. of Fish and Wildlife
PO Box 1401, Dover, DE 19903
(302) 739-5297; (302) 653-2079 **BW, F, H**

DISTRICT OF COLUMBIA
ROCK CREEK PARK
National Park Service
3545 Williamsburg Lane, NW
Washington, D.C. 20008
(202) 282-1063
Day-use area; permit required for picnic
BT, BW, CK, GS, H, HR, I, MT, PA, RA, T, TG

THEODORE ROOSEVELT ISLAND
National Park Service
George Washington Memorial Pkwy.
Turkey Run Park
McLean, VA 22101
(703) 285-2598
Guided tours by appt. only
BW, CK, F, H, MT, T

MARYLAND
APPALACHIAN NATIONAL SCENIC TRAIL
National Park Service
Appalachian Trail Conference
PO Box 807, Harpers Ferry, WV 25425-0807
(304) 535-6331
Backpack camping; no motorized vehicles; no horses
BW, C, F, H, MT, PA, RC, S, XC

ASSATEAGUE ISLAND NATIONAL SEASHORE
National Park Service
7206 National Seashore Lane
Berlin, MD 21811
(410) 641-3030; (410) 641-1441
BT, BW, C, CK, F, GS, H, I, MB, MT, PA, RA, S, T

ASSATEAGUE ISLAND STATE PARK
Maryland State Forest and Park Service
7307 Stephen Decatur Hwy.
Berlin, MD 21811-9741
(410) 641-2120
No pets allowed
BW, C, CK, F, GS, H, PA, S, T

BATTLE CREEK CYPRESS SWAMP SANCTUARY
Calvert County Natural Resources
c/o Courthouse, Prince Frederick, MD 20678
(410) 535-5327 **BW, GS, I, MT, PA, T, TG**

BIG RUN STATE PARK
Maryland State Forest and Park Service
349 Headquarters Lane
Grantsville, MD 21536
(301) 895-5453 **BW, C, CK, F, H, MT, PA, T**

BLACKWATER NATIONAL WILDLIFE REFUGE
U.S. Fish and Wildlife Service
2145 Key Wallace Dr., Cambridge, MD 21613
(410) 228-2677 **BT, BW, CK, F, GS, H, I, MT, T, TG**

L Lodging	**PA** Picnic Areas	**RC** Rock Climbing	**TG** Tours, Guides
MB Mountain Biking	**RA** Ranger-led Activities	**S** Swimming	**XC** Cross-country Skiing
MT Marked Trails		**T** Toilets	

CALVERT CLIFFS STATE PARK
Maryland State Forest and Park Service
c/o Southern Maryland Recreational Complex
11704 Fenno Rd.
Upper Marlboro, MD 20772
(301) 888-1410; (800) 784-5380
  Seasonal closures; digging into cliffs prohibited; carry drinking water; camping for youth groups only
  BW, H, I, MT, PA, T, TG

CATOCTIN MOUNTAIN PARK
National Park Service
6602 Foxville Rd., Thurmont, MD 21788
(301) 663-9388
  No motorized vehicles; check fishing regulations
  BW, C, F, GS, H, HR, I, MT, PA, RA, T, XC

CEDARVILLE STATE FOREST
Maryland State Forest and Park Service
c/o Southern Maryland Recreational Complex
11704 Fenno Rd.
Upper Marlboro, MD 20772
(301) 888-1410; (800) 784-5380
  Camping for youth groups only
  BT, BW, F, H, HR, MT, PA, T, XC

CHESAPEAKE AND OHIO CANAL NATIONAL HISTORICAL PARK
National Park Service
PO Box 4, Sharpsburg, MD 21782
(301) 739-4200
  Fee at Great Falls   **BT, BW, C, CK, F, H, HR, I, MB, MT, PA, RA, T, TG, XC**

CHOPTANK WETLANDS PRESERVE
The Nature Conservancy of Maryland
2 Wisconsin Circle, Suite 600
Chevy Chase, MD 20815
(301) 656-8673
  Accessible by boat from Kingston Landing; no pets allowed
  BW, CK, H, MT

CRANESVILLE SWAMP NATURE PRESERVE
The Nature Conservancy of Maryland
2 Wisconsin Circle, Suite 600
Chevy Chase, MD 20815
(301) 656-8673
  Day-use area; no pets allowed
  BW, H, MT

CRYSTAL GROTTOES CAVERNS
19821 Sheperdstown Pike
Boonsboro, MD 21713

(301) 432-6336
  Call in advance winter weekdays; rock and mineral shop   **T, TG**

CUNNINGHAM FALLS STATE PARK
Maryland State Forest and Park Service
14039 Catoctin Hollow Rd.
Thurmont, MD 21788
(301) 271-7574   **BW, C, CK, F, GS, H, MT, PA, RA, S, T, XC**

DAN'S MOUNTAIN WILDLIFE MANAGEMENT AREA
Maryland Wildlife Division
HCR 13, Box 71
Flintstone, MD 21530
(301) 478-2525   **BW, H, XC**

DEAL ISLAND WILDLIFE MANAGEMENT AREA
Maryland Wildlife Division
c/o Wellington WMA
32733 Dublin Rd., Princess Anne, MD 21853
(410) 543-8223
  Primitive camping
  BT, BW, C, CK, F, H, MB, MT

DEEP CREEK LAKE STATE PARK
Maryland State Forest and Park Service
898 State Park Rd.,Swanton, MD 21561
(301) 387-5563   **C, F, H, MT, PA, S, T**

EASTERN NECK NATIONAL WILDLIFE REFUGE
U.S. Fish and Wildlife Service
1730 Eastern Neck Rd.
Rock Hall, MD 21661
(410) 639-7056
  Day-use area   **BW, F, I, MT, PA, T**

ELK NECK DEMONSTRATION FOREST
Maryland State Forest and Park Service
130 McKinnytown Rd.
North East, MD 21901
(410) 287-5675
  Pit toilets only   **BW, C, H, HR, PA, T, XC**

ELK NECK STATE PARK
Maryland State Forest and Park Service
4395 Turkey Point Rd.
North East, MD 21901
(410) 287-5333   **BW, C, CK, F, GS, H, MT, PA, RA, S, T, TG**

FINZEL SWAMP NATURE PRESERVE
The Nature Conservancy of Maryland

BT	Bike Trails	**CK**	Canoeing, Kayaking	**F**	Fishing	**HR**	Horseback Riding
BW	Bird-watching			**GS**	Gift Shop		
C	Camping	**DS**	Downhill Skiing	**H**	Hiking	**I**	Information Center

2 Wisconsin Circle, Suite 600
Chevy Chase, MD 20815
Day-use area; no motorized vehicles
BW, H

FLAG PONDS NATURE PARK
Calvert County Natural Resources
c/o Courthouse, Prince Frederick, MD 20678
(410) 535-5327; (410) 586-1477
Entrance fee; reserve in advance for
guided tours
BW, F, GS, H, I, MT, PA, T, TG

GAMBRILL STATE PARK
Maryland State Forest and Park Service
South Mountain Recreation Area
21843 National Pike, Boonsboro, MD 21713
(301) 791-4767 **BT, BW, C, F, H, MB,
MT, PA, RA, T, XC**

GARRETT STATE FOREST
Maryland State Forest and Park Service
Rte. 3, Box 9305, Oakland, MD 21550
(301) 334-2038
Includes Muddy Creek and Herrington
Creek Watersheds
BT, BW, C, F, H, HR, MB, MT, PA, RA, XC

THE GLADES
The Nature Conservancy of Maryland
2 Wisconsin Circle, Suite 600
Chevy Chase, MD 20815
(301) 656-8673
Limited public access **BW, H**

GREEN RIDGE STATE FOREST
Maryland State Forest and Park Service
HCR 13, Box 50,Flintstone, MD 21530-9525
(301) 777-234 **BT, BW, C, CK, F, GS, H,
HR, I, MT, PA, RA, TG, XC**

GUNPOWDER FALLS STATE PARK
Maryland State Forest and Park Service
PO Box 5032, Glen Arm, MD 21057
(410) 592-2897
Entrance fee at Hammerman; camping
for youth groups only **BT, BW, CK, F, H,
HR, I, MB, MT, PA, S, T, XC**

**HARPERS FERRY NATIONAL
HISTORICAL PARK**
National Park Service, PO Box 65
Harpers Ferry, WV 25425
(304) 535-6298; (304) 535-6029
Registration required for rock climbing
BW, F, GS, H, I, MT, PA, RA, RC, TG

HERRINGTON MANOR STATE PARK
Maryland State Forest and Park Service
Rte. 5
Box 2180
Oakland, MD 21550
(301) 334-9180
BW, CK, F, GS, H, I, L, MT, PA, S, T, XC

HORSEHEADS WETLANDS CENTER
Wildfowl Trust of North America
PO Box 519
Grasonville, MD 21638
(410) 827-6694
No pets; no feeding of birds
BW, CK, GS, I, MT, PA, T, TG

JANES ISLAND STATE PARK
Maryland State Forest and Park Service
26280 Alfred Lawson Dr.
Crisfield, MD 21817
(410) 968-1565 **BW, C, CK, F, GS, I,
L, MT, PA, RA, S, T, TG**

MARTINAK STATE PARK
Maryland State Forest and Park Service
137 Deep Shore Rd.
Denton, MD 21629
(410) 479-1619
BW, C, CK, F, MT, PA, RA, T

**MCKEE-BESHERS WILDLIFE
MANAGEMENT AREA**
Maryland Wildlife Division
11960 Clopper Rd.
Gaithersburg, MD 20878
(301) 258-7308 **BW, H, HR**

MERKLE WILDLIFE SANCTUARY
Maryland State Forest and Park Service
c/o Southern Maryland
Recreational Complex
11704 Fenno Rd.
Upper Marlboro, MD 20772
(301) 888-1410; (800) 784-5380
Some trails closed during wildlife feed-
ing and nesting periods
BT, BW, F, GS, H, HR, I, MT, PA, RA, T

MOUNT BRIAR WETLANDS PRESERVE
Washington County Recreation and Parks
Dept. 1307
South Potomac St.
Hagerstown, MD 21740
(301) 791-3125
Gates opened by appt. only; walk-in
traffic permitted **BW**

L Lodging	**PA** Picnic Areas	**RC** Rock Climbing	**TG** Tours, Guides
MB Mountain Biking	**RA** Ranger-led Activities	**S** Swimming	**XC** Cross-country Skiing
MT Marked Trails		**T** Toilets	

NASSAWANGO CREEK PRESERVE
The Nature Conservancy of Maryland
2 Wisconsin Circle, Suite 600
Chevy Chase, MD 20815
(301) 656-8673; (410) 632-2032
Open year-round; Furnace Town and
facilities closed in winter; fee to enter
Furnace Town

BW, CK, GS, H, I, MT, PA, T

NATIONAL WILDLIFE VISITOR CENTER
National Biological Survey
10901 Scarlet Tanager Loop
Laurel, MD 20708-4027
(301) 497-5760

BW, GS, H, I, MT, T, TG

NEW GERMANY STATE PARK
Maryland State Forest and Park Service
349 Headquarters Lane
Grantsville, MD 21536
(301) 895-5453

**BT, BW, C, CK, F, GS, H, I, L,
MB, MT, PA, RA, S, T, TG, XC**

PATUXENT ENVIRONMENTAL SCIENCE CENTER
North Tract Visitors Contact Station
National Biological Survey
230 Bald Eagle Drive
Laurel, MD 20724
(410) 674-3304   **BW, F, H, I, T**

PATUXENT RIVER PARK, JUG BAY NATURAL AREA
Maryland National Capital Park and
Planning Commission
16000 Croom Airport Rd.
Upper Marlboro, MD 20772
(301) 627-6074

BW, C, CK, F, H, HR, I, RA, T, TG

PATUXENT RIVER STATE PARK
Maryland State Forest and Park Service
c/o Seneca Creek State Park
11950 Clopper Rd.
Gaithersburg, MD 20878
(301) 924-2127
Undeveloped; no hiking during hunting
season

POCOMOKE RIVER STATE FOREST
Maryland State Forest and Park Service
3461 Worcester Hwy.
Snow Hill, MD 21863
(410) 632-2566

Includes Pocomoke River State Park

BW, F, H, HR, MT, TG

POINT LOOKOUT STATE PARK
Maryland State Forest and Park Service
Rte. 5, Box 48, Scotland, MD 20687
(301) 872-5688; (301) 872-5389
Includes nature center; seasonal operation

**BW, C, CK, F, GS, H, I,
MT, PA, RA, S, T, TG**

PURSE STATE PARK
Maryland State Forest and Park Service
Southern Maryland Recreational Complex
11704 Fenno Rd.
Upper Marlboro, MD 20772
(301) 888-1410; (800) 784-5380
Undeveloped; check with office during
hunting season   **BW, F**

ROBINSON NECK/FRANK M. EWING PRESERVE
The Nature Conservancy of Maryland
2 Wisconsin Circle, Suite 600
Chevy Chase, MD 20815
(301) 656-8673
Self-guided nature trail; surrounded by
hunting areas, caution during season

BW, H, MT

ROCK CREEK REGIONAL PARK
Montgomery County Dept. of Parks
6700 Needwood Rd.
Rockville, MD 20855-1699
(301) 948-5053 park info.
(301) 762-9500 boating/fishing info.
(301) 924-4141 nature center
Includes Meadowside Nature Center;
day-use area

BT, BW, CK, F, H, MT, PA, T, TG, XC

ROCKS STATE PARK
Maryland State Forest and Park Service
3318 Rocks
Chrome Hill Rd.
Jarrettsville, MD 21084
(410) 557-7994   **BT, BW, CK, F, H, HR,
MB, MT, PA, RA, RC, S, T**

ROCKY GAP STATE PARK
Maryland State Forest and Park Service
Rte. 1, Box 90, Flintstone, MD 21530
(301) 777-2138; (301) 777-2139
Pontoon boat tours

**BW, C, CK, F, GS, H, I,
MB, MT, PA, RA, S, T, TG, XC**

BT	Bike Trails	CK	Canoeing, Kayaking	F	Fishing	HR	Horseback Riding
BW	Bird-watching			GS	Gift Shop		
C	Camping	DS	Downhill Skiing	H	Hiking	I	Information Center

SANDY POINT STATE PARK
Maryland State Forest and Park Service
1100 East College Parkway
Annapolis, MD 21401
(410) 974-2149
BT, BW, F, GS, H, MT, PA, RA, S, T

SAVAGE RIVER STATE FOREST
Maryland State Forest and Park Service
349 Headquarters Lane
Grantsville, MD 21536
(301) 895-5759; (301) 895-5453
BT, BW, C, CK, F, H,
HR, I, MT, PA, RA, S, T, TG

SIDELING HILL CUT
Maryland State Forest and Park Service
c/o Fort Frederick State Park
11100 Fort Frederick Rd.
Big Pool, MD 21711
(301) 842-2155
I, PA, T, TG

**SIDELING HILL WILDLIFE
MANAGEMENT AREA**
Maryland Wildlife Division
Indian Springs Work Center
14038 Blairs Valley Rd.
Clear Spring, MD 21722
(301) 842-2702
BW, CK, F, H

**SOLDIERS DELIGHT NATURAL
ENVIRONMENT AREA**
Maryland State Forest and Park Service
5100 Deer Park Rd., Owings Mills, MD 21117
(410) 922-3044
Day-use area; bicycles and horses pro-
hibited
BW, H, I, MT, RA, T, TG

SOUTH MOUNTAIN STATE PARK
Maryland State Forest and Park Service
South Mountain Recreation Area
21843 National Pike
Boonsboro, MD 21713
(301) 791-4767
Includes portion of the Appalachian
Trail; year-round access
BW, C, H, MT, RC, XC

SUGARLOAF MOUNTAIN
Stronghold, Inc.
7901 Comus Rd.
Dickerson, MD 20842
(301) 874-2024
BW, H, MT, PA

SUSQUEHANNA STATE PARK
Maryland State Forest and Park Service

3318 Rocks Chrome Hill Rd.
Jarrettsville, MD 21084
(410) 557-7994
BT, BW, C, CK, F, H,
HR, MT, PA, RA, S, T, TG, XC

SWALLOW FALLS STATE PARK
Maryland State Forest and Park Service
Rte. 5, Box 2180, Oakland, MD 21550
(301) 387-6938, summer; (301) 334-9180,
off-season
BW, C, F, H, I, PA, T

TUCKAHOE STATE PARK
Maryland State Forest and Park Service
13070 Crouse Mill Rd.
Queen Anne, MD 21657
(410) 634-2810
Includes the Adkins arboretum; camping
for youth groups only by prearrange-
ment
BW, CK, F, H, I,
MT, PA, RA, T, TG

**WYE ISLAND NATURAL RESOURCE
MANAGEMENT AREA**
Maryland State Forest
and Park Service
632 Wye Island Rd., Queenstown, MD 21658
(410) 827-7577
BT, BW, F, H, HR, MT, PA, S

WYE OAK STATE PARK
Maryland State Forest and Park Service
c/o Martinak State Park
137 Deep Shore Rd.
Denton, MD 21629
(410) 479-1619
PA, T

ZEKIAH SWAMP
Zekiah Natural Environmental Area
Maryland State Forest and Park Service
c/o Southern Maryland
Recreational Complex
11704 Fenno Rd.
Upper Marlboro, MD 20772
(301) 888-1410; (800) 784-5380
Undeveloped
BW, CK, F

NORTH CAROLINA

ART LOEB TRAIL
Pisgah National Forest
Pisgah Ranger District
1001 Pisgah Hwy.
Pisgah Forest, NC 28768
(704) 877-3265
Primitive camping
BW, C, F, H, MT

L Lodging	**PA** Picnic Areas	**RC** Rock Climbing	**TG** Tours, Guides	
MB Mountain Biking	**RA** Ranger-led Activities	**S** Swimming	**XC** Cross-country Skiing	
MT Marked Trails		**T** Toilets		**267**

BOONE'S CAVE STATE PARK
North Carolina Div. of Parks and Recreation
c/o Morrow Mtn. State Park
Albemarle, NC 28001
(704) 982-4402
Includes access to the Yadkin River
Canoe Trail   **BW, F, H, PA**

BUXTON WOODS
Cape Hatteras National Seashore
PO Box 190
Buxton, NC 27920
(919) 995-4474
Stay on roads and trails; cottonmouth
snake and tick precautions
BW, C, F, H, HR, I, MT, PA, RA, T

CAPE HATTERAS NATIONAL SEASHORE
National Park Service
Rte. 1, Box 675, Manteo, NC 27954
(919) 473-2111; (919) 995-4474 (summer)
BW, C, CK, F, GS, H, I, MT, PA, RA, S, T

CAPE LOOKOUT NATIONAL SEASHORE
National Park Service
131 Charles St.
Harkers Island, NC 28531
(919) 728-2250
Closures of certain areas for turtles and
birds spring through fall
BW, CK, F, I, PA, RA, S, T

CAROLINA BEACH STATE PARK
North Carolina Div. of Parks and Recreation
PO Box 475, Carolina Beach, NC 28428
(910) 458-8206; (910) 458-7770
BW, C, F, GS, H, I, MT, PA, RA, T

CHIMNEY ROCK PARK
PO Box 39, Chimney Rock, NC 28720
(704) 625-9611; (800) 277-9611
Trails closed in winter
BW, GS, H, I, MT, PA, RA, T, TG

CLIFFS OF THE NEUSE STATE PARK
North Carolina Div. of Parks and Recreation
345-A Park Entrance Rd.
Seven Springs, NC 28578
(919) 778-6234
BW, C, F, I, MT, PA, RA, S, T, TG

CRABTREE MEADOWS RECREATION AREA
Blue Ridge Parkway
200 BB&T Bldg., Asheville, NC 28801
(704) 298-0398
BW, C, GS, H, MT, PA, RA, T, TG

CRAGGY GARDENS RECREATION AREA
Blue Ridge Parkway
200 BB&T Bldg., Asheville, NC 28801
(704) 298-0398   **BW, H, I, MT, PA, RA, T**

CROATAN NATIONAL FOREST
National Forests in North Carolina
141 E. Fisher Ave.
New Bern, NC 28560
(919) 638-5628
Plant removal prohibited
BW, C, F, H, MT, PA, S, T, TG

CROWDERS MOUNTAIN STATE PARK
North Carolina Div. of Parks
and Recreation
Rte. 1, Box 159, Kings Mountain, NC 28068
(704) 853-5375
Backpack camping
BW, C, CK, F, H, HR, MT, PA, RA, RC, T

DOUGHTON PARK
National Park Service
Rte. 1, Box 263, Laurel Springs, NC 28644
(910) 372-8568; (910) 372-8867
Permit required for backcountry camping
**BW, C, F, GS, H, I, L,
MT, PA, RA, T, TG, XC**

ELLICOTT ROCK WILDERNESS AREA
Nantahala National Forest
Highland Ranger District
Rte. 1, Box 247, Highland, NC 28741
(704) 526-3765
Primitive camping   **BW, C, F, H**

ENO RIVER STATE PARK
North Carolina Div. of Parks and Recreation
6101 Cole Mill Rd., Durham, NC 27705-9275
(919) 383-1686
Backpack camping only by permit
BW, C, CK, F, H, I, MT, PA, RA, T

FORT FISHER STATE HISTORICAL SITE
North Carolina Dept. of Cultural Resources
109 E. Jones St.
Raleigh, NC 27601-2807
(910) 458-5538   **BW, F, GS, I, MT, TG**

FORT FISHER STATE RECREATION AREA
North Carolina Div. of Parks and
Recreation
PO Box 475
Carolina Beach, NC 28428
(910) 458-8206; (910) 458-7770
BW, F, H, RA, S, T

BT	Bike Trails	**CK**	Canoeing, Kayaking	**F**	Fishing
BW	Bird-watching			**GS**	Gift Shop
C	Camping	**DS**	Downhill Skiing	**H**	Hiking

HR	Horseback Riding
I	Information Center

**GREAT SMOKY MOUNTAINS
NATIONAL PARK**
National Park Service
107 Park Hdqtrs. Rd.
Gatlinburg, TN 37738
(615) 436-1200
Free permit required for backcountry
camping; no pets on trails
**BT, BW, C, F, GS, H, HR,
I, L, MT, PA, RA, T**

GREEN SWAMP NATURE PRESERVE
The Nature Conservancy
North Carolina Chapter
S.E. Coastal Plain, Stewardship Office
321 N. Front St.
Wilmington, NC 28401
(910) 762-6277; (919) 967-7007
Public access limited; call office
BW, H, MT, TG

HAMMOCKS BEACH STATE PARK
North Carolina Div. of Parks and
Recreation
1572 Hammocks Beach Rd.
Swansboro, NC 28584
(910) 326-4881; (919) 393-8008 (water taxi
year-round)
Pets allowed on leash; no pets on summer ferry   **BW, C, CK, F, H, PA, RA, S**

HANGING ROCK STATE PARK
North Carolina Div. of Parks and Recreation
PO Box 278, Danbury, NC 27016
(910) 593-8480
BW, C, F, H, L, MT, PA, RA, RC, S, T

JOCKEY'S RIDGE STATE PARK
North Carolina Div. of Parks and Recreation
PO Box 592, Nags Head, NC 27959
(919) 441-7132
BW, H, I, MT, PA, RA, S, T, TG

JONES LAKE STATE PARK
North Carolina Div. of Parks and Recreation
Rte. 2, Box 945, Elizabethtown, NC 28337
(910) 588-4550
No camping in winter
BW, C, CK, F, H, I, MT, PA, RA, S, T

JORDAN LAKE STATE RECREATION AREA
North Carolina Div. of Parks and Recreation
280 State Park Rd., Apex, NC 27502
(919) 362-0586
Includes a marina with rental boats
BW, C, CK, F, H, I, MT, PA, RA, S, T, TG

JOYCE KILMER MEMORIAL FOREST
Nantahala National Forest
Cheoah Ranger District
Rte. 1, Box 16A, Robbinsville, NC 28771
(704) 479-6431   **BW, C, F, H, I, MT, PA, T**

JULIAN PRICE MEMORIAL PARK
Blue Ridge Parkway
200 BB&T Bldg., Asheville, NC 28801
(704) 298-0398
Includes Boone Fork Trail
BW, C, CK, F, H, HR, MT, PA, RA, T

LAKE WACCAMAW STATE PARK
North Carolina Div. of Parks and Recreation
c/o Singletary Lake State Park
6707 NC 53, Hwy. E
Kelly, NC 28448
(910) 646-4748; (910) 669-2828
Primitive camping   **BW, C, F, MT, T**

LINVILLE FALLS RECREATION AREA
Blue Ridge Parkway
200 BB&T Bldg., Asheville, NC 28801
(704) 298-0398
Falls can be dangerous; do not try to
walk across
BW, C, F, GS, H, I, MT, PA, RA, T

LINVILLE GORGE WILDERNESS AREA
Pisgah National Forest
Grandfather Ranger District
PO Box 519
Marion, NC 28752
(704) 652-2144; (704) 765-7550
Backcountry camping
BW, C, F, GS, H, I, RC, S, T

**MACKAY ISLAND NATIONAL
WILDLIFE REFUGE**
U.S. Fish and Wildlife Service
PO Box 39, Knotts Island, NC 27950-0039
(919) 429-3100
Day-use area; portions of refuge closed
seasonally
BT, BW, CK, F, H, I, MB, MT, T

**MATTAMUSKEET NATIONAL
WILDLIFE REFUGE**
U.S Fish and Wildlife Service
Rte. 1, Box N-2
Swan Quarter, NC 27885
(919) 926-4021; (919) 926-6751
No fishing or boating November–
February due to nesting birds
BW, CK, F, PA

L	Lodging	**PA**	Picnic Areas	**RC**	Rock Climbing	**TG**	Tours, Guides
MB	Mountain Biking	**RA**	Ranger-led Activities	**S**	Swimming	**XC**	Cross-country Skiing
MT	Marked Trails			**T**	Toilets		

MERCHANTS MILLPOND STATE PARK
North Carolina Div. of Parks and Recreation
Rte. 1, Box 141-A
Gatesville, NC 27938
(919) 357-1191
BW, C, CK, F, H, I, MT, PA, RA, T

MORROW MOUNTAIN STATE PARK
North Carolina Div. of Parks and Recreation
49104 Morrow Mtn. Rd.
Albemarle, NC 28001
(704) 982-4402
BW, C, CK, F, H, HR, I, L, MT,
PA, RA, S, T, TG

MOSES H. CONE MEMORIAL PARK
National Park Service
Rte. 1, Box 565; Blowing Rock, NC 28605
(704) 295-7591; (704) 295-3782
BW, F, GS, H, HR, I, MT, RA, T, TG, XC

MOUNT JEFFERSON STATE PARK
North Carolina Div. of Parks and Recreation
PO Box 48, Jefferson, NC 28640
(910) 246-9653
No toilet facilities in winter
BW, H, MT, PA, RA, T, TG

MOUNT MITCHELL STATE PARK
North Carolina Div. of Parks and Recreation
Rte. 5, Box 700
Burnsville, NC 28714
(704) 675-4611
BW, C, GS, H, I, MT, PA, RA, T, TG

MOUNT PISGAH
Pisgah National Forest
Pisgah Ranger District
1001 Pisgah Hwy., Pisgah Forest, NC 28768
(704) 877-3265
Primitive camping outside Blue Ridge
Pkwy. boundary   BW, C, H, I, MT, PA

**NAGS HEAD WOODS
ECOLOGICAL PRESERVE**
The Nature Conservancy
North Carolina Chapter
701 W. Ocean Acres Dr.
Kill Devil Hills, NC 27948
(919) 441-2525
Visitor hours vary by season; canoeing
by guided tour only
BW, GS, H, I, MT, T, TG

NANTAHALA GORGE
Nantahala National Forest

Wayah Ranger District
8 Sloan Rd., Franklin, NC 28734
(704) 524-6441
Parking fee
BT, BW, CK, F, H, MB, PA, RC, S, T

NANTAHALA NATIONAL FOREST
National Forests in North Carolina
PO Box 2750, Asheville, NC 28802
(704) 257-4200
BT, BW, C, CK, F, GS, H,
HR, I, L, MB, MT, PA, RC, S, T

NEW RIVER STATE PARK
North Carolina Div. of Parks and Recreation
PO Box 48, Jefferson, NC 28640
(910) 982-2587
Includes Wagoner Rd. Access Area; primi-
tive camping; park gates locked at sunset
BW, C, CK, F, H, MT, PA, RA, T, TG

PEA ISLAND NATIONAL WILDLIFE REFUGE
U.S. Fish and Wildlife Service
PO Box 1969, Manteo, NC 27954
(919) 473-1131; (919) 987-2394
BW, F, GS, H, I, MT, RA, S, T, TG

PEE DEE NATIONAL WILDLIFE REFUGE
U.S. Fish and Wildlife Service
Rte. 1, Box 92
Wadesboro, NC 28170
(704) 694-4424
Best time to view waterfowl November–
January   BW, F, H, MT

PETTIGREW STATE PARK
North Carolina Div. of Parks and Recreation
2252 Lake Shore Rd.
Creswell, NC 27928
(919) 797-4475
BW, C, CK, F, H, I, MT, PA, RA, T

PILOT MOUNTAIN STATE PARK
North Carolina Div. of Parks and Recreation
Rte. 3, Box 21
Pinnacle, NC 27043
(910) 325-2355   BW, C, CK, F, H, HR,
I, MT, PA, RA, RC, T, TG

PISGAH NATIONAL FOREST
National Forests in North Carolina
PO Box 2750, Asheville, NC 28802
(704) 257-4200
Includes Shining Rock Wilderness Area
BT, BW, C, CK, F, H,
HR, I, MB, MT, PA, RC, S, T

BT	Bike Trails	**CK**	Canoeing, Kayaking	**F**	Fishing	**HR**	Horseback Riding
BW	Bird-watching			**GS**	Gift Shop		
C	Camping	**DS**	Downhill Skiing	**H**	Hiking	**I**	Information Center

RAVEN ROCK STATE PARK
North Carolina Div. of Parks and Recreation
Rte. 3, Box 1005
Lillington, NC 27546
(910) 893-4888
Includes Cape Fear Canoe Trail;
backpack camping only
BW, C, F, H, HR, I, MT, PA, RA, T

ROAN MOUNTAIN GARDENS
Pisgah National Forest
Toecane Ranger District
PO Box 128
Burnsville, NC 28714
(704) 682-6146   **BW, H, I, MT, PA, T, XC**

ROAN MOUNTAIN MASSIF
Pisgah National Forest
Toecane Ranger District
PO Box 128, Burnsville, NC 28714
(704) 682-6146
BW, H, I, MT, PA, RA, T, XC

SHUT-IN TRAIL
Blue Ridge Parkway
200 BB&T Bldg., Asheville, NC 28801
(704) 298-0398   **BW, H, MT**

**SOUTHERN NANTAHALA
WILDERNESS AREA**
Nantahala National Forest
Wayah Ranger District
8 Sloan Rd., Franklin, NC 28734
(704) 524-6441
Primitive camping   **BW, C, F, H, MT, S**

SOUTH MOUNTAINS STATE PARK
North Carolina Div. of Parks and
Recreation
Rte. 1, Box 206-C
Connelly Springs, NC 28612
(910) 433-4772
Primitive camping   **BT, BW, C, F, H, HR,
I, MB, MT, PA, RA, T, TG**

STONE MOUNTAIN STATE PARK
North Carolina Div. of Parks and Recreation
Rte. 1, Box 15
Roaring Gap, NC 28668
(910) 957-8185
C, F, H, HR, I, MT, PA, RC, T

TANAWHA TRAIL
Blue Ridge Parkway
200 BB&T Bldg., Asheville, NC 28801
(704) 298-0398   **BW, H, MT**

**TURNBULL CREEK EDUCATIONAL
STATE FOREST**
North Carolina Div. of Forest Resources
Rte. 2, Box 942A, Elizabethtown, NC 28337
(910) 588-4161
Closed mid-November–mid-March
BW, H, MT, PA, RA, T, TG

UWHARRIE NATIONAL FOREST
National Forests in North Carolina
Rte. 3, Box 470, Troy, NC 27371
(910) 576-6391
Some trails closed for bald eagles; call
office   **BW, C, CK, F, H, HR, MT, PA, T**

**WEYMOUTH WOODS/SANDHILLS NATURE
PRESERVE**
North Carolina Div. of Parks and Recreation
1024 N. Fort Bragg Rd.
Southern Pines, NC 28387
(910) 692-2167
Permit required for plant collection
BW, H, I, MT, RA, T

WHITEOAK BOTTOMS BOG
Nantahala National Forest
8 Sloan Rd., Franklin, NC 28734
(704) 524-6441
No foot travel permitted into bog   **BW**

WHITESIDE MOUNTAIN
Nantahala National Forest
Highland Ranger District
Rte. 1, Box 247, Highland, NC 28741
(704) 526-3765   **BW, H, MT, RC, T**

WHITEWATER FALLS SCENIC AREA
Nantahala National Forest
Highland Ranger District
Rte. 1, Box 247, Highland, NC 28741
(704) 526-3765
Falls are dangerous, use caution
BW, H, MT, PA, T

VIRGINIA

ABINGDON TO DAMASCUS TRAIL
Town of Abingdon
PO Box 1776, Abingdon, VA 24210
BT, BW, C, F, H, HR, L, MB, MT, S, XC

**APPOMATTOX-BUCKINGHAM
STATE FOREST**
Virginia Dept. of Forestry
Rte. 3, Box 133, Dillwyn, VA 23936
(804) 983-2175   **BW, F, H, HR, I, PA**

L	Lodging	**PA**	Picnic Areas	**RC**	Rock Climbing	**TG**	Tours, Guides
MB	Mountain Biking Marked Trails	**RA**	Ranger-led Activities	**S**	Swimming	**XC**	Cross-country Skiing
				T	Toilets		

BACK BAY NATIONAL WILDLIFE REFUGE
U.S Fish and Wildlife Service
4005 Sandpiper Rd.
Virginia Beach, VA 23456
(804) 721-2412
Call office for seasonal trail closures
BT, BW, CK, F, H, I, MB, MT, RA, T

BALL'S BLUFF REGIONAL PARK
Northern Virginia Regional Park Authority
5400 Ox Rd., Fairfax, VA 22039
(703) 729-2596; (540) 352-5900
Day-use area   **BW, F, H, I, MT, PA, RA**

BEAR CREEK LAKE STATE PARK
Virginia Div. of State Parks
Rte. 1, Box 253, Cumberland, VA 23040
(804) 492-4410
Includes the Willis River Trail
**BW, C, CK, F, GS, H,
I, MT, PA, RA, S, T, TG, XC**

BETHEL BEACH NATURAL AREA PRESERVE
Virginia Dept. of Conservation and Recreation
Div. of Natural Heritage
1500 E. Main St., Suite 312
Richmond, VA 23219
(804) 786-7951   **BW**

BIG BLUE TRAIL
Potomac Appalachian Trail Club
118 Park St., S.E., Vienna, VA 22180
(703) 242-0315; (540) 242-0965   **H, MT**

BIG SCHLOSS
U.S. Forest Service
Lee Ranger District, 109 Molineu Rd.
Edinburg, VA 22824
(540) 984-4101
Primitive camping; noted for peregrine
falcon viewing   **BW, C, F, H, MB, MT**

BLUE RIDGE PARKWAY
National Park Service
200 BB&T Bldg.
Asheville, NC 28801
(704) 298-0398   **BW, C, F, GS, H, HR, I,
L, MT, PA, RA, RC, T, TG, XC**

BREAKS INTERSTATE PARK
Virginia Div. of State Parks
Rte. 80, Breaks, VA 24607
(540) 865-4413; (800) 982-5122
White-water rafting October weekends
**BW, C, CK, F, GS, H, HR,
I, L, MT, PA, RA, S, T, TG**

BULL RUN REGIONAL PARK
Northern Virginia Regional Park Authority
7700 Bull Run Dr.
Centreville, VA 22020
(703) 631-0550
Most of park closed December to mid-
March   **BW, C, GS, H, I, MT, PA, RA, S, T**

CALEDON NATURAL AREA
Virginia Div. of State Parks
11617 Caledon Rd.
King George, VA 22485
(540) 663-3861
Visitor center open summer only
BW, GS, H, I, MT, PA, RA, T, TG

**CHINCOTEAGUE NATIONAL
WILDLIFE REFUGE**
U.S. Fish and Wildlife Service
PO Box 62
Chincoteague, VA 23336
(804) 336-6122
Day-use area; no pets allowed
**BT, BW, F, GS, H, HR,
I, MB, MT, PA, RA, S, T, TG**

CLAYTOR LAKE STATE PARK
Virginia Div. of State Parks
Rte. 1, Box 267, Dublin, VA 24084
(540) 674-5492
BW, C, F, GS, H, I, L, MT, PA, RA, S, T

CUMBERLAND STATE FOREST
Virginia Dept. of Forestry
Rte. 1, Box 250
Cumberland, VA 23040
(804) 492-4121   **BW, F, H, I, MT, PA**

DOUTHAT STATE PARK
Virginia Div. of State Parks
Rte. 1, Box 212
Millboro, VA 24460
(540) 862-8100
Includes Goshen Pass Natural Area
**BW, C, CK, F, GS, H,
I, L, MB, MT, PA, RA, S, T**

DYKE MARSH WILDLIFE PRESERVE
National Park Service
George Washington
Memorial Pkwy.
c/o Turkey Run Park
McLean, VA 22101
(703) 285-2598
Day-use area
BT, BW, CK, F, MB, MT, PA, T

BT	Bike Trails	**CK**	Canoeing, Kayaking	**F**	Fishing	**HR**	Horseback Riding
BW	Bird-watching	**DS**	Downhill Skiing	**GS**	Gift Shop	**I**	Information Center
C	Camping			**H**	Hiking		

**EASTERN SHORE OF VIRGINIA
NATIONAL WILDLIFE REFUGE**
U.S. Fish and Wildlife Service
5003 Hallett Circle
Cape Charles, VA 23310
(804) 331-2760   BW, GS, H, I, MT, T, TG

FAIRY STONE STATE PARK
Virginia Div. of State Parks
Rte. 2, Box 723
Stuart, VA 24171
(540) 930-2424
    Entrance fee   BT, BW, C, F, GS, H,
                          I, L, PA, RA, S, T

FALLS RIDGE PRESERVE
The Nature Conservancy, Virginia Chapter
1233A Cedars Ct.
Charlottesville, VA 22947
(540) 382-2220
    Entry by prior permission only
                          BW, H, MT, TG

FALSE CAPE STATE PARK
Virginia Div. of State Parks
4001 Sandpiper Rd.
Virginia Beach, VA 23456
(804) 426-7128
    Includes Wash Woods Environmental
    Education Center; no motorized vehi-
    cles; 6 miles of ocean beach; primitive
    camping; pit toilets
                          BT, BW, C, CK, F,
                          H, MT, PA, RA, S, T

**FISHERMAN ISLAND
NATIONAL WILDLIFE REFUGE**
U.S. Fish and Wildlife Service
5003 Hallett Circle
Cape Charles, VA 23310
(804) 331-2760   BW, TG

FRASER PRESERVE
The Nature Conservancy, Virginia Chapter
1233 Cedars Court
Charlottesville, VA 22903
(804) 295-6106
    Call ahead for permission to visit
                          BW, H, I

GRAND CAVERNS REGIONAL PARK
Upper Valley Regional Park Authority
PO Box 478, Grottoes, VA 24441
(540) 249-5705
(540) 249-5729
          BT, GS, H, MT, PA, S, T, TG

GRAYSON HIGHLANDS STATE PARK
Virginia Div. of State Parks
Rte. 2, Mouth of Wilson, VA 24363
(540) 579-7092
          BW, BT, C, F, GS, H, HR,
          MB, MT, PA, RA, RC, T, TG, XC

**GREAT DISMAL SWAMP NATIONAL
WILDLIFE REFUGE**
U.S. Fish and Wildlife Service
PO Box 349, Suffolk, VA 23439-0349
(804) 986-3705
    Hike or bike 4 miles to Lake Drum-
    mond; boat access from Corps of
    Engineers land; very buggy in summer
          BT, BW, CK, F, H, I, MB, MT, RA, T

GREAT FALLS PARK
National Park Service
PO Box 66, Great Falls, VA 22066
(703) 285-2966
    Canoeing and kayaking in designated
    areas only
          BT, BW, CK, F, GS, H, HR, I,
          MB, MT, PA, RA, RC, T, XC

**G. R. THOMPSON WILDLIFE
MANAGEMENT AREA**
Virginia Wildlife Division
1320 Belman Rd.,Fredericksburg, VA 22401
(540) 899-4169
    Primarily a hunting area, caution during
    season; primitive camping
          BW, C, CK, F, H, HR, I, MT

HELENA'S ISLAND PRESERVE
The Nature Conservancy
Virginia Chapter
1233 Cedars Court
Charlottesville, VA 22903
(804) 295-6106
    Call ahead for permission to visit   CK

**HOG ISLAND WILDLIFE
MANAGEMENT AREA**
Virginia Wildlife Division
5806 Mooretown Rd.
Williamsburg, VA 23188
(804) 253-4180   BT, BW, F, H, MB

HOLLIDAY LAKE STATE PARK
Virginia Div. of State Parks
Rte. 2, Box 622
Appomattox, VA 24522
(804) 248-6308   BT, BW, C, CK, F, GS, H,
                  I, MB, MT, PA, RA, S, T

L Lodging	**PA** Picnic Areas	**RC** Rock Climbing	**TG** Tours, Guides
MB Mountain	**RA** Ranger-led	**S** Swimming	**XC** Cross-country
Biking	Activities	**T** Toilets	Skiing
MT Marked Trails			

HUNTLEY MEADOWS PARK
Fairfax County Park Authority
3701 Lockheed Blvd.
Alexandria, VA 22306
(703) 768-2525
Includes 4 observation platforms
BT, BW, H, I, MT, RA, T, TG

JAMES RIVER PARK SYSTEM
City of Richmond
Dept. of Recreation and Parks
700 Blanton Ave.
Richmond, VA 23221
(804) 780-5311 **BT, BW, CK, F, H, I,
MT, PA, RA, RC, S, T, TG**

LAKE ANNA STATE PARK
Virginia Div.of State Parks
6800 Lawyers Rd.
Spotsylvania, VA 22553-9645
(540) 854-5503
BW, F, H, I, MT, PA, RA, S, T

**MACKAY ISLAND NATIONAL
WILDLIFE REFUGE**
U.S. Fish and Wildlife Service
PO Box 39, Knotts Island, NC 27950-0039
(919) 429-3100 **BW, CK, F, H, I, MT**

MASON NECK NATIONAL WILDLIFE REFUGE
U.S. Fish and Wildlife Service
14344 Jeff Davis Hwy.
Woodbridge, VA 22191
(703) 690-1297; (540) 491-6255
Includes Woodmarsh Trail; pets on
leashes allowed **BW, H, MT, T**

MASSANUTTEN MOUNTAINS
U.S. Forest Service
Lee Ranger District
109 Molineu Rd., Edinburg, VA 22824
(540) 984-4101 **BW, F, H, I, MB, MT**

MICHAEL MARSH REFUGE
Virginia Wildlife Division
5806 Mooretown Rd.
Williamsburg, VA 23188
(804) 253-4180
Day-use area **BW, CK**

**MOCKHORN ISLAND WILDLIFE
MANAGEMENT AREA**
Virginia Wildlife Division
4010 West Broad St.
Richmond, VA 23230-1104
(804) 253-4180 **BW, F**

MOUNTAIN LAKES WILDERNESS
U.S. Forest Service
Blacksburg Ranger District
110 Southpark Dr., Blacksburg, VA 24060
(540) 552-4641
Primitive camping **C, H, MT**

**MOUNT ROGERS NATIONAL
RECREATION AREA**
U.S Forest Service
Rte. 1, Box 303
Marion, VA 24354
(540) 783-5196; (800) 628-7202
**BT, BW, C, F, GS, H, HR, I,
MB, MT, PA, RA, S, T, XC**

NATURAL BRIDGE OF VIRGINIA
PO Box 57, Natural Bridge, VA 24578
(540) 291-2121 **GS, H, I, L, PA, S, T, TG**

NATURAL CHIMNEYS REGIONAL PARK
Upper Valley Regional Park Authority
Rte. 1, Box 286, Mt. Solon, VA 22843
(540) 350-2510
BT, BW, C, GS, H, PA, S, T

NATURAL TUNNEL STATE PARK
Virginia Div. of State Parks
Rte. 3, Box 250, Duffield, VA 24244
(540) 940-2674
Chairlift to tunnel area
**BW, C, F, GS, H, I,
MT, PA, RA, S, T, TG**

NEW RIVER TRAIL STATE PARK
Virginia Div. of State Parks
Rte. 1, Box 81X, Austinville, VA 24312
(540) 699-6778 **BT, BW, CK, F, H, HR, I,
MB, MT, PA, T, TG, XC**

**NORTH LANDING RIVER
NATURAL AREA PRESERVE**
Virginia Dept.of Conservation
and Recreation
Div. of Natural Heritage
1500 E. Main St., Suite 312
Richmond, VA 23219
(804) 786-7951
Fishing from canoes **BW, CK, F**

PEAKS OF OTTER
Blue Ridge Parkway
200 BB&T Bldg., Asheville, NC 28801
(540) 298-0398
No information center or tours in winter
BW, C, F, GS, H, I, L, MT, PA, RA, T, TG

BT Bike Trails	**CK** Canoeing,	**F** Fishing	**HR** Horseback
BW Bird-watching	Kayaking	**GS** Gift Shop	Riding
C Camping	**DS** Downhill	**H** Hiking	**I** Information
	Skiing		Center

PINNACLE NATURAL AREA PRESERVE
Virginia Dept.of Conservation and Recreation
Div. of Natural Heritage
1500 E. Main St., Suite 312
Richmond, VA 23219
(804) 786-7951 — BW, F, H, MT

RAGGED ISLAND WILDLIFE MANAGEMENT AREA
Virginia Wildlife Division
5806 Mooretown Rd.
Williamsburg, VA 23188
(804) 253-4180 — BW, CK, F, H, MT

RAMSEY'S DRAFT WILDERNESS AREA
U.S. Forest Service
Deerfield Ranger District
Rte. 6, Box 419, Staunton, VA 24401
(540) 885-8028 — BW, F, H, MT, PA, T

ROCKY KNOB RECREATION AREA
Blue Ridge Parkway
200 BB&T Bldg., Asheville, NC 28801
(704) 298-0398
Camping May–October
BW, C, F, H, I, L, MT, PA, T

SAXIS WATERFOWL MANAGEMENT AREA AND REFUGE
Virginia Wildlife Division
PO Box 11104
Richmond, VA 23230
(804) 367-1000 — BW, CK, F

SEASHORE STATE PARK AND NATURAL AREA
Virginia Div. of State Parks
2500 Shore Dr.
Virginia Beach, VA 23451
(804) 481-4836; (804) 481-2131
Maximum 6 per campsite; pets on leashes; 1 handicapped-accessible trail
BT, BW, C, F, H, I, L, MB, MT, PA, RA, S, T, TG

SHENANDOAH NATIONAL PARK
National Park Service
Rte. 4, Box 348, Luray, VA 22835
(540) 999-3500; (540) 999-2266
Includes the Appalachian National Scenic Trail; entrance fee; winter road closures; registration required for camping along the Appalachian Trail
BW, C, F, GS, H, HR, I, L, MT, PA, RA, T, XC

SKYLINE CAVERNS
PO Box 193, Front Royal, VA 22630
(540) 635-4545; (800) 296-4545
GS, I, PA, T, TG

SKY MEADOW STATE PARK
Virginia Div. of State Parks
11012 Edmonds Lane
Delaplane, VA 22025
(540) 592-3556
Parking fee; hike in; primitive camping
BW, C, F, H, HR, MT, PA, RA, T, TG, XC

VIRGINIA COAST RESERVE
The Nature Conservancy
Virginia Chapter
PO Box 158
Nassawadox, VA 23413
(804) 442-3049
Accessible by boat only — BW, F

VIRGINIA CREEPERS NATIONAL RECREATION TRAIL
Virginia Creepers Trail Club
PO Box 2382, Abingdon, VA 24210
(540) 783-5196 (Mt. Rogers NRA)
BT, H, HR, MT, XC

VIRGINIA HIGHLANDS HORSE TRAIL
Virginia Horse Council
PO Box 72, Riner, VA 24149
(540) 783-5196 (Mt. Rogers NRA) — HR

WESTMORELAND STATE PARK
Virginia Div. of State Parks
Rte. 1, Box 600, Montross, VA 22520
(804) 493-8821 — BW, C, F, GS, H, I, L, MT, PA, RA, S, T, TG

YANKEE HORSE OVERLOOK TRAIL
Blue Ridge Parkway
200 BB&T Bldg., Asheville, NC 28801
(704) 298-0398 — H, MT

YORK RIVER STATE PARK
Virginia Div. of State Parks
5526 Riverview Rd.
Williamsburg, VA 23188
(804) 566-3036
Includes York River Environmental Education Center; canoeing through interpretive programs only
BT, BW, CK, F, GS, H, HR, I, MB, MT, PA, RA, T, TG

L Lodging	**PA** Picnic Areas	**RC** Rock Climbing	**TG** Tours, Guides
MB Mountain Biking	**RA** Ranger-led Activities	**S** Swimming	**XC** Cross-country Skiing
MT Marked Trails		**T** Toilets	

The Atlantic Coast and Blue Ridge

INDEX

Numbers in **bold** indicate illustrations; numbers in ***bold italics*** indicate maps.

Index

A

Abingdon to Damascus Trail, 161, 271
alders, 109, 110, 195
 seaside, 78
 speckled, 29
alexanders, golden, 150
alligators, 13, 196
American redstart, 154
anole, green, 103
Appalachian National Scenic Trail, 34, 263
Appomattox-Buckingham State Forest, 117, 271
arbutus, trailing, 50
arrow arum, 62, 74, 98, 134
Art Loeb Trail, 244, 267
ash, 42, 146, 207
 green, 195
 mountain, 242
aspen, bigtooth, 224
Assateague Island National Seashore, 82, 84, 263
Assateague Island State Park, 82, 84, 263
Assawoman Wildlife Area, 82, 262
Atamasco lily, 206, **206**
Augustine Wildlife Area, 67
avens
 Appalachian, 251-52
 spreading, 224, 227
avocets, American, 58, 60-61
azalea, xiii, 146, 169
 flame, iv, vi, 228, **228**, 236
 pink, 170, **170**
 pink-shelled, 232
 swamp, 75, 125

Back Bay National Wildlife Refuge, 126-27, **128**, 129, 272
bald cypress, xvii, 10, 22, 50, **51**, 63, 75-76, **77**, 85, 88, **89**, 103, 108, 122, 125, 129, **130–31**, 132, 178, **180–81**, 195

Bald Cypress Nature Trail, 132
Ball's Bluff Regional Park, 110, 272
balsam, 152
 see also fir, Fraser
Barbour Hill Nature Trail, 127
barrens
 serpentine, 6, 24, 51
 shale, 18, 31-32, **32**
barrier islands, 4, 6, 12, **56,** 57, 62, 78, 82-91, 108, 127, 174-93, 196-99, 201, 254
bass
 largemouth, 67, 73, 195
 Roanoke redeye, 207
 smallmouth, 29, 117
 striped, xii, 63, 205
basswood, white, 146
Bat Cave, 243
Battery Park, 65
Battle Creek Cypress Swamp Sanctuary, 50, 263
bay
 see loblolly bay; red bay; sweet bay
bayberry, 78
 southern, 192
beach grass, 79
 American, **128,** 129
beach heather, 79
beach plum, 78
Beach Plum Island Nature Preserve, 78, 262
Bear Creek Lake State Park, 116, 272
Bearfence Mountain, 153
bears, black, 29, 126, 152, **152,** 153, 196, 216, 221, 227, 248
beauty-berry, 122, **122**
beavers, xvii, 41, 42, 71, 108, 113, 116, 139
beech, 47, 49, 67, 186, 207, 242, 252
 American, 134, 146
beetles
 glass shrimp, 47
 northeastern beach tiger, 91, 139
bellflowers, Virginia, 120
Bethel Beach Natural Area

Preserve, 134, 139, 272
Big Blue Trail, 172-73, 272
Big Hunting Creek, 35-36
Big Meadows, 153
Big Run State Park, 29, 263
Big Schloss, 173, 272
Big Spring Bog Natural Area Preserve, 155-56
Big Stone Gap, 161
Billy Goat Trail, 41
birch, 155, 229, 232
 river, 67, 116, 206
 yellow, 164, 166, 242, 252
bitterns
 American, 65
 least, 39, 52, 65
blackberry bushes, 165, 229
blackbirds, red-winged, 18, **20–21,** 39, 43, 75, 92
Blackbird State Forest, 67, **68–69,** 70, 262
black-eyed susans, 153
black gum, 76, 108, 122, 195
Blackwater National Wildlife Refuge, 18, **20–21,** 94-95, **96–97,** 263
bladderworts, 28, 201
blazing stars, 51
blindfish, 126
bloodroot, 150, 170, **170**
Bluebell Nature Loop, 115
bluebells, Virginia, 4, 104, **106–07,** 110, 115
blueberry bushes, 78, 153, **153,** 232
bluebirds, Eastern, 46, 224, **224**
bluefish, 193
bluegill, 67, 73
blue jays, 204
Blue Ridge Parkway, 154-55, 172, **172,** 272
Bluff Mountain, 224
boars, European wild, 248
bobcats, 29, 104, 126, 224
bobolink, 43, 75
bobwhite, 116
Bombay Hook National Wildlife Refuge, 13, **13,** 58, **60–61,** 70-71, **72,** 73, 262
Boone's Cave State Park, 210-11, 268
box huckleberry, 75
Brandywine Creek State

276

The Atlantic Coast and Blue Ridge

ACKNOWLEDGMENTS

The editors gratefully acknowledge the professional assistance of Susan Kirby and Patricia Woodruff. The following consultants also helped in the preparation of this volume: Richard Hoffman, Virginia Museum of Natural History; Wayne Klockner, Director, Maryland Chapter of the Nature Conservancy; Dallas Rhodes, Professor and Chair of Geology, Whittier College; Charles R. Roe, Executive Director, Conservation Trust for North Carolina; Charles R. Vicker, Delaware Division of Parks and Recreation, Land Preservation Office.

PHOTOGRAPHY CREDITS